T0213633

Procedural Generation in Game Design

Procedural Generation in Game Design

Edited by

Tanya X. Short and Tarn Adams

CRC Press
Taylor & Francis Group
Boca Raton London New York

CRC Press is an imprint of the
Taylor & Francis Group, an **informa** business

AN A K PETERS BOOK

CRC Press
Taylor & Francis Group
6000 Broken Sound Parkway NW, Suite 300
Boca Raton, FL 33487-2742

CRC Press is an imprint of Taylor & Francis Group, an Informa business
No claim to original U.S. Government works

Printed on acid-free paper

International Standard Book Number-13: 978-1-4987-9919-5 (paperback)
978-1-138-74331-1 (hardback)

This book contains information obtained from authentic and highly regarded sources. Reasonable efforts have been made to publish reliable data and information, but the author and publisher cannot assume responsibility for the validity of all materials or the consequences of their use. The authors and publishers have attempted to trace the copyright holders of all material reproduced in this publication and apologize to copyright holders if permission to publish in this form has not been obtained. If any copyright material has not been acknowledged please write and let us know so we may rectify in any future reprint.

Library of Congress Cataloging-in-Publication Data

Names: Short, Tanya X., author. | Adams, Tarn, author.
Title: Procedural generation in game design / authors, Tanya X. Short and
Tarn Adams.
Description: Boca Raton : Taylor & Francis, CRC Press, 2017. | Includes
bibliographical references and index.
Identifiers: LCCN 2016054480| ISBN 9781498799195 (pbk. : alk. paper) | ISBN
9781138743311 (hardback : alk. paper)
Subjects: LCSH: Level design (Computer science) | Compter games--Design.
Classification: LCC QA76.76.C672 S543 2017 | DDC 794.8/1536--dc23
LC record available at https://lccn.loc.gov/2016054480

Visit the Taylor & Francis Web site at
http://www.taylorandfrancis.com
and the CRC Press Web site at
http://www.crcpress.com

Contents

CHAPTER 17 ▪ Audio and Composition   175

BRONSON ZGEB

SECTION III **Procedural Narrative**

CHAPTER 18 ▪ Story and Plot Generation   187

BEN KYBARTAS

Preface

The term *procedural generation* sounds cold and uncaring—it invokes images of robots building things for practical use rather than for fun, aesthetics, or enlightenment. In practice, however, I've found that hand-made content can feel far more artificial than what an algorithm can produce. When game designers have total control over their creations, there's a strong temptation to overdesign and lead players around by the hand, making them feel less like a hero on an adventure and more like a child on a scavenger hunt. In that sense, a little bit of indifference toward the player can be a good thing. The real world, after all, doesn't care if there's anything of interest to us at our destination or even if we have a destination, and that makes it all the more exciting when something interesting does happen.

My first experience with procedural generation was with *Hack*, one of the first roguelikes released after *Rogue*. The game's ASCII graphics were primitive looking even by 1982's standards, but its smart design based around randomly generated dungeons made it deep enough to last a lifetime. Fast-forward to 2006: brothers Tarn and Zach Adams released the first version of *Dwarf Fortress*, a hybrid simulation/roguelike that procedurally generated not just dungeons but entire continents, populated by characters with histories stretching back centuries. Visually, the game was only a few steps above *Hack*, but the promise of never-ending fantasy worlds more than made up for it. At the time, I was sorely disappointed with the beautiful but restrictive titles that were coming out of the mainstream AAA. Games like *Dwarf Fortress* and *Hack* were so inspiring to me that I began experimenting with random-level generation myself, in a side-scrolling platform game called *Spelunky*.

I quickly realized how fun it is to build levels with procedural generation. Making small changes behind the scenes could lead to a cascade of new possibilities, and the randomization that made roguelikes so replayable to players also kept the game fresh for me even after years of working on it. My experience with *Spelunky* also taught me how much handiwork is involved in making algorithms that generate enjoyable levels. Using procedural generation doesn't mean that there's no human hand involved in the design, but only that the hand is less direct in its control. It's similar to how a painter might hold the paintbrush closer to the end of the handle to create looser, more painterly brush strokes.

That intersection between handiwork and procedure, art and science, still feels vast and wild. It took many years before the importance of roguelikes became widely accepted. Similarly, it will take some time before developers begin to fully realize the potential for procedural generation beyond dungeon building, for things like graphics, music, and storytelling. Thankfully, many of the creators who are thinking about those things are in this book, sharing their knowledge and experience.

Derek Yu

I

Procedural Generation

PROCEDURAL GENERATION IS A powerful tool and a great way to ruin your game design. A human artist wants to create compelling landscapes that aren't bland or messy. A human author wants to write an engaging story that isn't repetitive or nonsensical. Even better, they can do these things in concert, respecting the overall vision of the project. Procedural content can be difficult to control, and even when the output is tamed, it might add up to a costly result no better than a scripted one.

Yet the draw of procedural generation is undeniable. Unimagined visions, replayable levels, reactive music, and unique player-guided narratives are all within reach. Players can have their own personal journey but still have enough common experience to share their tales with others, working together to define what any given procedural game is and what it can become. Unexplored frontiers are somehow close at hand at every turn, and even beginning developers can jump right in to see what they can find.

In this first section, we discuss when to use procedural generation, and the many concerns that need to be addressed when using these techniques, whether game balance, object management, adhering to a vision, or handling broader obligations to the community that experiences what you create. Later sections offer specific techniques and solutions, while here we will consider the purpose and utility of generation as a tool, providing a foundation for future explorations.

CHAPTER 1

When and Why to Use Procedural Generation

Darren Grey

Roguelike Radio

PROCEDURAL GENERATION (PCG) TECHNIQUES are now used widely through game design and development, from content drafting to on-the-fly generation, graphical effects to responsive narrative. This chapter examines the motivations behind including PCG in your development process, as well as important issues that may hold you back and the risks when deciding to delve into the depths of generative processes.

PLANNING WHEN TO USE PROCEDURAL GENERATION

Making a game can be an intensive process, and if not planned properly, it can easily run hugely over budget. A worry with any project is scheduling, and at what point in your process to instigate risky endeavors like procedurally generated content. In game development, this partly comes down to what way you're using PCG in your game's design.

Integral

In the most well-known cases, the choice to make use of PCG is wrapped up in the initial design of the game. Most of the games that make extensive use of PCG also rely on it entirely to be the type of games they are. Games with significant random content, such as *Rogue* and *Spelunky*, depend on PCG to deliver their core gameplay. Games using PCG to include a vast amount of content, such as *Elite* and *No Man's Sky*, are similarly dependent on PCG to achieve their vision. The decision to use procedural content was integral to the decision to make that type of game.

It is vital in these cases to consider the scope of PCG involvement in achieving the aims of the game. The amount of time it takes to produce the majority of game content by procedural means cannot be underestimated. This can have a massive impact on project planning. Any changes to your project direction (which are far from unusual in game development) will have vast implications for your codebase.

Your algorithms will need to be drafted and redrafted multiple times, with the rest of the game's content built around them. Work on this will continue throughout the project life cycle, and this should be carefully considered when planning resources for development. The debugging and tweaking of the game's procedural systems will continue after the game's release, and with the nature of these games, every little change can have wide-reaching impact on every aspect of the player's experience.

Holistic use of procedural content needs tight development from cradle to grave.

Drafting Content

PCG is often used in game development to produce a large amount of content that is then polished later. The typical example of this is an open-world game, such as *Skyrim*, which has a vast explorable map. Major sections of this are produced using procedural techniques and are then adjusted and polished by hand later. Other examples include puzzle games where a generator can produce hundreds of examples of solvable puzzles, and then a human manually picks out or sorts the more interesting ones.

In these cases, the decision to use PCG comes early, but isn't needed from the project inception. Typically, the code used doesn't need a huge amount of finesse, and doesn't need to be as carefully honed to fit the rest of the project. A landscape generator for an RPG just needs to produce some rough drafts, with the important detail that the player really interacts with filled in by hand. Because of this, the project timescales are more predictable.

The use of PCG in these areas both starts and finishes early. Once the generator has done its job, it is locked down, and the flesh-based designers get to work on honing the outputs to their needs.

Modal

Some games rely little on PCG, but have a special mode of play that makes use of procedurally generated content. This is sometimes called an "infinity mode" and is a special piece of side content to the main game. Examples include the Ancient Cave in *Lufia II* and procedural maps in *Rust*.

Since these are separate modes, they can be created later in the development process, perhaps released as downloadable content (DLC) after the game's initial release. It can even be something the game's modding community produces, if your game allows them such flexibility.

A procedural mode that mimics the core game may prove to be less resource-intensive to develop, as the designer already has a clear vision of how the output should look and how the mechanics will work in this environment, and many of the assets will already be in place. However, this also tends to restrict the potential for interesting and innovative content, leading to content that is more random than procedural. Many games that implement this mode of play end up simply relying on waves of randomized enemies rather than putting the extra work into having engaging, procedurally driven gameplay.

Segmented

Certain segments of a game can be squared off from the rest of the game's design to use PCG. A linear, hand-designed game could still have procedural music, for instance. A certain graphical effect could have interesting randomized elements. A specific room in a single area of the game may have some special procedural rules in place.

These individual elements of the game can vary widely in scope, but they tend to be segmented from the rest of the game design. Thus, the "when" of using PCG comes down purely to when this feature needs implementing. And because of the lack of knock-on implications from these sections, they typically don't run a heavy risk of overrun on time. If there is a problem implementing PCG in these instances, then as a contingency you can simply revert to hand-generated content instead.

WHEN PCG IS A BAD IDEA

PCG comes with a warning label. It can be a black hole, a slippery slope, a project risk, and a dark abyss. It's important to understand these risks when looking to integrate PCG into your game, and to realize all the implications and impacts of PCG across your project.

Quality Assurance

One of the most prominent blockers to the use of PCG in mainstream games, in particular AAA games, is quality assurance (QA). A PCG game may not be guaranteed to work as intended 100% of the time. There is no way of having testers go through every single iteration of the procedural content. The generator may have serious bugs in 0.1% of its levels that are never picked up until it gets released to a wide playerbase.

I have heard multiple first-hand accounts of developers making a procedural generator for a game, showing their boss how it can make 100 levels in an instant, and the boss saying, "Just send those 100 levels to the QA team, but we're not having the generator live in the game." The perceived risk of losing control to a procedural system is too great.

The risks can be mitigated with various controls and automated tests. Connectivity tests for level generators are vital, for instance, but one can also include minimum difficulty tests or put in further constraints to have a more controlled experience. This is usually good design too! However, there is a chance you lose the variety PCG brings to the game, with over-constrained, "samey" levels. It's also a lot more work.

One area of PCG that tends to pass this QA test is quilted-content PCG using premade blocks of content, meshed together on the fly for a varied experience. This is how the *Diablo* games make their levels. But it often produces the least varied experience, as the player gets to recognize the content blocks and the patterns produced by the generator. Over repeated plays, it can produce repetitive and stale gameplay.

Concern over QA is one of the reasons we see the most experimentation in this field from independent developers. Indies often have no one to report to, little reputation to sacrifice, and are more willing to take risks. But indies are also often the ones with the least resources and time to build well-constrained systems or automated testing scripts.

Time Restrictions

PCG is often touted as a time-saver, but there is no guarantee this is the case. Designing the generator may prove harder and more nuanced than initially expected, especially in an area for which there isn't a lot of existing code to rely on. Work on it may also continue after completion, as constant tweaking is needed to adapt to other developments.

It's important to assess how much a reliable time frame is needed for your project. A handcrafted process takes a more predictable amount of time. You might hope that making a level generator will take less time to make than hand-designing 10 levels, but you don't *know* that, and in the end, it might be that 10 levels is just fine for your game.

If money and time are particularly restricted for your game, then think twice about using significant amounts of PCG, and factor in plenty of contingency to your budget should it not go according to plan.

Authored Experience

In many games, the designer wishes to produce a highly authored experience. This is particularly notable in story-based games, where you wish the player to encounter various parts of the game in a linear way. These types of games benefit less from PCG, and may be made worse if the generated content doesn't fit neatly to the authored experience the developer has in mind.

This *can* be made to work, though. In particular, a thorough and well-crafted procedural game can take into account the player's actions and integrate their impact into the content produced. This sort of integration can create a far more effective feeling of an authored experience than a traditional linear game. It also requires a lot of work and great design to get right.

Another authored experience where PCG is unsuitable is reaction-based games that present specific timed and placed challenges. The likes of *Super Meat Boy* expect the player to fail and repeat the same content over and over until they master that authored part of the game. They can also include "gotcha" moments or clever pieces of design that take the player's thought processes into account, which are harder to reproduce through procedural means.

Multiplayer

Control of game balance in PCG isn't always easy, but it becomes an especially difficult issue in competitive multiplayer games. In particular, the likes of maps in real-time strategy games can present challenges, with starting positions, resources, threats, and topography all affecting how each player performs. A small difference in balance in a generator can give one side sufficient advantage to win far more often. This is unacceptable in games with highly competitive audiences.

Imbalance can be mitigated by having symmetrical maps, but this isn't always desired for aesthetic or other reasons.

Just Random

If you don't have the time and resources to make interesting procedural content, then typically you end up with something just random. As noted in Chapter 2, this is often boring and repetitive and doesn't make for a good play experience. Bland, samey content should be avoided, and if you're not able to do PCG properly, then reconsider its use in your game.

Overreliance on PCG

PCG has become a common term in game design and even in game marketing, with games advertising the immense possibility spaces they offer. But it absolutely cannot be a crutch the game solely relies on. Sheer variety, even well-designed variety, is not enough if you do not have the core mechanics and interactions to let the player have fun with what's on offer.

No Man's Sky in particular has received criticism for promising "Every Atom Procedural" but ultimately falling short, causing some to accuse it of shallow gameplay, despite a massive and beautiful universe. Procedural content should not be relied on to make your game special, and you should never lose sight of core gameplay experience.

WHY USE PROCEDURAL GENERATION?

Why should you use PCG in game design?

There are utilitarian, level-headed reasons. Perfectly sensible, logical points in favor of you using PCG. But there are also fun reasons, motivations for using PCG that are entirely unique to the process. And while every developer will tell their boss or producer (or themselves) that they have those level-headed reasons, in the back of their minds they are dreaming of playing with infinity.

Utilitarian

A few very practical reasons to generate include the following:

- *Time-saving*: With PCG, you can produce huge amounts of content far faster than a manual process. Many geographically extensive games, such as *Skyrim*, rely on this to generate their massive worlds, although they polish details by hand afterwards. The two main processes involve either procedural world gen followed by polish, or manual world gen followed by using procedural tools to generate varied content (trees, grass, buildings, etc.). Note that time-saving is sometimes a myth—one can end up spending far more time balancing and debugging a procedural system than one would spend on simply making things by hand.

- *Expandable*: Generators are usually designed in a modular fashion. Every time you add a new feature, it gets integrated across the generator's output. Each bit of hand-designed polish you add doesn't affect just one item—it affects a countless number of possible outputs. This means that extra work is multiplied immensely in impact across your game.

- *Replayability*: One generator can produce many instances of similar but varied content. Roguelikes and roguelike-inspired games in particular make use of this to produce highly replayable gameplay. It would be impractical to hand-produce enough varied content to suit thousands of instances.

- *Reusable code*: Generators can get reused between applications. A desert landscape generator from one game can have a few variables tweaked to produce icy mountains in another. Modular elements of generators can be swapped between applications—a visual effect can be copied from one series of an image processing tool to a tool that produces an entirely different end effect, but still relies on that same stage. A fire simulator in one game can make a disease spreader in another. When doing big projects in succession, this sort of reusable code is invaluable.

- *Rules enforcement*: Generators can be built with rules enforced, ensuring connectivity between elements or certain standards maintained across all output. The code, assuming it is bug-free and correctly designed, will be far more rigorous in applying these rules than a human designer. Architects rely on this now to ensure that building standards (and the laws of physics) are enforced in new projects. Game designers can include restrictions on difficulty balance, connectivity, solvability of puzzles, and many other vital features.

- *Modeling reality*: Often, simulationist techniques are used in procedural generators, reproducing the wearing of terrain or a naturalistic spread of life. Cell-based generators are inspired by life, and can be eminently effective at producing details that are similar to the messiness of reality. *Dwarf Fortress* is the undisputed king of this, incorporating an insane number of real-world physical laws (or approximations thereof) into its gameplay and world generation.

- *Scales and detail hard to do by hand*: Whole galaxies, fractal details, truly endless content. Games like *Elite: Dangerous* and *No Man's Sky* are nearly impossible to make by hand. PCG stretches the realm of possibility to scales beyond the conception of our limited little minds. This sort of potential can be of primary importance for small teams with big ambitions.

- *Overcome technical limitations*: Early in the history of video games, PCG techniques were used to produce levels of content that would be impossible to store on the media of the time. *Frontier: Elite II* had a whole galaxy of stars and planets stored on one 720 KB floppy disk—smaller than a single graphical texture in a modern three-dimensional (3D) game. These days, there are demo challenges to produce interesting content, such as visualizations and music from tiny codebases. This may seem pointless with modern computing hardware, but could prove to have great potential in the use of wearable devices, integrated electronics, and other emerging hardware.

Unique
There are also softer, more subjective reasons to prefer generation:

- *Individual experiences*: PCG opens up the potential to give every user a unique experience. A piece of music no one has ever heard before, or ever will. A gameplay challenge that only they will ever truly experience, and only in that instance. Slices of infinity that make the experience stand out in ways static content cannot reach. Reactive PCG can make it tailored to the user, producing a personalized experience. With an interactive medium like gaming, this is immensely powerful, and makes the gameplay experience both more memorable to the player and more worth talking about with others.

- *New gameplay/interaction modes*: Replayable games are just the beginning of how PCG opens up new gameplay types. Master *Spelunky* players learn how to game the generators, predicting patterns and turning PCG into a new gameplay element to be played with. Living procedural effects, such as Conway's *Game of Life*, demand the user's attention in ways repeated patterns do not. PCG involves rules, and they can be gameplay rules, as well as simple generative rules—something the player can interact and play with. This opens up a gigantic field of new gameplay opportunities.

- *Player input*: Mushroom-11 uses procedural content in a truly innovative way, having the player control a swarm of cells that regrow based on simple cellular automata rules. This gives the player a new form of gameplay through manipulation of PCG techniques. The player must internalize the behavior of the cellular automata to control the swarm and overcome the challenges in the game.

- *Unpredictable*: Even the designer does not know what to expect from the generators he or she creates. This can be scary, especially from a QA perspective, but for a creator, it can also be thrilling. It allows you to experience and enjoy your work in the same way as a normal end user—something most designers never get to enjoy.

- *Living system*: Procedural techniques can produce living, reactive effects. Fire, floods, lava, weather systems, populations, civilizations, diseases, cultures, life at every level. Hand-designed content will always appear repetitive when compared with a wild and changing procedural system. Certain techniques, like neighbor-based decision making, are tremendous at producing intricate and changing effects at scale. These feel real to us, because often they are following patterns similar to those that exist in the real world.

- *Inhuman creativity*: The outputs of PCG can be bizarre. They can produce things no human might ever think of, from unusual level designs to unreal animations. YouTube is awash with recordings of buggy procedural animations in 3D games, producing horrific and hilarious creations that astound our meat-based brains. Computers do not think about things in the same ways we do, and sometimes they come up with logical extremes that are wholly outside the realm of our imagination.

- *Reflections and refractions of humanity*: Procedural content is almost always based on human designed content, even if from small base blocks. What they produce is a reflection or refraction of our own creativity. What do we see when we stare into the abyss of Twitterbots and novel generators? And what do these twisted shadows and shapes have to tell us about ourselves? Combine this with a system that changes based on the player's input and you can develop some thought-provoking content generation. What would a game based on the player's Twitter account and followers look like?

- *Inspiration of infinity*: Infinity is a hard concept for us to grasp, but playing with generators of infinite content lets us try to straddle it, or get delightfully lost in it. A well-constrained generator will make a dungeon level that fits tidily with your expectations, and can make you feel the master of an infinite set of dungeons. A wild, unconstrained terrain generator will produce forests and fields beyond your imagination that put you in awe of all that infinity can produce.

- *Fun*: Ultimately, playing with procedural generators is really quite fun. To click a button and have a new creation brought into being. To change a number and click the button again, and the old creation is replaced by something quite different. To toy, to fiddle, to poke and prod and experiment, to see what interesting and novel things come out the other end. Dice and cards have entertained us for millennia, but now we have computers filled with millions of dice, and we can make them dance to our own strange tunes. Our living toys, our endless fun, our design of designers to make more than we could ever achieve alone. What greater than to create a creator?

CHAPTER 2

Managing Output

Boredom versus Chaos

Kenny Backus
Independent

H UMANS ARE NATURAL PATTERN-FINDING machines, and a procedural generation algorithm is often a pattern-creating machine. A central conflict of procedural generation is to subvert this pattern-matching urge without merely providing completely random output, output that will often become its own pattern of "oh, here's another thing that's completely and bizarrely random, lacking any interesting traits."

What's usually the aim of any generator is to mask the fact that it's a generator; we don't think of human authors as automatons who endlessly create a bunch of slightly varied versions of the same thing until they get something they like, despite the fact they sometimes do. We want generators to make something a human would make, or more precisely, something we didn't expect would be made, a spark of genuine creativity. We want to be pleasantly surprised. This "pleasant surprise" disarms the pattern-matching apparatus and steers us away from the quagmires of boredom and chaos, but it also happens to be very hard to accomplish with any consistency. Your ability to accomplish this with your own generator is not entirely in your control since the audience gets to decide if it's been pleasantly surprised or not. It will also require you to take a long, hard look at how your game *actually* works and how the content you want to generate lives inside it.

A common pitfall for beginners to procedural generation, even ones who do plenty of research in procedural techniques and design, is to

---

13

think that procedural content, a replacement for content creation, is also a replacement for content design. There's faith that the system, due to the fact that even a naive one will create unexpected results, will create pleasantly surprising results of high quality. Again, even a naive system will create these infinitely, so the assumption is that there will be an infinite procession of pleasantly surprising content.

This pitfall is born from two often unspoken unknowns: an ignorance of what makes a game's design actually compelling and an ignorance of the traits and requirements of content that will work best with that design. Simply put, novice developers are tempted to start creating a content generator before they even know what content they want, or before they even know what their game *really* is. The siren song of infinitely varied levels, items, and enemies is most enthralling when you don't actually have any idea of what levels, items, and enemies should be in the game and you'd rather just have a program do it for you.

An excellent starting point for when you don't know what you want to create is to figure out what you *don't* want to create. You almost always will need to introduce *constraints* to your generator that provide *guarantees* for the sort of content it can or cannot create.

If you're randomly choosing enemies for a level at the beginning of your game, for example, you should probably constrain the enemy set so it won't contain endgame bosses or elite enemies. If you have themes or biomes to your levels (forests, caves, deserts, etc.), you should also constrain the enemy set to only those sorts of enemies that fit with the environment or the intended difficulty level. Constraints are incredibly powerful, and perhaps the first concept any procedural generation novice becomes familiar with. You'll also quickly become familiar with the danger of overconstraint: say you've constrained your enemy set so much that only one type of enemy ever spawns. This is where boredom sets in, revealing that constraints aren't a complete cure and that boredom and chaos is more of a balancing act to be mediated than a conflict to be won.

The best approach to avoid this pitfall, of not actually understanding your content before creating a generator, is to actually know in clear terms what you want to generate before you write your generator. Create, by hand, a set of levels, items, enemies, or smaller pieces of them, and explore what's best and what's worst for that content, and you'll actually know when your not-yet-created generator is actually making good content. In simpler terms, make what a human content designer would create, and then try to make your generator create similar content. Life is never black and white, but shades of gray, so it's actually best to merely be toward the "prepared" end of this "prepared–unprepared" spectrum. There are also always exceptions to the rule: when you want to make a game so systematically driven that having a clear idea of what content should live in it actually limits the system, you should start making a generator sooner rather than later that will actually inform the game and content design, rather than the other way around. If you are pursuing this method wholeheartedly, you should investigate "novelty search," or algorithms that focus on creating things that haven't already been created in the absence of a specific objective.

From a game design standpoint, it's very interesting to create a generator that then actually guides your game design (which then feeds back into the generator, now that you know what you want), but it often means you'll feel painted into a corner if you end up with a design that's just not the best and leads to generated content that's not very pleasantly surprising.

The island generation in *Sky Rogue* (Figure 2.1), namely, the spawning and placement of enemies, is an example of this iterative process and gradual discovery of constraints on generated content. *Sky Rogue* is an action flight simulator where most of the gameplay occurs on a series of small, procedurally generated islands or island chains. When starting a new mission, the player is sent to one of these islands, where a multitude of air enemies are buzzing around in packs above clusters of lucrative ground targets with surrounding ground defenses. The player must destroy a specifically chosen set of ground or air targets to proceed to the next island, although they are free to engage or ignore the other enemy targets spawned on or above the island.

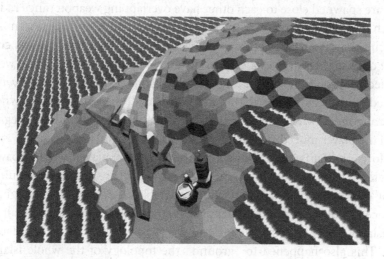

FIGURE 2.1 Image of *Sky Rogue*.

This was an attempt to model the level-driven topology of classic rogue-likes, a "dungeon in the sky," but adapt it to a flight simulator where there are no corridors, rooms, or walls to provide obstacles to the dungeon's exit. *Sky Rogue*'s design explicitly forbade any sort of floating power-ups or other in-flight pickups, so as not to veer too far from "simulation" territory into "arcade" territory, and thus the usual discovery and equipping of items in classic roguelikes was relegated to an interisland setup menu. The lack of these actually made the level design incredibly difficult, because there was such little material to work with when you couldn't forcibly obstruct a player or provide the item-driven exploration and risk taking that the genre depends on. It also meant the island terrain that was actually generated was only of minor consequence: beyond a few hills that might obscure your approach from ground targets when flying low, the terrain simply has very little effect on the gameplay, something that makes perfect sense in a flight simulator but simply comes off as boring in an action game.

Given these challenges, the island generation relies almost entirely on the placement of enemies and targets as its means of level design. It began completely naively: a certain number of ground targets would be generated, with a certain number of ground defenses a tile away, and a certain number of flying enemies were spawned in the air (more on what "a certain number" really means later). It very quickly ran into the double-edged sword of randomness: sometimes enemies were evenly spaced, and sometimes they were all clumped together. This only created difficulties because enemies that are spawned close to each other have overlapping weapon range radii, which means they can attack the player simultaneously and are thus more difficult than if they were more evenly spaced. A new constraint was created: only spawn enemies a certain distance from each other. There were immediate problems with air targets: fighting one of them at a time, evenly spaced, wasn't as interesting as fighting squadrons, so I now spawned "patrol zones," where squadrons of airborne enemies would congregate until the player moved close enough to be detected and attacked.

More problems were found: occasionally, the player would spawn directly in front of the mission target, making the bare minimum requirement of completing an island highly variable. A simple, albeit slightly nuanced solution: make sure they always spawn on the "northern" half of the island, where the player is spawning at the very edge of the "southern" half. This also happened to "ground" the topology of the whole island in the player's mental map. Sometimes, especially in more difficult later islands, squadrons of enemies would be spawned practically on top of the player, such that they'd be thrown into a defensive battle immediately. This broke a core rule of randomness: "random circumstances, not random outcomes." Again, a simple two-pronged solution: make sure they don't spawn too close, and make them ignore the player for the first 10 seconds of the mission. On later islands, ground defenses were so numerous and evenly placed that there was no "breathing room" in the island design, so the island size in later levels was increased slightly and the placement of ground targets was changed so that they would form "sites" of clustered, heavily defended ground targets. This meant the objective of having breathing room was achieved, and with negative space, the existence of positive space becomes that much more apparent, giving rise to actual "points of interest" on the island. From here, a design subspace was discovered: how to create a really interesting point of interest or set piece.

Again and again, through iterating on the island generator's design, it was revealed that managing distances between enemies or, more accurately, distances between weapon radii was a core pillar of *Sky Rogue*'s level design. I would have discovered this much earlier in development if I had just made a few prototype levels to feel out the sort of experience I wanted the player to have at each stage of difficulty in the game.

Another case of managing boredom and chaos is a melee weapon generator that I made for an aborted action-RPG project (Figure 2.2). The weapon generator followed an approach similar to the *Borderlands* series: given a weapon family, type, and quality level (e.g., hafted weapon, axe, or masterwork), choose from a constrained set of pieces for that weapon that would both look appropriate and avoid patterns enough that a new

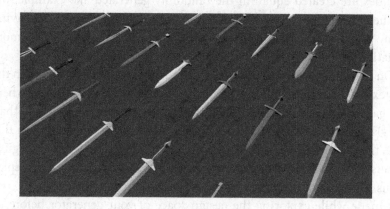

FIGURE 2.2   Grid of swords.

weapon would be visually enticing in a loot-driven game. Here, combining premade pieces to create a unique whole is an incredibly powerful way of providing enough possibilities that the player will never find the same weapon twice. Given a weapon made of three parts (grip, cross-guard, and blade) and five handmade instances of each part type, the generator creates 125 possibilities. Given the quality level, the generator then colors each part within a constrained set: low-quality weapons look dark and dull, while high-quality weapons look bright and vibrant. Given three colors for each of three quality levels, per part, this multiplies the possibilities even more than having a fourth part type ($5 \times 9 \times 5 \times 9 \times 5 \times 9 = 91{,}125$, rather than $5 \times 5 \times 5 \times 5 = 625$) because the handmade instances have been slightly modified by the generator itself. Compare this number with an average amount of weapons a player might see in a playthrough, and you can start to reason mathematically about the possibility that the player would see the same weapon twice.

This sort of run-time modification of premade content (a parametric method) is also seen in *Spelunky*, where a handmade level chunk is slightly modified by a few tiles, giving rise to an incredible amount of diversity, a powerful assault in the war against pattern matching that benefits from the control and ease of use of partial human authorship.

It's important to remember, though, that even combinatorially driven procedural content can run out of steam after the player has seen hundreds of combinations and discovered your premade pieces. The pattern-matching human brain kicks in, and the illusory curtain of uniqueness disappears: your artist-in-a-box is revealed for the pattern assembler it is rather than the infinitely surprising creator it strives to be. Not all possibilities are created equal: in the randomly generated axe example, the axe head provides a great deal of the weapon's visual identity, so having many variations of it will give you a lot more mileage than having more variations of handles.

On a similar note, you could have visually surprising content, but in the context of a numbers-driven, "crunchy" loot-driven sort of game where the gameplay properties of content are perhaps more important than the visuals, your visual excellence is undermined by your design. In this case, the player will likely discard each incredibly unique item in disgust, because it's practically the same as what she's already found in gameplay terms. Hopefully, this can easily be avoided in the human-authored content made while exploring the design space of your generator before its actual creation. In this case, it's best to try and surprise yourself: allow the generator to add a diverse set of properties (fire damage, ice damage, fire–ice damage, bonus vs. birds?) that can then be cleaned up or balanced by your generator.

This puts a lot of pressure on the generator to actually understand the game design, though: Is a sword that does 100 base damage really equal to a sword that does 50 fire damage and 50 ice damage? If not, just how unequal is it? Is fighting a dire wolf and a death knight at the same time more difficult than fighting them one at a time, and by how much? Quantifying properties like power, difficulty, or value in a way the generator can use accurately becomes a necessity, something that's usually left to trial-and-error-driven iteration in handmade content.

Ultimately, it comes back to promising a pleasant surprise and carefully avoiding predictable output. Knowing how to create a convincing illusion of appropriate randomness is as challenging as generating content in the first place, but simply knowing that before diving in avoids a lot of pain. Keep in mind how your players see your generator, rather than seeing the generator for what you know it is, and try to discern repetitive features of content that you know is technically unique. From the right perspective, a million unique items can seem like the same item repeated a million times. If patterns can form, find ways to break them, keep the player guessing about what's coming next. If the player stops guessing, if they feel like they can predict the output even if they essentially can't, you've lost the battle of human versus machine.

Beyond high-level advice, there are a lot of practical, reusable ways to break up patterns and introduce a bit of chaos to your boredom:

- *Avoid grid patterns when possible.* This is more difficult than it sounds, because grids are excellent for easily organizing environments and necessary for smooth gameplay in turn-based games. For games where the player has no need to see the underlying grid, try and move static objects by tiny amounts to break up the pattern.

- *When spawning pieces of your environment, randomly rotate static objects to make them seem less similar to one another.* For example, if you have three types of rock, rotate them randomly, and clump them together in irregular patterns. The player will have a very hard time picking out patterns without closely studying the rock formations. Compare this to having the same three types that are evenly spaced and always presented at the same angle.

- *When constructing an environment out of tiles, try using nonstandard shapes instead of squares.* Herringbone Wang tiles are a great example that aren't too hard to implement; you can find more information at http://nothings.org/gamedev/herringbone/index.html.

- *When creating heightmaps or other maps with Perlin or other kinds of noise, try multiplying each pixel by several layers of other noise (also multiplied by a scalar to adjust the other noises' intensity), using either a different seed or an entirely different algorithm.* This is a quick way of breaking up a lot of the patterns you might be unhappy with in your current generator.

- *Spawn characters with randomized looks.* Use props, clothing, hair, or palette swaps, and give them slight variations in scale where possible. These can influence gameplay or be purely visual, but go a long way to break up patterns when the player sees packs of completely identical characters onscreen. This might not be a quick fix depending on how visually complex your characters are.

- *Random circumstances, not random outcomes.* Players are generally comfortable with, or even prefer, being thrown into an unpredictable environment, with an unpredictable starting point in terms of location or equipment. These are circumstances that can lead to new strategies to either deal with their limitations or exploit their advantages: you know, feeling smart. What they don't like are random outcomes: a die roll they can't influence that just didn't go in their favor, or a randomized start point or starting equipment so influential that it might as well be an outcome. In these cases, they lack choice, by explicitly being given either no choice (die roll) or a false choice (bad start point).

- *Be careful with "pure" randomness.* There's not much connection between the statement "this enemy should appear 20% of the time" and the enemy appearing at what actually feels like 20% of the time. Saying something should happen "3 times out of 10" brings with it a subconscious expectation that after seven tries with no luck, it will certainly happen on the eighth try. This specific technique of loading the dice should be in your toolkit, but this particular example of randomness actually being random digs deeper at an expectation of variety or fairness that players have. Pure randomness always seems like a good idea when the dice are in your favor. The statement "there's a 33% chance a mini-boss will spawn each level" in practice is often better implemented as "a mini-boss will spawn every 2, 3, or 4 levels, with the highest probability being 3."

CHAPTER 3

Aesthetics in Procedural Generation

Liam Welton

Failbetter Games

T HE KEY TO CREATING satisfying aesthetics is the creation of a collection of guides and rules that enable you to maintain a coherent look and feel across an entire project. This requires the development of a language that you will use to communicate the themes, sense of place, and story of your game to the player.

When working as a solo developer, these rules also serve as a guiding principle that will help ensure the work you are producing today matches the work of the day before, or the days to come. The aesthetic guides you put in place set parameters within which you know you can safely experiment and improvise without creating something completely inappropriate for your game.

When you are working in a team, it becomes even more important to have a visual and aural design that everybody knows they are working toward. This makes sure that everyone's individual contribution can add together to form a coherent whole.

When establishing the style for your game, and translating it into a set of design rules, it is also important to bear in mind the strengths and weaknesses of your team. You might find someone's technical execution lends itself to a slightly different aesthetic approach than that originally envisaged. Factor in that a team member's skill set may lead them to interpret your rules and guides in a way you did not predict, if you are insufficiently precise. Establishing good aesthetic rules involves making allowances for, as well as even embracing, the creative differences that are inevitable when working with a team.

In this respect, it can be useful to imagine your procedural generation engine as a member of your team that works alongside your other artists and designers, taking into consideration its own strengths and weaknesses. The engine is going to be contributing work based on rules that you have established for it. It'll even be granted some creative freedom, although admittedly this is usually simulated by introducing a degree of randomness. The procedural generation engine is a team member that can follow hard-and-fast rules to the letter, but can fall short when it comes to making judgments in less strictly defined areas.

It is possible to work around this, as long as you identify the strengths and weaknesses of your procedural generation engine in advance of using it, and plan your aesthetic design accordingly. Work out where it will need help and grant more control to your other team members there.

ATMOSPHERE IN *SUNLESS SEA*

When we began development on *Sunless Sea*, it was clear from the outset that atmosphere and exploration were going to be every bit as important to the core experience of the game as survival and danger. *Sunless Sea* is a game about setting off from the familiar and traveling out into the unknown. We wanted the world to provide both a challenge and a sense of threat, and didn't want these to be lost as the player became familiar with the setting. To accomplish this, we decided the map should vary each time a new game was started. This would ensure each new journey was different and the sea it took place on never felt like an entirely safe place.

But it needed to be balanced. A sense of challenge and freshness would only add to the atmosphere and thrill of exploration up to a point. We didn't want the player to feel they gained no skill or understanding despite spending significant time in the game, or for journeys to feel entirely arbitrary. To create the sense of a long, strange journey through the darkness, we needed to induce the feeling of gradually passing from the familiar into the alien. This meant that the world of *Sunless Sea* had to be a coherent one—while every discovery should feel exciting and fresh, it should also feel natural to the player in hindsight. Discoveries needed to build on the expectations players would have developed from exploring areas adjacent to them. Our greatest fear when designing our procedural generation process was that we would expose the players to tonally jarring contrasts that would throw them out of the world, rather than draw them deeper in.

ESTABLISHING THE RULES

We decided on a grid-and-tile-based approach toward map generation. The advantage of this approach was that the rules for tile placement could be simple enough for everyone working on the project to understand, not just the designers and coders. As originally envisaged, the system would involve laying out an 18 × 18 grid of tiles, each of which would contain content (a creature, an island, a geographical feature, etc.). The design rules would determine the type of tile that could be placed to the north and east of each tile. Tiles were organized into categories, and each category had a particular style and difficulty level. Blue tiles were placed to the north of the map and featured icebergs and snowstorms, while purple tiles would generally be to the far east of the map and feature our most alien flora and fauna.

While working within this system, we found occasional aesthetic dissonance between the tiles. To avoid this, we began creating ever more specific subcategories, but this reduced the sense of variety and randomness we were achieving. We spent a long time working out the best way to make the moment-to-moment play experience feel harmonious, while still allowing for variation on a larger scale when crossing the map.

We found ourselves naturally designing areas in 3 × 3 chunks, as this provided enough space to create a sense of a coherent location. You would have a few islands, some aquatic features, a sea beast or two, and then you would move on to the next area. We therefore decided to reduce our grid size from 18 × 18 to 6 × 6 (Figure 3.1). We retained the region-sorted tiles, ensuring tiles were placed next to those with a complementary theme and design, but the decrease in the number of tiles meant that we could be a lot more lenient with their placement. Finally, to make sure that areas of

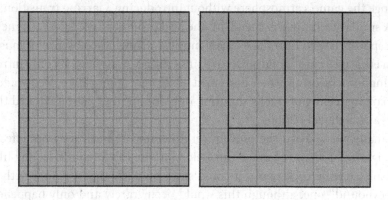

FIGURE 3.1   Before (18 × 18) and after (6 × 6).

the map that would conflict aesthetically could never be placed next to one another, we made sure there were neutral, bridging regions between them so that they would never adjoin.

Eventually, we wound up with a grid of 36 tiles, 24 of which were split into five regions and 12 of which were located in a fixed position. Each tile could be placed anywhere within its corresponding region of the map, allowing for much greater variety than the earlier ruleset allowed. Restricting tile type to only five regions, rather than subdividing them further by specific areas, also meant our procedural generation code had a greater likelihood of creating exciting combinations.

We also established a series of unifying rules around the use of color, lighting, sound, and music. These are essential for any game, but we found them particularly helpful. By adhering to stylistic rules, we could avoid maps being generated with clashes between the atmosphere generated by the sound and by the visuals. This, combined with the fact that the game, by design, has long stretches of open water between inhabited areas, meant that we were able to avoid some of the uglier issues that can arise when using procedural generation for environment design.

BLURRING THE BOUNDARIES

The tile rules meant that areas wouldn't align discordantly. However, tiles from different region categories would still be placed next to each other. Easing the transition between tiles helped to smooth over the joins. When the player travels from tile to tile, we determine their intention—whether it's to continue into the tile or to move back into the previous tile (zigzagging back and forth between tile boundaries). If they do continue into the tile, we will slowly alter the color of the sea beneath them, allowing us to change the game's atmosphere without introducing a jarring transition.

A similar technique is used with the background music to determine if it is appropriate to introduce a new musical theme. The absence of music is an effective way of building and maintaining atmosphere. By only introducing underscoring when it seemed absolutely appropriate, we avoided the jarring feeling of tracks shunting into one another as you crossed the map and changed regions.

Finally, we allowed the procedural generator to create weather effects that ignored tile boundaries. This helped to prevent each tile feeling like an isolated little rock pool—it could snow on a tile that wasn't strictly a "snowbound" one, although this would occur rarely and only happened when such a tile was adjacent to one of the northern ones.

THE RESULT

In the end, the tile-based approach we took to procedural generation in *Sunless Sea* was successful. It enabled enough variation to keep the challenge fresh for players, while allowing us to retain sufficient aesthetic control to craft the experience we wanted. However, the approach wasn't without drawbacks. Treating each tile as a puzzle piece that could be slotted into various locations meant that more time had to be taken designing them to fit in every arrangement. We made this easier to accomplish by providing our procedural generation engine with pieces that were visually and aurally coherent. If you were to put each asset in a line, you would see evolution and subtle variation, but they would all be of a piece. The color palette is restrained and harmonious, contrast levels are consistent, and shapes and sizes are fairly uniform.

One decision we regret was the attempt to introduce more variety by creating handcrafted variants of each of these individual tiles and randomly assigning one per play session. This was time-consuming, prone to human error, and very difficult to debug, which taught us the valuable lesson that sometimes it is better to accept the limitations of your approach to procedural generation than to patch over them with manual solutions. For Failbetter Games's expansion to *Sunless Sea*, *Zubmariner*, we used a solution that attempts to accomplish a similar effect, but through procedural logic rather than manual placement.

In *Zubmariner*, players are given the opportunity to explore underwater in a submarine. This involves creating an entire subsurface level to the play area—and would be a daunting task if attempted by hand. Instead, we are using the rules already established for our surface tiles and handing over even more control to our procedural generation engine. It picks from a predefined list of atmospherically appropriate pieces of terrain and decorations and places them in unoccupied areas of the map at a density our artist can adjust.

In this way, we can hand over the task of decorating large areas of the map to the procedural generation engine. We have taken the time to establish the rules it applies and ensured that all the assets it is using are well crafted and visually coherent. Now we get to sit back and enjoy the work that our silent, stalwart team member produces.

CHAPTER 4

Designing for Modularity

Jason Grinblat
Freehold Games

MODULES AND GESTALTS

Modularity is the use of discrete units, called *modules*, to assemble larger structures, which we'll call *gestalts*. Our motivation for investigating modular design comes from the combinatorial magic that modularity conjures. We design a few modules, along with an assembly mechanism, and we inherit a plethora of gestalts for free. And gestalts are what matter. They're the artifacts our players encounter and care about, be they dynamic puzzles, dungeon levels, or dialog trees. Modularity multiplies our work, often bearing novel results in the process.

Modular design has an extensive presence across the genealogy of game systems. Consider one canonical example—equipment in an RPG. Here, the modules are the individual pieces of armor. The assembly mechanism is the player's choice of equipment, within the constraints prescribed by each piece's coupling to a particular body part. The gestalt is the entire equipment loadout. When a fortunate player has amassed more gear than they can wear and must decide how to outfit themselves, it's modularity that gives the system its play. I'm using a particular definition of *play* here, namely, "the free space of movement within a more rigid structure."[1] When we talk about play in this chapter, we mean the range of interesting possibilities prescribed by our system's rules.

In the context of designing systems that leverage procedural generation, we limit our consideration to modular designs that satisfy these two qualities:

1. The assembly mechanism includes some degree of randomness.

2. The gestalt space is too large to craft every possible gestalt by hand.

The aim of the modular designer, then, is twofold. Craft modules that assemble into desirable gestalts, and design an assembly mechanism to manifest them. The gestalts themselves are out of our direct reach, and that's why it's a challenging problem. Of course, what counts as desirable depends on the aesthetics of the designer. But we assume the designs that give our system the most play are the favorable ones, especially those that contribute to our thematic goals for the system.

This chapter sets out to develop a model for the modular paradigm. We introduce language to help conceptualize the pieces at play, and we familiarize ourselves with the underlying math. Then we suggest an approach to designing for modularity. We examine material systems as examples, but we don't get into the idiosyncrasies of specific applications, such as level generation or dynamic puzzles. We leave those challenges to later chapters.

ASSEMBLY MECHANISMS AND GESTALT SPACES

A gestalt space is the set of all possible gestalts that can be assembled from a set of modules, by a given assembly mechanism. When designing modular systems, it's useful to think about the sizes and shapes of their gestalt spaces. In fact, we can restate the aim of the modular designer in terms of gestalt spaces: we want to craft modules and an assembly mechanism that yield a sufficiently large gestalt space with a high proportion of desirable gestalts.

There's no generic metric to assess gestalt desirability. We have to decide what a desirable gestalt looks like for each of our modular systems. For equipment in an RPG, it might look like a set of equipment with synergistic bonuses. Desirability is often graded on a spectrum, with ideal gestalts on one end and unworkable gestalts on the other. When a gestalt crosses a certain threshold of undesirability, we say it enters the *null zone* of our gestalt space. This is a useful concept that we'll revisit later.

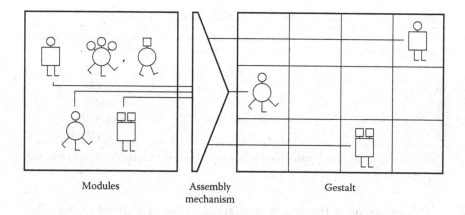

Modules   Assembly   Gestalt
                 mechanism

FIGURE 4.1   Monsters (modules) are chosen by the dungeon populator (assembly mechanism) to populate a dungeon room (gestalt).

Most assembly mechanisms produce gestalt spaces within a certain size class. Let's look at an example to illustrate this point. Say we're populating a dungeon room with three monsters from a set of five monster types. Each monster type can be chosen multiple times. Our population algorithm is simple: choose a monster at random from the set and add it to the room, and then do it again, and then again. For simplicity's sake, assume that the monsters' positions in the room don't matter. In this example, the monster types are the modules, the population algorithm is the assembly mechanism, and the dungeon room is the gestalt (Figure 4.1).

How many ways can the dungeon populator choose monsters to populate the room? The answer is $5 \times 5 \times 5 = 125$. Note that this is a different question than how many gestalts there are. That's because in this scenario, the order that the dungeon populator chooses monsters doesn't matter. Whether the algorithm picks an orc or a goblin first, we don't care, as long as they both end up in the room. A gestalt that cares about order is called a *permutation*, and one that doesn't care is called a *combination*.* Out of the 125 ways the assembly mechanism can populate the room, there are 35 distinct gestalts.†

Without getting into the nuances of the math, we can note how quickly the size of the gestalt space grows as we increase the number of monster types or the number of monsters we populate a room with. Table 4.1 shows some examples.

---

* Technically, since we're allowing each monster type to be chosen multiple times, it's *permutation with repetition* and *combination with repetition*.
† The number of r combinations of a set of size n with repetition allowed is $[(r + n - 1)!]/[r!(n - 1)!]$.

TABLE 4.1   Populating a Dungeon Room with Monsters Chosen at Random

Number of Monster Types to Choose From (Modules)	Number of Monsters Chosen (Assembly Mechanism)	Number of Possible Dungeon Room Populations (Gestalts)
5	3	35
10	3	220
25	3	2,925
25	5	118,755
25	10	131,128,140

Note: The size of the gestalt space grows very quickly when we increase the values of the parameters.

This explosion is the combinatorial magic we mentioned earlier. The precise numbers change as we vary our assembly mechanism, and variations are limitless. They include algorithms that, for example, care about the order modules are chosen, choose modules from a number of different sets, or weight the choice of future modules based on modules chosen previously. But in nearly all cases, even a modest number of modules yields a big gestalt space.

Now that we have a feel for the size of this gestalt space, let's examine how certain design decisions can affect swaths of the space. Our goal is to understand how interactions between our modules propagate through our gestalt space. In the dungeon room example, let's contrive two monsters: a fire imp and a water elemental. Whenever a fire imp spawns in the same room as a water elemental, its attack instantly annihilates the elemental. This is undesirable behavior, so let's say any dungeon room containing both a fire imp and a water elemental is undesirable.

As it turns out, 5 of our 35 dungeon rooms contain both monsters.* Therefore, our decision to include both the fire imp and water elemental among our monster types confines 5 of our 35 gestalts to the null zone. At this point, we have a few choices. We can live with this proportion, or we can add a constraint that ensures the two monsters don't spawn together, or we can revisit our monster design. Whatever we decide, the mathematical context we get from examining our gestalt space enables us to make better design decisions and work toward enabling play.

---

* Lettering the monsters *a*, *b*, *c*, *d*, and *e*, the following combinations comprise all the gestalts that include two arbitrarily chosen monsters, *a* and *b*: *aab*, *abb*, *abc*, *abd*, and *abe*.

ENABLING PLAY

What makes a set of modules and an assembly mechanism conducive to producing desirable gestalts? As mentioned earlier, our goal is to give our system as much play as possible. Again, by giving our system play, we mean enabling players to explore the greatest amount of the compelling space created by the rules of our system, within some thematic constraints. Let's examine three principles of modular design that work toward enabling play. We'll use examples from *Sproggiwood*, a roguelike game I designed and released in 2014 with Freehold Games, to illustrate the principles in practice.

Mechanics as Shared Substrates

If certain combinations of modules assemble into desirable gestalts, then it stands to reason that there's some definable relationship between modules that assemble desirably. Consider this straightforward example of such a relationship: two pieces of equipment that each grant some bonus when the other is worn. This design pattern occurs regularly in RPGs in the form of set pieces. From the assembly of these two modules, we get a desirable gestalt, in this case the equipment loadout and its corresponding set bonus. But this relationship tightly couples the two modules, and in doing so, it prevents either of them from assembling meaningfully with other modules. While we gain a desirable gestalt, we lose a big swath of our gestalt space to the null zone. For this reason, I contend that direct relationships like this one are detrimental to the goal of enabling play. Accordingly, I dislike the design of set pieces.

Instead, we can relate modules indirectly by using the language of our game's mechanics to define them. Each mechanic acts as a substrate for our modules to act in. For example, consider the following two pieces of equipment for an RPG. The first piece is a lance that deals bonus damage equal to your movement speed. The second piece is a pair of boots that increases your movement speed by 20%. We can see how the assembly of these two modules produces a desirable gestalt. But they aren't tightly coupled, and so we haven't confined other potential gestalts to the null zone. Each module can be combined with other modules that are defined in the language of the game's movement mechanics to produce more desirable gestalts. By avoiding the prescriptive design of set pieces, we give our players more options for meaningful combinations.

The key to this approach is choosing a suitable suite of mechanics to act as substrates. The more central a mechanic is to our gameplay, the more play we can enable by designing modules in the language of that

FIGURE 4.2   Typical dungeon layout in *Sproggiwood*.

mechanic. For *Sproggiwood*, turn-based movement is a central mechanic. Dungeons are laid out on a grid and populated procedurally with monsters (Figure 4.2). On each turn, the player can either move one tile in any of the four cardinal directions, attack an adjacent monster, use a power, or use an item. After the player acts, each monster acts.

Since movement is so crucial to *Sproggiwood*'s gameplay, we designed several traps and monsters whose powers constrain or coerce movement on the grid. For this system, the traps and monsters are the modules, the dungeon populator is the assembly mechanism, and dungeon rooms are the gestalts. A dungeon room that's tactically challenging is a desirable gestalt. Since so many of the modules are designed on top of the shared substrate of movement, the number of dungeon rooms that present novel tactical challenges is enormous. Figure 4.3 shows an example.

In this scenario, the player recently killed a black jelly monster, which left behind a puddle of jelly (1). Jelly puddles must be walked over within seven turns, or they spawn another jelly monster. The frog (2) uses its tongue to attack every few turns by pulling the nearest creature to a tile adjacent to the frog. Next to the player, the lily pad (3) provides an escape route; it teleports anything that steps on it to another lily pad in the dungeon.

Players have an interesting choice here. They can move toward the jelly puddle and risk getting pulled to the frog, or they can escape via the lily pad. Or, if they possess a power that also acts on the movement substrate—say, by letting them move multiple tiles in one turn—they can get to the jelly puddle immediately. By designing our modules in the language of grid movement, a

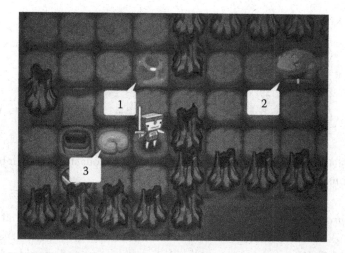

FIGURE 4.3 The dungeon populator (assembly mechanism) combined three traps and monsters (modules) into a tactically challenging dungeon room (gestalt).

core mechanic in *Sproggiwood*, we enabled the assembly of colorful gestalts like this one without nullifying a big swath of our gestalt space.

Orthogonality

In the context of a modular design and a set of game mechanics, orthogonality refers to the partitioning of the design into modules that don't overlap and whose gestalts span the space of gameplay prescribed by the mechanics. It's easy to see why that second part—spanning the space of gameplay—works to enable play. The first part is a little trickier, though, so let's examine it.

When the majority of the designs for two modules overlap, the gestalts that include either module have the potential to counterfeit each other, meaning they replicate each other's place in the gestalt space and effectively reduce the number of distinct, desirable gestalts. Let's revisit the example dungeon room with the black jelly puddle, frog, and lily pad. Remember that the jelly puddle spawns another jelly unless the player walks over it within seven turns. Imagine we had designed another type of jelly monster that leaves behind a similar puddle—say, a purple one that spawns two jellies unless walked over within nine turns. The example dungeon room and the dungeon room that includes the purple jelly puddle counterfeit each other. They present challenges that are virtually identical. Moreover, these designs compromise each other's thematic identity, muting the resonance each has with the player.

FIGURE 4.4   *Sproggiwood*'s assortment of jellies in various stages of their bounce animations.

In *Sproggiwood*, we designed six different jelly monsters that leave behind different puddles or otherwise affect the grid when they die (Figure 4.4). We tried to give each a distinct identity and considered how the gestalts they assembled into might counterfeit each other.

- Yellow jelly—leaves behind a puddle that causes walkers to slip one tile

- Blue jelly—leaves behind a puddle that causes walkers to slip one tile, and deals poison damage

- Red jelly—explodes in a cross pattern one turn after it dies and damages anything it hits

- Black jelly—leaves behind a puddle that causes walkers to slip, and must be walked over within seven turns or spawns another jelly

- Purple jelly—leaves behind a puddle that causes walkers to slip, and shoots a lightning bolt that triggers other purple puddles

- Ice jelly—explodes in a cross pattern one turn after it dies and freezes anything it hits

Note that we didn't achieve total orthogonality. The yellow jelly's puddle is subsumed by all the other puddles, and the red and ice jellies present very similar challenges. It's difficult to get all the way there, both because some overlap is inevitable when designing thematic monsters and because spanning the space of gameplay, or even articulating the whole space, can be challenging. However, it's useful to let orthogonality play a role in your design decisions.

Equivalence of Impact

An overshadowing module is one whose impact is so powerful that it distorts the gestalts it gets assembled into. Similar to how overlapping module designs can counterfeit gestalts, overshadowing modules can flatten the dimensionality of gestalts by compelling so much action that other modules can't compete. Think of the negligible effect other massive bodies on Earth have on the planet's gravitational pull. No matter what the bodies are or how they're positioned, they're dwarfed by Earth's monumental force.

It's unrealistic and undesirable to expect all our modules to converge to a single impact value, but it's a reasonable goal for *most* of our modules to fall within a certain impact range. We can adhere to this principle by designing modules with roughly equivalent impact values and by ensuring our assembly mechanism rarely combines modules whose impact values are wildly disparate. Note that it's not enough for the *average* impact values of our gestalts to be similar if the impact values of our modules are distributed unevenly. This is because an outlier module can render the gestalt undesirable even if the gestalt has a suitable average value.

For an example of an overshadowing module, let's look at how out-of-depth encounters work in *Sproggiwood*. The dungeon populator in *Sproggiwood* has a chance to produce an out-of-depth encounter, where a difficult monster from a later dungeon appears in an earlier one. These encounters add spice to the dungeon population mix, but they do so at the potential cost of overshadowing the other modules in their gestalts. The easiest way to illustrate this point is to imagine entering a dungeon room at one-fourth your total hit points and seeing an out-of-depth monster. No matter how interesting a tactical situation the other challenges in the room might present, the presence of the big baddie compels us to flee (Figure 4.5). This is a principle we understand from other spheres of design insight; an unbalanced encounter can be unfun. But it's useful to consider it in terms of the effect it has on our gestalt space.

In *Sproggiwood*, far out-of-depth encounters are rare. We engineered the dungeon populator to produce out-of-depth monsters at a clip that adds spice without compromising too much gameplay. Another option is to tweak your assembly mechanism to pair out-of-depth encounters with out-of-depth rewards. For example, a difficult monster might guard a powerful sword. This approach still runs the risk of flattening the

FIGURE 4.5 A yeti looms over the battlefield. No matter how interesting the rest of the encounter is, we're forced to flee.

dimensionality of the gestalt, but it also adds a new dimension that could be worth the compromise in the right situations.

PLOTTING DESIRABLE GESTALTS

Now we have some principles to guide us in the design of our modules. But how do we translate an initial gameplay idea into a modular design that yields the desired gameplay? After all, gameplay in modular, procedural systems is emergent. It's operating on the level of the gestalts, whereas we—as designers—are operating on the level of modules and assembly mechanisms. We stated previously that the gestalts are out of our direct reach, that we can't hope to articulate the whole gestalt space of our design. But we can envision individual gestalts that typify our ideal gameplay and use them to inspire our design. This powerful approach acts as a bridge between our vision and the parameters that enable it.

Look to envision gestalts across the spectrum of your rule systems, from common interactions to rare ones. Think about a story one of your players might excitedly tell their friends about how they took advantage of a rare confluence of events to narrowly escape a deadly situation. Now think about a more common occurrence, say, a particular strategy a savvy player might repeat over and over again for some minor benefit. Once we have a number of desirable gestalts, we can interpolate between them to develop modules and an appropriate assembly mechanism.

We used this approach to design the faction system for our roguelike/RPG *Caves of Qud*, released in Steam Early Access in 2015. *Caves of Qud* is set in the far future, long after an apocalypse of unknown origin, where mutations have uplifted certain animals to human-level intelligence and beyond. In our original design, players would find animals from several different species in the same zone. Most of the animals would act aggressively toward the player and ignore each other. We wanted to add interspecies conflict to give the world more thematic texture and dynamism. Specifically, I imagined a scenario where a player stumbles on a fight between a troop of baboons and a herd of goats, two groups that often inhabit the same zones in *Caves of Qud*. I also imagined that occasionally these groups would be fighting for a ridiculous reason; I wanted to match the tone of the game's frequent forays into the absurd (Figure 4.6). I thought, "What if a named baboon leader was hated by goats for some esoteric reason that no baboon or goat would normally care about? And what if that dispute triggered a battle?"

This imagined gestalt led to the design of a faction system where animal groups' behavior patterns get modified by the procedural histories of their faction leaders. When a faction leader is generated, they're given a small backstory with one to three procedurally chosen factions. That backstory determines whether the factions like or dislike the leader, which in turn governs an animal's behavior when it's generated in the same zone as the leader.

The system ultimately expanded on this idea and yielded many more interactions than I initially conceived. Animal factions find strange allies in each other, and players can share water with faction leaders to alter their reputations with the factions that like or dislike the leader. The exercise of plotting desirable gestalts gave me a kernel to design around and pushed the design into unexpected territory.

FIGURE 4.6 A baboon leader angers goatfolk with its radical ideas about mathematics.

INSERTING MEMORABLE ASYMMETRY

In closing, let's examine a pitfall inherent to the paradigm outlined in this chapter. The approach of neatly partitioning systems into modules that enable play is a powerful one. Designs that use mechanics as shared substrates and adhere to the principles of orthogonality and equivalence of impact tend to form elegant, symmetric systems. But games are more than elegant systems, and the beauty of the design shouldn't be privileged over the experience of the player. If we lose our way in the weeds of systemization, we can end up with a system that loses touch with its thematic inspirations. Make sure to leave room for thematic overrides that violate the principles of enabling play where appropriate. Asymmetry can disrupt the balance of elegantly designed systems, but in the right doses, it can do so in memorable and favorable ways.

We ran into this pitfall in the design for *Sproggiwood*'s weapons. I had decided early on that I wanted a concise suite of weapons for the player to find as loot. Each weapon would offer a different tactical tool and would act on the substrates of grid movement and monster health. I created three classes of weapons that implemented three nearly orthogonal ideas: freezing, flaming, and vampiric. Freezing weapons freeze enemies for a single turn. Flaming weapons deal bonus fire damage. Vampiric weapons drain monsters' life and give it to the player. Within each class, I designed a few tiers that elaborated on each theme by producing its effect in different shapes on the grid or dealing various amounts of damage. I intentionally decoupled the weapon classes from the six player classes so that any player class could find a freezing, flaming, or vampiric weapon.

From the perspective of enabling play, this precise systemization and decoupling was very effective. When a warrior equipped a freezing sword, the combination of the sword's attack and the warrior's powers produced a desirable gestalt. The same thing happened when a wizard equipped a freezing staff. Furthermore, the freezing warrior and freezing wizard gestalts played very differently and maintained distinct personalities. But in the roguelike genre, looted items—and weapons in particular—have a tradition of juicing up gameplay. Our overwrought systemization caused some of our players to note that our weapons felt "samey" and lifeless (Figure 4.7).

To fix this problem in our 2015 mobile release of *Sproggiwood*, we inserted a dash of asymmetry into our weapon design. In addition to the standard weapon classes, we created unique weapons that were coupled

FIGURE 4.7 Three identical weapons for three player classes. The repetition diluted the thematic impact of the weapons and made them feel boring.

to the player classes. For example, the farmer class got a grappling pitchfork that could be shot at walls to slide the player along the grid toward the wall. Even though we lost out on desirable gestalts by confining that effect to the farmer class, the benefit of an exciting, thematically resonant weapon made up for it.

Ultimately, your adherence to the principles of enabling play should be in service to your vision for your game. When the principles run afoul of that vision, don't be afraid to subvert them.

REFERENCE

1. Salen, K., and Zimmerman, E. 2004. *Rules of Play: Game Design Fundamentals.* Cambridge, MA: MIT Press.

CHAPTER 5

Ethical Procedural Generation

Dr. Michael Cook

Independent

THERE ARE A WHOLE bunch of different things to worry about when you make a procedural generator. Will my generator ever make a mistake? Does it produce a lot of boring things? How much time does it need to generate something? Sometimes, it can be so tricky to get your generator to work that simply getting it to produce anything feels like a huge accomplishment. Worrying about what it's producing, why it's producing it, or what others might think about it can get lost in the huge relief and satisfaction of finally seeing little dungeons, poems, or stories coming out of your computer.

As generative software grows in popularity, we're seeing its ideas used by more people in lots of novel ways, and for lots of exciting new uses. These developments are encouraging and inspiring, but it also makes it even more important that we take the time to think about the broader impact of this technology on people and society. In this chapter, we look at the ethical issues that can arise when making procedural generators, and give you some things to keep in mind when you're making your next generator. They won't all apply to every person and every project, and you may not agree with every single thing we suggest, but hopefully just reading through this chapter will give you a new perspective on procedural generation, and help you think about this awesome art form in a different way. Along the way, we're going to travel to some pretty extreme parts of the generative world, and pose some open-ended questions about what we should let generators do, how we should talk about them, and how we should let them talk about the world.

TALKING IN CODE

A procedural generator encodes a lot of different ideas and knowledge into a tiny package of rules and procedures. Each time we run it, those rules and procedures unpack bits and pieces of the knowledge we fed in, and reassemble them into something new. Some of the ideas we feed into our generator are technical, and a lot of this book is given over to the broad and complicated technical challenges that surround procedural generation. We've already seen some of this in earlier chapters about modular design and balancing chaos with predictability. Other ideas are aesthetic or artistic in nature. Procedural generators encode our ideas about how we think games should be designed: they represent what we think a good dungeon looks like, how a good story should end, or what makes a beautiful color scheme. They're little digital apprentices that we train and then trust to finish bits of our artwork in the homes of the people who view them.

Creating a procedural generator is a bit like making a work of art—some of the things we put on the canvas are intentional, but other things we paint on might be unconscious acts we don't give much thought to. Some might simply be mistakes. When we tweak the maximum size parameter of our dungeon generator, we most likely know the effects it will have on our level difficulty, or how long our game takes to play—that's an example of a conscious decision. But there are lots of ways in which we can introduce accidental features to our generators, sometimes without even thinking. The tricky thing about this is that it can be very difficult to realize this has happened, because generators are often quite complicated, and are designed to generate huge quantities of content. If there's something wrong in the system, it might be hard to tell without looking at thousands and thousands of examples.

Let's explore an example of a system that ends up with an unexpected feature in it. Suppose we're making an RPG level set in a spooky graveyard, and we want the player to be able to read randomized inscriptions on each tombstone. We decide to do this using a few simple patterns, so we write a few templates for gravestone patterns, like "#NAME lies here, died #YEAR." Our templating system knows that when it sees #YEAR, it replaces it with a random four-digit number, and when it sees #NAME, it generates a random name by sticking a first name and a last name together.

We give it a try and it works great—random names appear with random years attached. We're getting bored of the templates we've written, though, so we add one more, an inscription for couples buried together. It reads: "#NAME and #NAME, reunited in love once again, #YEAR." As a quick exercise, you can imagine a few possible outputs for this template in your head, or maybe write them down.

This template is a bit more interesting than the ones with only one name. Take a moment and imagine how we might implement the #NAME generator. You don't need to think about it in terms of code—imagine how you might do it with pen and paper. Depending on how we think about relationships, gender, and sexuality, our first instinct might be to write two lists of names: one list of names that sound like they might be associated with male identity, and another list of names that sound like they might be associated with female identity. Another approach is to simply have one big list of names and not worry too much about separating it out into a binary of any kind. You might not even think about this distinction—maybe you just used one list because it was quicker and you wanted to save time. But this decision, whatever you do, is going to have an impact on what this graveyard says about sexuality and gender in your game.

To see how, let's continue through our example. Suppose we use our two separated name generators for our new couples' template, and generate a gravestone or two. The individual examples will make sense. "Jack and Jane, reunited in love once again, 2016." They'll look fine, and you might even read a dozen or so while walking around. But "Jack and John" or "Jane and Lucy" will never appear—name pairings that might suggest nonheterosexual relationships. Because of the way we've structured the data in our generator, our graveyard is now presenting our game world in a way that implies that only heterosexual relationships exist.

Of course, this might be exactly what you want for your game! Perhaps you want to show the player that only heteronormative couples are afforded a proper burial in this town, and it becomes an important part of the plot. What matters here isn't the message sent by the generator (although for what it's worth, we highly recommend the single namelist approach). What matters is whether you as a creator realize what message your generator is broadcasting, because that means that you're in charge and able to assess whether that message is something you're happy with sending out into the world. Procedural generators can be powerful tools—they can amplify our ideas thousands of times for every single person who plays our games. But it's important to know what it's amplifying, and our little gravestone example is a case where we might be sending a message we didn't expect to.

How can we stop these undesired features from appearing in our generators, or find them when they appear? For this specific kind of problem, where the structure of our data or code is to blame, a good rule of thumb is to simply never introduce distinctions that don't mean anything in your game. If gender doesn't affect your player or your game mechanics, there's no reason to build it into the systems of your game. The more variables you introduce, the more likely there will be something you didn't plan for, so if something doesn't need to be defined in code, it's safer to simply sidestep it.

In general, though, there isn't a hard-and-fast rule from preventing these things from happening. Video games are big, complicated pieces of art and technology all mixed together, and part of the fun and excitement of making games is seeing things you didn't predict. The best thing you can do is always be thinking about what you make, always try to be critical of what you do, and be prepared to fix mistakes when they happen. Everyone working in procedural generation is learning something new every day, and no one should feel bad for not seeing something coming. Each surprise is another learning experience.

THE BIG WIDE WORLD

A lot of the time our generators don't need to know much about the real world in order to do their job. *Spelunky*'s level generator doesn't need to know anything about how caves are formed, who Indiana Jones is, or where a dog is most likely to hide if it gets stuck underground. All it needs is a big pile of level chunks, and the rules for how to stick them together to make levels.

Sometimes we want our generators to have a little bit more information and knowledge in them. Maybe we want our recipe generator to name itself after random places from the real world, or maybe we want to look up the symbolic meanings of colors for our flag generator. Whether it's knowledge we simply don't have ourselves, or it's faster and more flexible to do it automatically, procedural generators can easily be fed information from the Internet or other sources to make them more clever and more powerful.

One way of doing this is to use static databases of knowledge, like Wikipedia, for information. *Argument Champion*, a 2012 game about debating, used an online resource called ConceptNet to generate content for its game. ConceptNet is a database of facts and relationships designed for use by software, especially artificial intelligence (AI) programs. Some of its knowledge is input by hand, while others are automatically scraped from other sites and formatted for ease of use.

The results can seem fairly impressive, especially at first. Type in "cat," and ConceptNet can tell you that cats are capable of hunting mice, that they have four legs and whiskers, and that they like playing and drinking milk. These are represented as a pair of concepts linked by a relationship, so, for example, "cats" and "whiskers" are connected by the "has" relationship. *Argument Champion* uses these to connect topics together, allowing a debate to shift focus from schools to computers, from computers to keyboards, and from keyboards to pianos.

You might have noticed in that last connection that the sense of "keyboard" changed from something you type on to something you play music with. ConceptNet isn't perfect, and often conflates concepts (a janitor is a custodian; The Janitors are a noise rock band). If your game made these connections, the player might find them at worst a little confusing, but might actually find them entertaining. Unfortunately, that isn't all ConceptNet thinks. If you type "woman," one of the facts you retrieve is "women are sluts." *Argument Champion* might not come up with that connection, but the next game to use ConceptNet could well make that mistake, and most players probably won't find that quite as entertaining, to say the least.

In fact, they might even find it as offensive as if you'd said it yourself. As humans, we tend to respond to software being intelligent by expecting it to behave in increasingly intelligent ways. When we see a game making clever connections between computers and keyboards, or cats and milk, we often assume that the software understands the meaning of what it's doing, when in practice it likely does not. That means that when it does something wrong, we don't just see it as an accident—we treat it as if it was a genuine statement, and that the software knew what it was doing. This is a great reason why, as developers and designers, we need to think very carefully about the systems we build.

One approach that can solve some of these problems is using a ban list for language. Darius Kazemi, a well-known Twitterbot creator who has done a lot of work with generative software, maintains various ban lists designed to catch words that might lead to offense being caused. These lists are often designed to be additionally cautious, under the thought that it's better to accidentally filter out too much than to not filter out enough. One bad incident is generally all you need to ruin someone's day.

Ban lists are great if you're working with language because they work by filtering the output of your generator, which means they can catch mistakes in generators that you might not ever have predicted. The original *Elite*, released in 1984, had a name generator for star systems that would stick together small collections of letters to make long words. The developers spent some time tweaking this system to make sure it never generated anything rude—a ban list can help by checking the output of even the most random words and strings of letters. But they don't solve everything, and data from the outside world can be a real source of danger when building experimental procedural generators. To give you an idea of why, we're going to look at another game that, like *Argument Champion*, used online data. This game was called *A Rogue Dream*, and was originally made in 2013 for the 7-Day Roguelike jam (Figure 5.1).

The principle behind the game was quite simple—the player types a noun into the game at the beginning, and the game procedurally generates a theme for itself so that the main character of the game is the noun the player input. So, for instance, if the player types in "cat," then they control a little cat sprite, avoiding droplets of water, eating grass, searching for cardboard boxes, and using powers called "Scratch" and "Sleep."

The way the game did this was by using a technique called "Google milking," coined by researcher Tony Veale. Google milking works by reverse engineering the language of question—asking to get information about the world. When someone asks Google, "Why do doctors wear white coats?" a likely reason for them asking the question is that they believe it to be true. They're looking for a reason, but the fact that doctors wear

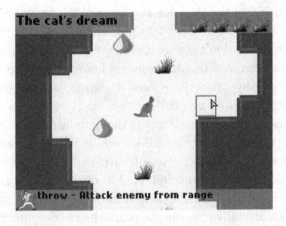

FIGURE 5.1 Screenshot of *A Rogue Dream* where the player is controlling a cat.

white coats is considered something true—we can extract the factual part out of the question and use it as knowledge about doctors.

The more people ask a question, the more people presumably believe the facts of the question to be true—but how do we know which questions are popular? Google autocomplete can tell us, because it's trained to give us the most popular search queries. So if we type "why do doctors" into Google, the search queries it suggests are the most common things people ask about doctors. Why do doctors wear white coats? Why do doctors say stat? Why do doctors prescribe steroids? Our game might not know the answer to these questions, but it can use these things to understand more about what a doctor is.

So if you type "why do cats hate …" into Google, you get "water" as an autocompletion; if you type "why do cats eat …," you get "grass," and so forth. Each of these specialized queries is used by the game to generate its enemies, pickups, goals, and ability names. *A Rogue Dream* is entertaining to play, because unlike many knowledge databases, like ConceptNet, Google is packed with popular culture, everyday observations, and slang. If you choose to be a ninja, you'll be fighting pirates. If you choose to be a musician, you'll be fighting music sensation Kenny G. If you choose to be a nihilist, your health packs are floating clouds of darkness.

But you might be sensing a problem here, and indeed, *A Rogue Dream* did not get very far in development before unfortunate things started happening. While a lot of the most generic, innocent queries produced fun game themes, others carried more weight. If you typed in "priest," as the player character, one of your abilities would be "abuse child." If you typed in "man," your enemies were women. If you typed in "Muslim," your abilities included "kill." People don't just type into Google things that they've directly observed—they type in stereotypes, rumors, misconceptions, hate speech, conspiracy theories, and worse. *A Rogue Dream*, unable to tell the difference between people who see cats eating grass and people who think French people are lazy, ends up collecting all this information and using it as fact.

It's difficult to throw away work, and it's hard to admit an idea is bad. *A Rogue Dream* was almost developed into a museum exhibit for children to interact with and learn about procedural generation. But after weeks of trying to filter the system, improve its understanding, limit its search capabilities, or change its purpose, it was abandoned. Now it's mostly used as an example of how procedural generators with the best of intentions can end up being harmful—which, as it turns out, is quite useful. Hopefully, it's also a great reminder of why it's important to think about the ramifications of the systems we build from an ethical standpoint.

YOU ARE WHAT YOU EAT

As an addendum to the previous section, we should also talk about another way that generators can find bad things out there in the world. Previously, we focused on real-world data that we might find and want to use in our game—live data like Google results, knowledge bases like ConceptNet—and the things we might want to be wary of when doing this. Just as dangerous is opening our generator up to real people and giving them some control over the content it creates.

Outside of games, Microsoft learned this lesson the hard way in 2016 when it released Tay, a Twitterbot that interacted with users and learned words and phrases from them. Tay had a lot in common with a procedural generator in a game: it created things for other people to look at and enjoy, from a catalog of data it could intelligently chop up and rearrange. But Microsoft wanted Tay to interact more closely with its users and to appear as intelligent as possible, so it allowed Tay to learn things from people who spoke to it. This had the unexpected (or perhaps completely expected, depending on your perspective) effect of turning Tay into a mimic for anything anyone told it, from hate speech to pure nonsense. Tay was shut down within hours of launching, and led to a lot of reflection from engineers and artists about how to create systems that learn from other people.

Tay might seem like it doesn't have too much for us to learn from, but a number of trends in game design and development are leading in the direction of more human involvement in the games that we play. Games like *Stellaris* have built-in mod tools that allow players to edit, upload, and share data lists for the in-game procedural generation, which means that the game's procedural generator is partly designed by someone who may not be thinking about the game and content generation in the same way that the game's designer was. Of course, in the case of modding, players are able to choose what they install and what they ignore. But other trends—like taking game input from the chat messages on streaming services such as Twitch—open up the game to unpredictable, hard-to-filter input from a large quantity of people. If anything, these inputs are likely to be even more problematic for a generative system than Tay's Twitter followers were.

Getting input from people can produce much more interesting and varied content; they can add a dose of human creativity into a rigid system, and they can help make a generator feel personalized and unique for a particular player. But we always run the risk of encountering the worst side of human creativity with this, and that can be something that is hard to recover from. Just because opening up our generators is potentially dangerous doesn't mean we shouldn't try to experiment and see what new systems and games we can build. But we need to be aware that these problems are out there, and do what we can to design our systems to limit these bad outcomes. One way we can experiment in this area while limiting the bad outcomes is to restrict the ways we take input into our generator. If our generator can be given strings of words, then instead of letting our users have totally free input, we can limit them to a set of a few hundred words to express themselves with. If our generator uses artwork, we can let our users snap shapes together instead of allowing them completely freeform drawing. People will always try to circumvent whatever systems you give them, but a few restrictions here or there will make life easier and your generator safer.

Before we close out this section, let's dwell a moment longer on Tay, because in many ways the story of Tay is a good explanation of why this chapter matters, and why it might have an impact on your game. One of the reasons why the response to Tay was so negative and so critical was that once a piece of software is given bad patterns of behavior, the people who see it repeat those patterns don't think about who taught them to it. They only focus on what the software is doing. If our generator starts producing offensive or other kinds of bad content, people won't blame Twitch chat—they'll blame our generator. It's a totally reasonable response, and something that should motivate us to do our best to be responsible in what we build, who we let it talk to, and where we let it do its work.

TALKING THE TALK

Most of this chapter was dedicated to all the things that can go wrong with our software. It can be taught bad things, it can find out bad things all on its own, it can spread ideas (both good and bad) far and wide. Of course, as the designer of that software we are responsible for what it does. But sometimes we're more directly responsible for the issues surrounding our procedural generators, and so before we move on from this chapter back into technical and aesthetic concerns, let's take a minute to think about how we talk about procedural generation with the wider world.

Promoting games—or anything else for that matter—is really hard. Even if money isn't involved, simply getting people to look at something you made is really difficult. A lot of advice is offered to developers about how to promote games in particular: advice about who you should talk to, what you should talk about, and how you should phrase it. Even if you've never read a thing about promotion, you'll probably have noticed common patterns in the way other people talk about their games or describe them in stores. It's important to summarize things, to focus on the most important points, to get across the essence of what it is that you've made, and to emphasize what makes your game special. What sets it apart? What makes it unique and worth talking about?

Procedural generation is still a powerful selling point for video games. Steam has a tag dedicated to it, and many curators recommend games solely for the presence of procedural generation in them, but games with generators have been popular for a very long time. "The heart of *Diablo* is the randomly created dungeon," states the very first page of the original *Diablo* design document, "providing a new gaming experience every time *Diablo* is played." Even though it can feel like so many games have procedural generation these days, people are still interested in it. So it's natural for it to come up when talking about games.

It's also very easy to get carried away when describing something amazing that you've created and are proud of. So when we talk to people about procedural generators, often we say things that express how excited we are, without thinking about what they really mean. Let's go back to that statement from the *Diablo* design document for a second: "a new gaming experience every time *Diablo* is played." What does that actually mean? Does it mean the game mechanics change? If you've played *Diablo*, you'll know that's definitely not the case—you're clicking on zombies and casting spells no matter what happens. Does it mean the levels change? Well, sort of. They look different and have different layouts. You couldn't memorize a level and run it twice, certainly. But you're always going to the same places—the same caves, the same villages. They are shaped differently but painted the same.

That might sound unfairly harsh on *Diablo*, because we know what they *really* mean by "a new gaming experience." It's a euphemism, like a lot of language about procedural generation is: "limitless gameplay," "infinite replayability," "endless variety." These are all phrases we see used to describe algorithms that are usually doing the computer equivalent of shuffling a deck of cards and dealing you a new hand. Over time, we've grown so used to these turns of phrase that we probably don't think much about the language any more—we instinctively know what the person speaking them means, so we don't think about how they sound to people who are less familiar with these ideas.

Relying on people to "know what we mean" when we talk about our work isn't a very good idea. People might learn over time, but all we're really doing is passing the problem on to a new community of people who will make the same mistakes. More importantly, as this book shows, new ideas are coming out of the procedural generation world every day. When we try to explain or sell these ideas to people, there will be hardly anyone who knows what you mean. You'll be deciding how people understand your work, and what expectations people have when they buy your game.

A good example of this is the idea of "uniqueness" in procedural generation. A lot of games try to count how many different dungeons or items their game has, and use it to illustrate how big their procedural generator is. The 2009 shooter *Borderlands* proudly stated the game's 17.5 million guns as a key part of its marketing campaign—it even managed to find its way into the *Guinness Book of World Records* with this award. But if we made a copy of a gun in the game and added one point to its damage, most people wouldn't consider the two very different except in the most legal, technical sense. Even if we kept adding damage points until it felt different, we'd probably end up in a situation a little bit like *Diablo*'s dungeons—they're distinct from one another, but not unique.

What's wrong here? We're not specifically lying; we're just being a little misleading or unclear with how we're talking about the game. It probably comes from a good place, from a feeling of excitement and positivity the developers have about their game. When we put a big number in front of someone, though, we're leaving it up to them to guess at what percentage of that number will be interesting, useful, fun, or relevant. If they're familiar with procedural generation in games and its limitations, they probably won't mind! But if they're less experienced, or perhaps you're offering something new, then there's more of an opportunity for misunderstanding.

That doesn't mean we can't be passionate and excited about our work, of course! It just means that we should think carefully about what we say and write about what we make. Sometimes it can be as simple as changing the kind of language you use. In *Spelunky*, the game tells you "the walls are shifting" as a new level is generated. It's a small and elegant phrase, but it tells you everything you need to know: the levels are being shuffled around; they aren't entirely new, but they're different to what you just saw. It doesn't promise too much, and it slots neatly into the game's theme.

Another approach is to think more carefully about what makes your procedural generator fun. In many ways, advertising millions of guns or billions of levels doesn't really make much sense—the average player will probably only see a few thousand. So what is it that makes our generator cool? What does it do that makes us smile or want to see more of what it produces? Maybe it actually produces a lot of rubbish, and maybe that rubbish is what makes the rare discoveries of something good so wonderful and exciting. Instead of avoiding these ideas, we can play into them and build our game to be more strongly based around these ideas of rarity and surprise.

Everyone will have their own idea of how to talk about their procedural generation, what kind of language they feel comfortable using, and what story they want to tell people about their game. Don't feel like you need to take everything we've discussed here at face value, but do bear some of these ideas in mind the next time you tell someone about a procedural generator.

THE FUTURE

One of the great things about working in procedural generation is how fresh and unexplored most of the field is. Although games have had procedural generation for many decades now, we've spent a lot of that time doing the same things over and over. We're getting really good at them now, but there are a lot of things that people have never even thought of yet, let alone actually attempted. This book will give you a lot of inspiring ideas to consider and experiments to try, and hopefully inspire some things that we've never seen before!

With that excitement of pioneering comes the responsibility of being the first people in a strange new land. It means we should tread a little more carefully in case something unexpected happens, and that we should be prepared to think in new ways and break old traditions if the situation demands it. It also means that the things that we do now, the problems we decide to solve, the issues we consider important—these become examples that are set for the people who come later. All the ethical topics in this chapter do matter, even if they seem trivial right now, because by valuing these issues, we make them valuable for the generations of procedural generation enthusiasts who will follow us.

Each reader will have a different response to this chapter, agreeing with some things, ignoring others. All that really matters is that you've thought about these things long enough to decide what they mean to you, and what you want to do in response. We hope you'll bear some of them in mind as you enjoy the inspiring chapters in the rest of this book, and as you build generators of your own in the future.

II

Procedural Content

THE MANY DOMAINS OF potential design expertise can be reflected in algorithms we use to build our games. Where one designer chooses to generate a mountain range, another experiments with generating a brush-stroke and a third interrogates the variables in generating a suitably challenging opponent. The skills of the designer and the artist can be applied across a stunning variety of procedural generators.

From *Rogue* to *Minecraft*, the most famous examples of "procedural games" apply generation to their explorable physical spaces. We therefore begin with procedural level design. From there, this section wanders the many ways that generation may be employed to create content, whether audio, visual, or abstract. Specific case studies, broader approaches, and modes of thinking are explored.

This section allows discovery of different methods of implementation, as well as a breadth of philosophies of what can define an "asset" in a procedurally generated game. Although no encyclopedia of game content can claim to be all-encompassing, the reader may find the best inspiration comes from cross-disciplinary study. The following chapters provide diverse examples serving to illuminate the vast field of possibility and spark the imagination.

CHAPTER 6

Level Design I

Case Study

Chris Chung
Independent

CATLATERAL DAMAGE IS A casual physics-based three-dimensional (3D) first-person shooter game where, instead of shooting, you make messes as an ordinary house cat. In it, you play as a cooped-up cat on a rampage and use your paws to knock as many of your owner's possessions onto the floor as possible. The game features a variety of levels within which to wreak havoc, including several different house types, a supermarket, a museum, and a mad scientist's laboratory. When you play the timed "Objective Mode," there is a set goal to complete (e.g., knock a total of 150 physics objects onto the floor) to progress to new levels, along with an optional secondary objective (e.g., knock 15 blue books onto the floor). All these levels and objectives are procedurally generated. You can also save the unique numerical value used to generate the level (its seed) to regenerate and replay it in the untimed, objective-free "Litterbox Mode."

Early in development, I had planned to build each level manually. After several months, it became apparent that, for a solo developer like myself, procedurally generating the levels would save time in the long run and would also allow for many more arrangements than I could possibly make by hand, thus increasing replayability. I had never built a procedural level generation system before and was still fairly new to game programming, so this system is pretty basic and has room for improvement. However, I am quite satisfied with how the system works and the results it produces.

OVERVIEW

What does a suitable level for *Catlateral Damage* look like? Since the game is a cartoony simulation of a realistic scenario (mischievous house cats making messes), the levels should be simplified versions of somewhat real-world interior locales. Each locale is a one-floor interior space divided into rooms that serve specific purposes. For example, a standard house should have a bedroom, bathroom, kitchen, and living room, and each room should contain certain objects that are appropriate for the room (Figure 6.1). Levels should have lots of different physics objects for the player cat to interact with in places where the player can reach. Therefore, furniture should be spread out around the rooms at tiered heights (so they act as platforms for the player) and covered with objects. An easy way to think about levels is that each one is a building divided into rooms that are filled with furniture with physics objects on top. Objectives should obviously be achievable within a reasonable amount of time for all generated levels, too.

Generating levels happens in three steps. First, a big rectangular area is cut up into smaller rectangles for rooms with open doors between them. Then, each room has appropriate furniture placed within it according to the type of room (e.g., the refrigerator is only placed in the kitchen). Finally, the physics objects that the player will interact with are placed on top of the furniture. Once the level generation is complete, the level's objective and time limit is generated based on the makeup of physics objects that were placed. When everything is ready, the player is placed in one of the rooms and can start making a mess!

FIGURE 6.1   Standard bedroom from the first level of the game.

THE RULES

The rules of the procedural level generation system were designed around the core mechanics of the game (enhanced, cat-like, first-person shooter movement mechanics and knocking around physics objects) and what ideal locations for a destructive cat would be. A couple of limitations were decided on early on: levels will only be interior spaces (buildings), and each one will be a single floor. Constraining levels to interior spaces simplified the level creation process and made levels feel nicely contained. Outside gameplay was not the intended direction for this game; indoor spaces seemed like they would be more fun. There are also the additional considerations of what the boundaries of an exterior space would look like, how to limit it without making it feel too constrained, and if there would actually be enough objects to knock down. Focusing on a single floor was entirely to keep level creation simple, specifically to not have to handle generating additional floors and the placement of stairs.

With the building limitations decided, the rooms that fill the building were considered next. There should be at least one room in a building, they should take up space based on their intended function, they should be able to limit how many doors are connected to them, and each one should know what furniture is allowed inside of it. For the sake of simplicity, only functional rooms (e.g., bedrooms, kitchens, and bathrooms) are put in buildings; spaces like entryways, hallways, and closets are not included due to their specific placement requirements and typically small sizes. The room rules all exist to make the level feel more believable rather than completely random. Being able to specify how much space each room should take up allows the system to create more suitable rooms; living rooms, kitchens, and dining rooms should be fairly large, while bathrooms should be quite small. Limiting the number of doors connected to a room restricts private rooms (bathrooms and bedrooms) to only one door while allowing public rooms (living rooms and kitchens) to have multiple. The list of furniture allowed in each room is vital for conveying the purpose of each room to the players while they are playing in the level.

While the building and room rules exist mostly for aesthetic reasons, furniture rules exist primarily for gameplay reasons. Furniture should be placed in a visually interesting way, but the main concern is to not hinder the players' movement or block their completion of the objective. Typically, a real room layout addresses both of these since furniture is usually spread out around the room and does not block other functional aspects of the room or other furniture (e.g., room doorways and wardrobe doors). The procedural furniture rules try to follow these standard real-world rules. Furniture objects should be placed either along the room's walls or somewhere in the middle of the room, furniture should be distributed within the room in such a way to not block doorways or other furniture, and there should be plenty of floor space visible so the player has room to knock physics objects onto it (i.e., rooms shouldn't be crammed with furniture). In addition to these rules, there are also self-imposed guidelines when creating the 3D models for furniture objects to ensure that they are at appropriate heights that the player can reach when jumping to and from them.

Just like how each room should have a list of furniture that can be placed within it, each piece of furniture should know what physics objects can be placed on top of it. While some objects, like books, can be placed in multiple places, certain others should only be placed on certain furniture, like pillows on a bed. Other information, like where on the furniture objects should be placed, the probability of each object appearing, and whether the objects should be rotated, is included with these rules. The rotation rule is very basic; it just specifies if a physics object should maintain the same rotation as the furniture (so objects like the TV face away from the wall) or should be given a random rotation to provide some visual variety.

The level's objective also has some rules. Of course, each level's objective should be attainable so the player can progress to new levels. The secondary objective, which requires a specific type of object to be knocked down, should only use physics objects that are present in the current level. The time limit should be enough for players to complete the objective, but not so long as to make the game too easy.

HOW IT WORKS

The rules of the procedural generation system are made up of several pieces of hard-coded data. The game takes this data, adds some randomness, builds a two-dimensional (2D) floor plan (Figure 6.2), and creates the 3D space. There is one data file for each level type that specifies how large the level is, what rooms are in the level, what textures to use for the walls, floor, and ceiling, and more. The generation code uses a squarified treemaps algorithm to take the big rectangle space and divide it up into smaller rectangular spaces (as close to squares as possible) with the values specified in the level's data file.

Each room in each level also has an associated data file. These files contain the list of furniture that can be placed within the room, with some information, like the maximum number of each type of furniture to be placed, the probability of the furniture being chosen, if the furniture

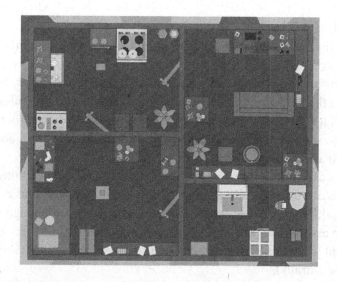

FIGURE 6.2 Top-down view of a level.

should be placed along a wall, and if the player will spawn there at the beginning. The furniture objects themselves consist of a model, physics colliders, an invisible rectangular bounding box (to prevent overlapping with or being placed too close to other furniture), and some rectangular surface area objects where physics objects can be placed.

In order for the system to know what physics objects to place, there is a script attached to the surface objects on each piece of furniture that contains the list of physics objects allowed on it, along with corresponding probabilities and rotation information. These surface objects are just rectangles on different areas of the furniture (e.g., the shelves on a bookcase) within which physics objects are placed based on the information included in the script. The generation code uses a rectangle packing algorithm to place the rectangular boundaries objects within the surface areas.

Once all physics objects are placed, the procedural system records and tallies all the physics objects in a dictionary and decides what the primary objective, secondary objective, and a bonus object that is worth more points will be. These are always a percentage of the total number of the objects in the level so the objectives are all attainable. The time limit for the level is simply calculated by multiplying the primary objective by a time estimate of how long each object takes an average player to knock down. Through testing, it was found that it took about 1.4 seconds for players to knock over 1 object on average, so an objective of 150 objects is given a time limit of 210 seconds, or 3 minutes, 30 seconds.

CONCLUSION

Overall, the procedural level generation system built for *Catlateral Damage* creates varied levels that both look natural and are enjoyable by players of all skill levels. The system not only creates desirable outcomes, but also has some flexibility for creating handmade content within the ruleset. For example, it's possible to group related furniture (e.g., a dining room table with chairs) or an arrangement of physics objects (e.g., a row of books) to be placed all at once.

Feedback from players indicates that most people don't notice that the levels are procedurally generated. This could be both good and bad, because although the system creates levels that are good enough for the player to assume they are handmade, they may also assume there is a lack of content (nine static levels rather than nine types of levels that are generated procedurally).

The system also isn't perfect. There are rare instances where furniture placement in some rooms is off, like when washers and dryers and the sink block the toilet in small, thin bathrooms. Minor polish items, like adding a permanently closed front door, and bigger functions, like multiple floors, would have been nice to have given more time and/or programming experience. Even so, this system works great for a silly and casual game like *Catlateral Damage*!

CHAPTER 7

Level Design II

Handcrafted Integration

Jim Shepard
Independent

B OLSTERING A PROCEDURALLY GENERATED play environment with handcrafted content can add variety and depth to your players' experience while at the same time guiding them to play and explore in a method that uses the best parts of your game system.

In *Dungeonmans*, I used this technique to create multiple different and varied adventure zones, such as graveyards, fallen castles, crypts, friendly towns, mighty towers, and the good old-fashioned dungeon. Here are a pair of examples that explain how I built these areas, and the goal behind the design.

STANDARD DUNGEONS

Goal: Expand standard "room and hallway" gameplay to include areas that make the best use of *Dungeonmans'* position and motion-based player powers and help the game's dynamic enemies shine.

Room data: The data is stored simply as text files, with ASCII characters representing tiles one to one (Figure 7.1). While the blocks of data are $x \times y$ bound rectangles, the actual room data may contain an irregular shape. This is important, as the process of placing and layering the rooms is much more interesting with nonrectangular shapes.

```
9,9,           12,10,          12,7,            First line: width and height of room
...W.W...      ...XXXXXX...    ...W...W....     x : Unused Space to help room shapes fit closely
..WW.WW..      ...XXXXXX...    ...d...W....     together.
.........      ...XXXXXX...    WWWW...W....     w : Wall Tile blocking wall tiles
....W....      ...XXXXXX...    ...wdWWWWdWW     . : Empty Tile open space to fill with loot and
..W.W.W..      .W.........W.   ......d.....     monsters.
....W....      .W.........W.   WWWWWWW.....     d : Door Tile an internal door
....W....      ...WWWWWW...    .......d.....
.WWWWWWW.      .....WW.....
.........      ...WWWWWW...
               ...XXXXXX...
```

FIGURE 7.1 How ASCII can be used to define playable worldspace.

Two things to note are

1. External room walls are not included, as the game adds those as part of the area gen code.

2. Data does not include enemy spawns or treasure locations. I didn't feel those were necessary for the game since the area gen code does a pretty good job of packing the rooms, and I didn't want treasure locations to feel stale. The standard dungeon is the bread-and-butter adventure area, and these locations would be seen often, so treasure locations shouldn't be static.

Standard dungeon area gen: The area gen code builds out a dungeon using a time-tested algorithm that extends new dungeon content from existing areas. This is an iterative loop that continues until you reach a desired room count or simply run out of dungeon space.

Starting environment: Define the size of your playfield, and define each tile as *unused space*. This is not the same as an empty floor tile; this is a block of undefined protodungeon, a blank slate ready for expansion.

Then, place down a starting room somewhere in that playfield. Generally, this room includes the stairs back up, unless you're feeling cruel. With a single room full of walls and floor tiles, you're ready to begin.

1. Take all existing wall tiles that

   • Have two neighboring walls along the same axis

   • Are exposed to unused space

   and make them into *candidates*. Take all these and throw them into a bag so you can pull them out at random, like delicious jelly beans.

2. Select a candidate from the bag, and decide if you want to add a room or a hallway. We'll build a room here. Select a random room

from the list of handcrafted areas, and then place the room against the candidate along any given alignment.

3a. If the room fits, excellent. Add a door at the candidate's old position, and recalculate your new candidates given the new shape of the dungeon.

3b. If it does *not* fit, that's ok. Don't place anything; just go back to Step 1 with your existing collection of candidates and rooms. It is possible to dynamically carve up rooms to fit, but there are two drawbacks. The first is that you naturally end up with more simple rectangular areas, and the second is that you lose whatever design value went into building the rooms in the first place.

4. Once you've placed a room, convert any unused space tile that is adjacent to a floor tile into a wall (Figure 7.2).

Take note of the second room fitting into the empty space around the first. Even though the data is stored in a rectangular format, building

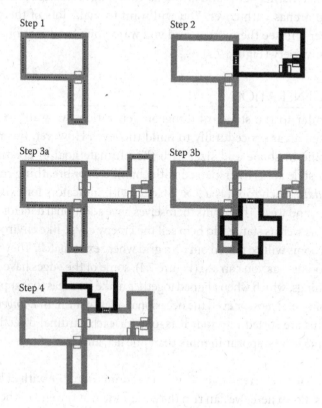

FIGURE 7.2   Potential generated floor map.

empty space into the data allows us to fit together rooms in a more interesting fashion.

Once this is done, you can optionally go back and spice up the environment a bit, such as

- Find walls that are between two rooms that don't have doors nearby, and add one. This creates the possibility of circular routes, which are excellent at reducing backtracking.

- Find doors along long empty walls and add a second (or third) door adjacent, to create a wider opening and prevent easy funneling of enemies into narrow areas.

- Secret doors! A staple.

The handcrafted rooms for standard dungeons exist to provide shapes that are fun places to fight in. A mixture of large areas and small, twisting paths and grand hallways, tight clusters of rooms and open arenas with cover. You will want to make lots of them, as the player will see them often, and you want your combinations to have great variety (Figure 7.3).

CRYPT GENERATION

Goal: Similar to the standard dungeon generation, we want to arrange handcrafted areas procedurally to build the level. However, the areas are very specific in shape and size, with the ultimate goal of creating tight catacomb-style areas interspersed with chambers for breathing room.

Room data: Each room is a 7×7 block, with indicators for exits: north, east, south, and west. The rooms themselves have additional data for treasure locations, as well as statues, to help sell the creepy crypt-like environment.

These rooms will be placed out on a grid where exits match. They won't all be solid rooms—as you can see (Figure 7.4), some of the edges have multiple loose openings, which when aligned together make for areas that appear to be larger rooms, endcaps, or even the occasional open atrium. In *Dungeonmans*, these rooms are sorted into four lists, one for each cardinal direction. This means some rooms appear in more than one list, and that's fine.

Step 1: Place a starter room. This is a random room tile with at least two exits. From here, we can run the code shown at the end of the chapter until we're satisfied (or dissatisfied!) with the results.

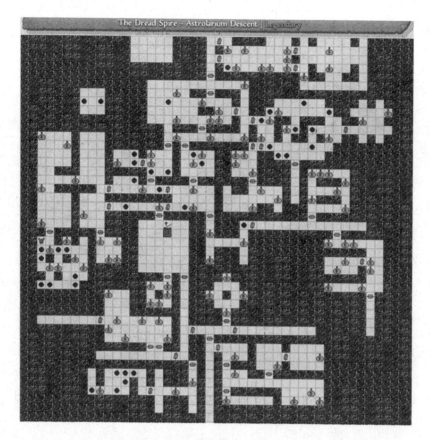

FIGURE 7.3   Screenshot of a generated map from *Dungeonmans*.

```
0100      1111      1011      1000
######    ###.###   ##..###   ###.###
######    #.....#   ...####   #.....#   #: Wall tile
###?...   #.#.#.#   ##.####   #C#.#C#   .: Empty tile
###?.#.   .......   ...####   ###.###   C: Coffin usable object
###?...   #.#.#.#   ##.####   #.....#   S: Statue art object
######    #.....#   ...####   #..?..#   P: Mysterious pool!
######    ###.###   ##..###   #######   ?: Random object from list
```

FIGURE 7.4   ASCII examples of crypt room designs.

Step 2: Pick a room placed in the level that has an open exit. Note the direction of that exit (i.e., north) and then draw from a list that has available exists in the south.

Step 3: Place that new room perfectly adjacent to the first. Recalculate rooms that have exits, and return to Step 2.

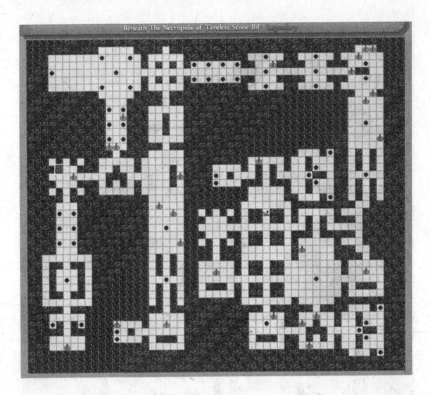

FIGURE 7.5   Screenshot of a generated *Dungeonmans* map, with crypts integrated.

Step 4: Once you have no rooms with available exits, you can evaluate the dungeon and see if you like the layout. For example, in *Dungeonmans* a crypt is invalid if it doesn't contain enough total room placements. In this case, it's tossed out and we start over from Step 1.

Crypt areas feel markedly different from standard dungeons, and this feeling is complemented by both the art in the crypt and the enemy styles: hordes that pressure down a hallway, and lots of ice enemies with controlling powers (Figures 7.5 and 7.6).

BEST PRACTICES

Here are some pertinent points gleaned over the development process of *Dungeonmans*.

Keep the data simple: Fast iteration was super important for these areas, as was the ability to create a multitude of them quickly. Simple text files managed in a simple text editor, loaded with a simple process.

FIGURE 7.6   Screenshot of a hero in a crypt area.

Dungeonmans is a tile-based game, and text files fit perfectly. Use the simplest possible data format for your project.

Keep the data lean and purposeful: Don't feel obliged to fill out every detail of your handcrafted areas, especially if they are being used as randomized pieces of area generation. Rely on your procedural systems to populate them with creatures, treasures, and traps. Too many specifics in your encounters will allow players to recognize every threat in an area upon entry, which is probably not desirable. If you do place specifics, make sure you're doing it for the right reasons.

Don't write an editor: Stopping your development flow to build a new editor by hand is the surest way to get lost in the weeds. Text files are easy to manipulate, and you can do so in Notepad, which may be nature's perfect fruit. If your game requires more complexity, first double-check that it actually does, and if so, look into one of the many already existing tools for data manipulation that are quick, clean, and well tested. Don't pour time and energy into a complicated system that will cause more frustration than it is worth.

DUNGEONMANS DUNGEON GENERATION PSEUDOCODE

```
{
    DetermineDungeonWidthAndHeight();
    PlaceStarterRoom();
    RoomCount = 0;
    GoalCount = 20;
    NumberTries = 0;
```

```
While(RoomCount < GoalCount && NumberTries < 1000)
{
        NumberTries++;

        //every wall tile with two adjacent wall tiles on
the same axis
        //and one side exposed to unused space
        RecalculateCandidates();

        Candidate c = GetRandomCandidateFromJellybeanBag();
        TestRoom room = GetCopyOfRandomRoomFromData();

        //don't actually place the room here, just
position it
        //and check for overlap with the existing rooms
        if( !TryPlaceRoomAdjacentToCandidateInOpenSpace(c,r
oom, out location) )
        {
                //oops we didn't succeed
                //delete the room if you aren't in a GC
language ^^
                continue;
        }

        ActuallyPlaceRoom(room, location);
        RoomCount++;

}
//now you can fiddle with the layout by introducing doors
//laying out traps and secrets too!
//then fill it with monsters
}
```

DUNGEONMANS CRYPT GENERATION PSEUDOCODE

```
{
    //During loadtime sort the room data into four lists
based on N, E, S and W exits.

    DetermineDungeonWidthAndHeight();

    //Pick a room with multiple exit directions for best
results.
    PlaceStarterRoom();

    RoomCount = 0;
```

```
    GoalCount = 40;
    NumberTries = 0;

    While(NumberTries < 1000 && HasExits)
    {
            NumberTries++;

            //A room placed in the level with an unmatched exit
            Room sourceRoom = GetRoomWithUnusedExits();
            if( sourceRoom == null )
            {
                    HasExits = false;
                    Continue;
            }
            Room nextRoom = GetRoomMatchingExit(sourceRoom, out
location);

            //Make sure your new room doesn't step outside the
bounds of the level
            //or any other consideration
            if( !CheckBounds(nextRoom))
            {
                    Continue;
            }

            PlaceRoom(nextRoom, location);
            RoomCount++;
    }

    //If we didn't make enough rooms, start over
    if( RoomCount < GoalCount )
    {
            Cleanup();
            Return E_DungeonInvalidTryAgain;
    }
    //Salt dungeon to taste
}
```

CHAPTER 8

Level Design III

Architecture and Destruction

Evan Hahn

Snowed In Studios

WINDFORGE IS A TWO-DIMENSIONAL (2D) action building block RPG, set in a floating island dieselpunk world (Figure 8.1). There is a huge emphasis on the player's freedom to explore and create within the game. Nearly everything in the world is destructible, and players are able to build new structures anywhere they choose. Functional flying airships can also be created, which typically serve as the primary way players will explore the world over long distances.

The world is almost entirely composed of blocks. These give substance to the world geometry, so that meaningful interiors can be revealed to the player as it is destroyed. These blocks can also be used as materials by players to build and craft things.

There are a lot of pros and cons to consider when it comes to deciding to put procedural content creation in your game, but this wasn't a difficult choice for *Windforge*. It wouldn't be practical to make a game like this without a least some amount of procedural content creation to make the world. It would be too time-consuming and tedious to get someone to build a world of any notable size by hand.

A significant portion of the world in *Windforge* is generated procedurally. In top-down order, these are the major aspects of the world that are procedural:

- Area definition and landmark placement
- Playable world areas

FIGURE 8.1   Screenshot from *Windforge*.

- Architecture

- Object placement

- Enemy placement and spawning

This chapter focuses on the architecture generation techniques we used in *Windforge*. These techniques were used to generate the explorable temples, dungeons, mines, and abandoned buildings that can be found in the world.

ARCHITECTURE GENERATION

We used a divide and conquer approach to generate our architecture. A complete building or dungeon will typically be complex as a whole, but fairly simple when decomposed into small individual sections.

The approach starts by determining the bounding area of the structure, which will then be divided into smaller regions using a recursive process. These regions provide a starting point where an algorithm can decide the high-level layout of the individual rooms and how they should be connected. Finally, the individual blocks and objects that will produce the end result will be placed using a number of techniques.

In total, there are seven main steps to this process:

1. Calculate the bounding box.

2. Split the box into regions.

3. Skim perimeter regions.

4. Place connections.

5. Assign region types.

6. Make adjustments.

7. Generate the regions.

Step 1: Calculate the Bounding Box

The bounding box defines where the architecture should be placed, and what its maximum dimensions should be (Figure 8.2). Most of the time, we wanted our architecture to be at least partially overlapping one of the floating islands in a world area. Our first step to figure this out was to choose one of these islands.

The selection process was based on what we wished to generate, but for essential landmarks, we typically chose the largest island in the given area.

Once the island was chosen, we generated a random bounding box based on the size of this island. Depending on the type of architecture we wanted to generate, we set up parameters to constrain the size and aspect ratio of the box. We also had parameters to control the placement and amount of overlap that should be used in relation to the island.

Step 2: Split the Box into Regions

We used axis-aligned binary splits to divide the space defined by the bounding box into smaller regions (Figure 8.3). This was a recursive process. Each time a region was divided, two smaller regions would be produced, which would be further divided as needed. We typically stopped dividing regions when one of their dimensions became too small.

FIGURE 8.2   Bounding box of a small dungeon.

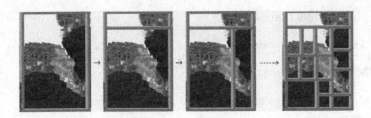

FIGURE 8.3 Recursive splitting at depths 0, 1, and 2, and the final result.

Occasionally, we would also stop dividing early in order to get a bit more variety and larger regions.

The approach used to choose the splitting axis will affect the result. Some simple approaches to dividing the region include:

- *Split along a random axis*: Generates the most variety, but it is the most unpredictable and sometimes produces undesirable results.

- *Always split the shorter axis*: Generates long narrow regions. This provides boring results if used alone, but it works well with hybrid solutions to provide more variety in region shapes.

- *Always split the longer axis*: The regions generated with this approach tend to be similar in size with somewhat square aspect ratios.

In *Windforge*, we created a hybrid of the approaches above using weighted random selection. We also introduced a chance of terminating the splitting process early in order to generate larger than normal regions (Figure 8.4).

Another important part of this step is maintaining the connection information between the regions with each split. This will be explained in more detail in Step 4.

Step 3: Skim Perimeter Regions

It would be a little boring if every structure found in *Windforge* were a perfect rectangle. We were able to achieve a variety of shapes by removing perimeter regions. Different results can be achieved by changing how these regions are removed.

For dungeons embedded into islands, we typically removed a random percentage of the regions along the perimeter of the bounding box (Figure 8.5).

To produce more building-like formations, we used an iterative process of removing regions from the top (Figure 8.6).

Finally, we were able to produce formations resembling mines and mazes by traversing over the region connections in a way that avoided

FIGURE 8.4   Hybrid splitting approach using weighted random selection and early termination.

FIGURE 8.5   Example of skimming regions from the perimeter before later generation steps.

FIGURE 8.6   Final result of a building generated using top-down region removal.

adjacent visited regions if possible, and then removed the regions that weren't visited (Figure 8.7).

The process of removing regions in this step can occasionally cause regions to float and become disjointed. These disjointed regions will be detected and removed when we process the region connections in Step 4.

Step 4: Place Connections

This step is responsible for connecting the regions we created in Step 2. To enable this process, we tracked and maintained all the possible connecting edges that regions shared after a split. This produced a graph where each region was a node that could be connected to zero or more other nodes (Figure 8.8). Each connection also carried information about its bounding region to make block and door generation easier later on (Figure 8.9).

This graph provided a straightforward way to ensure that players would be able to visit every region we generated without needing to break through walls. To place the connections, we did a random traversal over

FIGURE 8.7   Final result of a generated mine shaft using traversal-based region removal.

FIGURE 8.8   Visualization of the region nodes and their connecting edges.

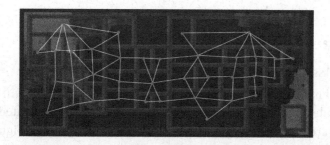

FIGURE 8.9   Graph formed using the region nodes and their connecting edges.

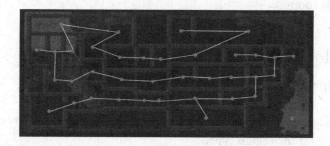

FIGURE 8.10   Region graph formed after random traversal. The traversal in this example was biased to favor horizontal movement.

the region graph, and assigned a weighted random connection type over each edge that was traversed (Figure 8.10).

This traversal can be configured to achieve different results. For instance, by changing the probability of choosing vertical versus horizontal connections, we were able to control the predominant axis a player would be traveling on to get through the structure.

After the traversal is complete, it will be possible to detect any disconnected regions that may have been produced by the region removal in Step 3. Any region that was not visited by the connection traversal will not be connected, and can be safely removed during this step if desired.

The connection types that are assigned will guide the generation process in Step 7. Some of the types we used in *Windforge* include

- Regular door
- Small opening
- Empty connection
- Trap door

- Boss door

- Treasure door

Step 5: Assign Region Types

This step is responsible for assigning each region a type that will specify the intended purpose of the region and how it should be generated.

These are some of the region types we assigned in *Windforge* (Figure 8.11)

- Treasure room

- Boss room

- Entrance room

- Hub region

- Trap region

We assigned these types in order of importance using a variety of rules, depending on the region type.

Example rules used to place types are

- Place the boss treasure room in a terminal region at a distance from the entrance.

- Place the boss room near the treasure room, so that you must travel through it to get to the treasure.

- Assign trap rooms to terminal regions with ceiling connections.

- Assign treasure and storage rooms to other terminal regions.

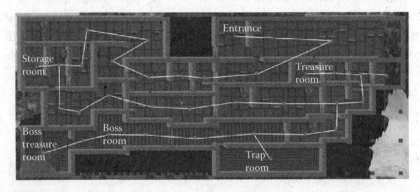

FIGURE 8.11   Region assignments.

Step 6: Make Adjustments

At this point, the high-level features of the architecture will be roughly in place. Further improvements can also be made by iterating over the region graph and making adjustments.

One of the most important adjustments we made here was to change the connection types to better match the connecting regions. Prior to this step, the connection types were chosen randomly. This was acceptable in many cases, but there were a few cases where we needed more control over how neighboring regions were connected.

Example connection adjustments made in *Windforge* are

- Use empty connections between adjacent boss rooms.

- Use trap doors for the connections with trap regions.

- Use treasure doors for the connections with treasure regions.

Step 7: Generate the Regions

In this step, we use the connection and region information produced by the previous steps, and generate blocks and objects for them. This is the first step that will produce results in the world that players will be able to see.

This step has two main responsibilities:

1. Generate the walls and connections between the regions.

2. Generate the contents of each region.

Generating the region contents is the most involved part of this process. This part is responsible for the background pattern generation, object placement, and platform placement. We managed the complexity of generating all this by further dividing the region into subregions (Figure 8.12).

This subdivision approach is similar to the region splitting covered in Step 2. This time around, the subdivision was more flexible and open-ended. We had a number of subregion types. Some of these types would divide themselves into other types, which could also be divided. We also had types that produced custom procedural patterns or structures, such as background decorations and stairs.

In addition to pattern generation, we used these subregions to guide platform and object placement. This worked well to ensure that the platforms and objects matched their background decorations, and it helped to

FIGURE 8.12 Final result of a region divided into subregions (left) and the same region with outlined subregions (right).

make the placement patterns more regular. Finally, as long as the selected objects were small enough to fit the dimensions of a subregion, we were able to guarantee that our objects would not be overlapping each other.

DISCUSSION

The techniques presented here were designed to seamlessly generate architecture in a larger procedural world. Many aspects of the game design guided the development priority of these techniques.

For example, *Windforge* is a very open-ended game where the player has the ability to easily create and destroy structures, as well as a variety of ways to traverse difficult terrain (e.g., by using grappling hooks and flyable airships). With this in mind, we put less emphasis on puzzle generation and platform placement than would likely be required in other games. Instead, our priority was to provide interesting places to explore with enough variety for a large open world.

The design of this approach made it relatively easy to extend and add new generation techniques as needed to create landmarks that feel unique and distinct from each other. We were also able to generate a variety of structure types just by changing the approaches used for certain steps. For example, changing how regions were removed in Step 3 allowed us to generate results suitable for dungeons, mines, small towns, and more.

Most of the architecture was generated on the fly each time a new area was visited. However, there were a few areas where it was more cost-effective to manually change the result. We did this with the major towns of the world and a few areas that required complicated quest-specific setup. These areas were created by using the usual generation techniques, and modifying them as needed.

CHAPTER 9

Cyclic Generation

Dr. Joris Dormans

Ludomotion

THERE ARE MANY DIFFERENT ways of generating dungeons for rogue-like games. The most popular method seems to be "drilling out" the dungeon from an arbitrary starting point. In this way, tunnels, corridors, and rooms are added to the expanding level. The big advantage of this method is that all areas are guaranteed to be accessible from the entry point. The big disadvantage, however, is that the structure of the generated dungeon essentially is a branching tree: it will have many dead ends and force the player to track back frequently.

A good example of this type of level generation can be found in *Brogue*. In an interview on Rock, Paper, Shotgun, *Brogue* developer Brian Walker explains that his way of getting around the branching problem is to ran-domly add doors between rooms in different branches of the tree.* This strategy seems effective enough; the quality of *Brogue*'s level generator is testimony to that. Yet, in this chapter I discuss a different approach I developed while working on *Unexplored*. This approach does not generate trees, but incorporates cycles from the get-go, allowing the generator to incorporate more sophisticated level design patterns.

Unexplored is a traditional roguelike in the sense that you traverse the Dungeon of Doom trying to retrieve the Amulet of Yendor and escape the dungeon with it. The main difference between *Unexplored* and games like *Rogue*, *NetHack*, or *Brogue* is that it is real time. The gameplay is mod-eled on top-down *Zelda* games, including real-time melee combat and lock-and-key puzzles. This difference in gameplay also means there are

* https://www.rockpapershotgun.com/2015/07/28/how-do-roguelikes-generate-levels/

different constraints on the levels generated for *Unexplored*. Levels tend to be smaller and more focused on a couple of themes (such as the presence of lava, water, or teleporters), and make more use of lock-and-key puzzles.

An example of one such level can be found in Figure 9.1. It illustrates how a combination of just a couple of design patterns can create a level that feels consistent and creates an exploration challenge beyond a series of individual monsters and hazards. In this case, the patterns are a larger lock-and-key cycle, with a large chasm in the middle, with an embedded gambit pattern. These patterns are discussed in more detail in the "Patterns" section.

CYCLES

The idea of using cycles for level generation arose during a research workshop on computational modeling in games,* and was inspired by previous research in architecture, urban planning, and hypertext structure. In the real world, branching trees are rare. In most cities, buildings, and parks, you can go around in circles. Cycles are also very dominant in handcrafted levels. Simply google dungeon maps for tabletop role-playing games and look for cycles in the most interesting ones. In fact, this is one way I harvested many of the patterns discussed below.

In *Unexplored*, cycles are created by connecting a starting point and a goal by two paths instead of one. Figure 9.2 illustrates how nesting these cycles often is much more effective in creating dungeon levels than simple branching.

There are many different ways of using a cycle. Both paths from the start to goal can offer different challenges to the player. Or maybe if one path is much shorter, it can be much more dangerous, or simply much harder to find. One path may actually only be traversable in one direction, creating a quick route back to the starting point (e.g., after the player has found a key). So far, I have identified a fair number of these types of patterns, which are discussed in more detail in the "Patterns" section.

USING GRAPHS TO EXPRESS CYCLES

Cycles are not easy to work with if your level is represented by a tilemap. In order to get around this problem, *Unexplored* uses graphs to represent level structure during the initial steps of the generation process. It is only halfway through that these graphs are converted to tilemaps.

---

* http://www.birs.ca/events/2016/5-day-workshops/16w5160

(1) You enter the level at a platform in the center of a huge chasm. (2) The door on the north is barred. The only open route is south. (3) Across the lava, you can spot the platform at 6, but you can not really reach it. (4) You can continue on or check out platform 6, which you might have seen earlier. (5) As you cross the bridge, it collapses. (6) If you make it to the platform, you are trapped there facing a giant rat. The chest contains a scroll of teleportation, which allows you to escape. (7) This door is also barred. (8) The narrow pathway is guarded by a patroling kobold spearman. (9) This section is protected by a sleeping goblin spearman. You can sneak past easily. But did you spot those triggers that set off an alarm? (10) Similar section. A trigger might wake up the goblin bowman. (11) Giant ants protect this area, but it also has two levers operating the doors at 2 and 7. (12) After visiting 11, you can now make your way to this platform and take the staircase down to the next level.

FIGURE 9.1   Pit-level walkthrough.

This process was inspired by the practice of model-driven engineering. In short, model-driven engineering advocates that automated processes use multiple steps to produce the final result. The output of each individual step is a model, preferably a model that makes some sort of sense on its own, that gets passed to the next step for further processing.

In general, when one is generating something as complex as a complete game level, it makes a lot of sense to break down the process into multiple

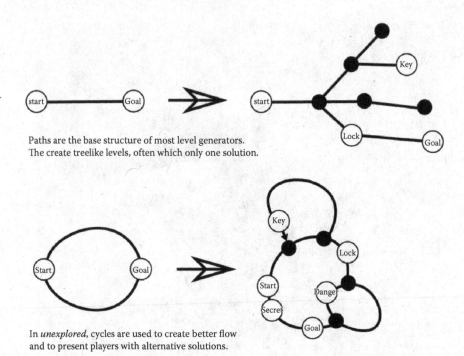

Paths are the base structure of most level generators.
The create treelike levels, often which only one solution.

In *unexplored,* cycles are used to create better flow
and to present players with alternative solutions.

FIGURE 9.2   Branching vs. nested cycles.

steps. In fact, I assume that all successful level generators do so. However, the advantages of multiple steps get hugely enhanced by using different types of models during the process. *Unexplored* initially uses graphs to represent level structure, as graphs are much better to retain structural information over distances. For example, Figure 9.3 shows one such graph showing connected rooms, containing obstacles, locks, and keys.*

At this stage, all nodes in the graph are deliberately generic. The exact nature and properties of most obstacles, locks, keys, and rooms are defined during later stages.

Unexplored manipulates graphs using transformational graph grammars. These grammars consist of rules that loom for particular patterns in a graph and suggest ways how these graphs can be transformed

---

* It is important to note that containment in this example is represented as a node embedded in another node. However, this is not different from a node connected with a special containment edge to its parent. In fact, that is exactly how it is implemented.

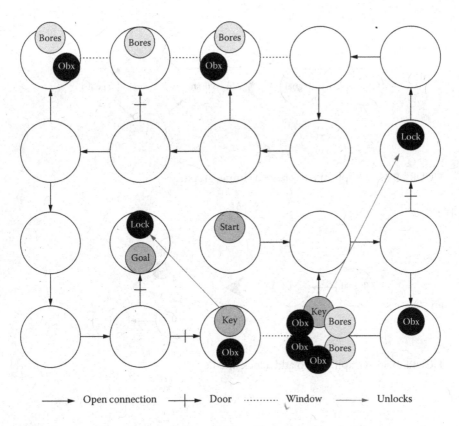

FIGURE 9.3 Graph of a level being generated, with explanations.

by replacing the found pattern with a different pattern. For example, Figure 9.4 illustrates a graph transformation rule that creates a simple cycle, while Figures 9.5 through 9.7 illustrate more rules and the graphs they can generate. It is important to note that the numbers in the rules are used to match up nodes on the left-hand side of the rule (the pattern to be replaced) and the right-hand side of the rule (what the pattern is replaced with).

PATTERNS

Graph transformation rules allow *Unexplored* to implement a number of design patterns. These patterns are common structures found across games. For example, adding a secret shortcut to a long and dangerous level is one such pattern. Each pattern has its own positive and negative effects;

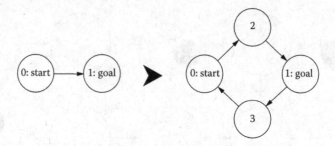

FIGURE 9.4   Graph rule to create a simple graph.

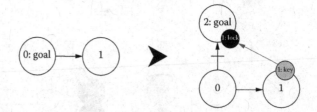

FIGURE 9.5   Graph rule to add a lock and key.

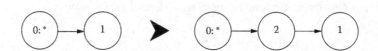

FIGURE 9.6   Graph rule to expand a cycle.

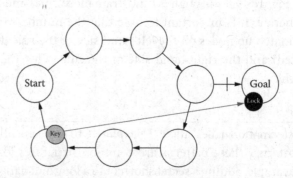

FIGURE 9.7   Sample of what can be generated from these rules.

in this case, the shortcut might be rewarding for players that take the time to explore thoroughly, but it can also bypass a large portion of an otherwise interesting level. However, the important point is that through transformational graph rules, the level generator is able to manipulate these patterns directly: it can make deliberate decisions about their use in order to maximize their positive effects and minimize their potential negative effects.

For example, most of the time, *Unexplored* starts a level by adding a starting point, a goal, and two paths. The first path, called *a*, initially leads from the start to the goal, while the second path, *b*, leads from the goal back to the start. Based on the relative and absolute lengths of *a* and *b*, a number of cycle patterns can be applied. For example, when *a* is short and *b* is long, it can place a locked door at the goal, and place the key at the end of *b* just before a spot where the player can cut back to the main path. This creates a level where players first encounter the locked door, and when they do find the right key, they do not have to go far to reach the door it unlocks. Obviously, this requires that the player cannot reach *b* from the cycle's entrance straightaway, although it might be interesting if they can already see *b* and the key. Figure 9.8 lists a couple more of these patterns.

IMPLEMENTATION

Of course, the devil is in details or, in this case, the implementation. Graph transformation and model-driven engineering are powerful methods, but to make them work in the way we wanted, we still had to add a couple of things. The most important addition to the graph transformation rules are attributes attached to nodes and edges in the graph. For example, a room node can have an attribute that specifies the room type or theme. The graph transformation rules in *Unexplored* can read and write to those attributes. In this way, the generator can activate a different transformation rule for rooms that are marked as a "shrine," "armory," "workshop," and so on.

Attributes turned out to be really important in generating lock-and-key mechanisms. For *Unexplored*, simply adding keys and locked doors was not going to work. There are several game elements that allow players to push ahead early and often involuntarily: they can jump in chasms to the level below, use a scroll of descend to similar effects, or use a scroll of teleportation to teleport to a random location in the level. As the objective

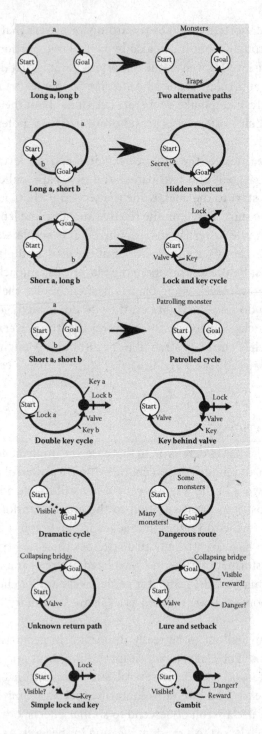

FIGURE 9.8   Level design patterns.

of the game is to get to level 20, retrieve the Amulet of Yendor, and make your way back up, this means that many of the lock-and-key puzzles need to be solvable in two directions.

A simple solution would have been to make all locked doors operated by levers and simply make sure there is a lever on both sides of the door. However, lock-and-key mechanisms can get boring very quickly, especially when there is little variation to their design. One design objective of *Unexplored* is to use as many game mechanisms as possible as lock-and-key mechanisms. For example, a potion of resist fire can serve as a key to a barrier of lava the player needs to cross. Unfortunately, the potion has a temporary effect, and you are never quite sure when the player will drink it, and it definitely will no longer work when the player is returning to the surface.

Using attributes to mark the structural function of different locks and keys proved to be a very useful way to avoid deadlocks and create variety in lock and keys at the same time. For example, locks can be marked as "conditional," indicating a lock for which the player must have a key to pass. The most typical conditional lock is an indestructible door that can be opened only with a particular key. An example of a nonconditional lock would be a room with turrets controlled by a lever. If the player has not found the lever, he or she can still risk running through the room. Nonconditional locks have the advantage of being traversable in two directions automatically, and it is often easier to involve different game mechanics in their design.

ASIDE: LOCK-AND-KEY ATTRIBUTES

Locks Might Be Conditional, Dangerous, or Uncertain

Typically, we think about locks as binary barriers: if you have the key, you can cross the barrier; if you don't have the key, you simply cannot. Locked doors, in whatever way they are unlocked or opened, are the typical example. Locks as binary barriers are conditional locks. However, locks do not need to function in that way. Some locks are barriers that might be navigated without a key, but this crossing the barrier might be uncertain or impose a certain risk. Keys for this type of lock make the crossing less dangerous, or more certain. A simple example of an uncertain lock would be a secret door, which is opened if one is able to find it (a certain matter of uncertainty). A dangerous lock could be a lake of lava that might be crossed at the expense of hit points (a certain risk). A scroll of magic mapping that reveals secret doors or a potion that protects you against fire damage can act as keys for those doors, making it easier to cross the lock in both cases.

Locks Are Permanent, Reversible, Temporary, or Collapsing

When you unlock a door, that door might remain unlocked forever (permanent), for a short period of time (temporary), or until it is relocked (reversible). Sometimes, a lock collapses after use, allowing the player only to pass once. Permanent locks are the safest to use, as once they are opened, nothing can go wrong. Temporary doors typically produce more gameplay at a certain risk; they can turn into valves (see the next section). Reversible locks can create problems, depending on the type of key you are using for them (see the following sections).

Locks Might Be Valves or Asymmetrical

Certain locks allow you to cross only in one direction (valves), while others can only be opened from one direction but traversed in two directions after they are opened (asymmetrical). Valves and asymmetrical locks tend to create more interesting conditional locks. They are frequently used in the patterns above to make sure the player cannot enter a part of the cycle that is intended as a route back. Valves do not always require a key. For example, jumping down a high ledge can be considered to be a valve, as it allows the player only to travel in one direction.

Locks and Keys Can Be Safe or Unsafe

A safe lock is guaranteed to have a solution, while an unsafe lock is not. To a certain extent, a dangerous or an uncertain lock is always safe. In general, you want to make sure all conditional locks on the main path through the game are safe. It is fine to use unsafe, conditional locks on optional paths, although if that lock is also temporary, collapsing, or a valve, you must make sure that the path back is safely locked (if it is locked at all).

Keys Can Be Single Purpose or Multipurpose

Single-purpose keys can only be used to open a lock, and for nothing else, while multipurpose keys can also be used in different ways. Even if a key can open multiple locks, it can be considered to be multipurpose. In general, it is better to make use of multipurpose keys, as single-purpose keys are more boring and frequently end up as dead weight in your inventory. The way *Zelda* dungeons frequently use the bow as a key by hitting switches from a distance is a good example of a multipurpose key. In fact, many of the best keys in *Zelda* also double as a weapons.

Keys Are Particular or Nonparticular

Particular keys are the only thing that unlocks a particular lock, whereas several nonparticular keys might unlock a single lock. Just as conditional locks tend to be more boring than dangerous or uncertain locks, particular keys tend to be more boring than nonparticular keys, often because nonparticular keys tend to be multipurpose as well (although they do not need to be). Particular keys function as do real-life keys. The small keys of *Zelda* are a good example of single-purpose, nonparticular keys. One effect of using nonparticular keys is that the players, for whatever reason, might have one when they encounter the lock. When you have not placed a nonparticular key for each lock you want it to open, this can make conditional locks feel less rigid.

Keys Might Be Consumed or Persistent

Keys that are destroyed somehow in the process of unlocking a door are consumable, while keys that are not are persistent. Keys that are consumed tend to be less safe than persistent keys, especially if those keys are also multipurpose and can be consumed to achieve other goals. Small keys in *Zelda* are consumed, as is a potion of resist fire that is placed as a key to pass a certain fire barrier. Like nonparticular keys, consumable keys might make a conditional lock less rigid, but also a lot less safe.

Keys Might Be Fixed in Place

Levers and switches are the best example of keys that are fixed in place (and typically single purpose and particular as well). One problem of fixed-in-place keys is that if there is only one key on one side of the lock, it makes the lock asymmetrical. Often, it is best to make the locks triggered by keys that are fixed in place open permanently, especially when the player can reach the key only once, which effectively would make the key consumable and probably unsafe as well. When using keys that are fixed in place, it is often important to give some sort of feedback on the status of the door, and to make sure the lock is permanent and not reversible (as often is the case with levers).

TILEMAPS

Another problem we ran into during the implementation of these techniques in *Unexplored*, but also in other games using similar ideas, is how to transform graphs into tilemaps. The problem is a generic one: during the initial stages of the generation process, graphs are used to represent the abstract structure of the level. Graphs are good for this, as they can include edges to represent the structural relationships between nodes. These relationships include adjacencies, but also which key unlocks what lock, what enemy patrols which rooms, and so on. However, at one point the generator needs to build a topological representation detailing the exact locations of wall, doors, keys, and enemies. In *Unexplored*, levels are represented as tilemaps.

Unfortunately, there is no standard solution to this problem. For *Unexplored*, we solved the issue by first creating a graph that is laid out as a grid and stored the topological information in the nodes' attributes (Figure 9.9). All graph transformations are then performed on this graph. This way, when the generator needs to make the transition from graph to tilemap, there are no issues in mapping the graph onto a two-dimensional tilemap. Initially, individual tiles correspond with nodes and edges directly, but the resolution of the tilemap is then increased to allow for

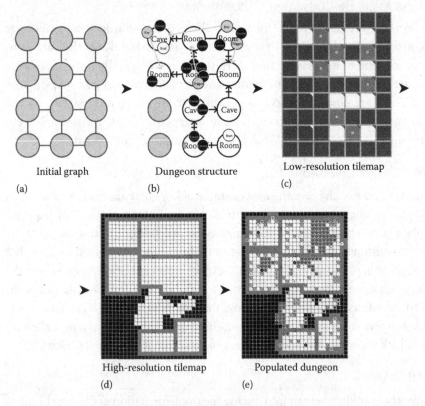

Initial graph
(a)

Dungeon structure
(b)

Low-resolution tilemap
(c)

High-resolution tilemap
(d)

Populated dungeon
(e)

FIGURE 9.9   Graph grid layout that any dungeon level starts from.

more details. During subsequent steps in the generation process, transformation rules, much like the graph transformation rules discussed in an earlier section, are used to expand rooms, add features as dictated by the graph, and decorate dungeons.

DISCUSSION

This chapter does not include every detail of implementation. For example, before even one dungeon level is generated, a plan for the dungeon is generated that specifies what themes, monsters, locks, and keys to use on each level. However, the general idea behind cyclic dungeon generation should be clear. The implementation in *Unexplored* relies heavily on the use of transformational grammars operating on graphs and tilemaps, but it is not hard to imagine that other generation techniques could also be used to generate dungeons based on cycles instead of branching paths.

For *Unexplored*, the advantages of cyclic dungeon generation are many. We have found that levels based on a couple of cycles are the most effective. Two to five cycles give each level a distinct and recognizable shape and character. This presents the player with a nice, but manageable navigational challenge. With just a handful of cyclic patterns, the number of possible combinations is still huge. Adding more cycles just seems to clutter the level.

The reason cyclic dungeon generation works well is that as a structure, cycles are able to express so many more interesting patterns than paths do. There is no reason to assume that this advantage is unique to cycles alone. Structures like T-joins or parallel, symmetrical branches might be able to achieve similar results in addition to, or independent of, cycles, but so far cycles are the most powerful and expressive structure we have come across.

In addition, cyclic generation is not restricted to the generation of sprawling dungeons alone. In fact, the research workshop from which the ideas behind cyclic dungeon generation emerged tried to come up with a good way to generate parks or meditative gardens. In such environments, cycles are also very useful: most people prefer a walk or hike that does not involve any backtracking. Similar ideas can be applied to open game spaces and world maps. Cycles can be drawn around obstacles such as forests, lakes, swamps, and mountains, with dangerous shortcuts connecting two sides of the cycle and prominent sites on locations where two cycles intersect. There are many opportunities that cyclic map generation offers that remain unexplored—for now.

CHAPTER 10

Worlds

Dr. Mark R. Johnson

Independent

T HE PROCEDURAL GENERATION OF entire worlds is surely one of the most compelling possibilities of algorithmic content. We are so used to the standard terraqueous world map we see on the news screen that the creation of entirely new planetary terrain—and, in most such games, the gradual discovery of that terrain through the virtual reenactment of exploration and voyage—brings with it a moment of excitement that is never quite lost, no matter how many games of *Civilization*, *Alpha Centauri*, *Dwarf Fortress*, or *Ultima Ratio Regum* one plays. Such games bring with them new and uncharted deserts, vast expanses of tundra and taiga, dense jungles, open plains, and mountains and ridges and valleys, and even, in some cases, procedural climates, ranging from heaviest of rainfall to the driest of lands, and even procedural flora and fauna.

In procedurally generating a world, world elements at both the macro- and the microscales require modeling (depending on the intended simulation granularity of the game itself), necessitating either a top-down approach that builds continents and mountain ranges, and then fills in the intervening land appropriately, or a system that models natural phenomena such as rainfall, tectonic plates, and weather patterns, and allows a world to emerge from these processes. If a mere world seems insufficient, one can go significantly grander in scope and generate solar systems, or even entire galaxies, if so inclined. At time of writing, I know of no game that has attempted to procedurally generate a universe, complete with its own set of algorithmically determined natural laws that differ from playthrough to playthrough, and percolate down into the creation (or not) of galaxies, stars, and planets, but I throw this out there as a challenge.

Alternatively, for games that don't need entire planets and certainly don't need entire solar systems, galaxies, or branes, world generation can readily be separated into components that function perfectly well in their own right—one might choose to generate a nation, or a smaller-than-a-world area of terrain, or cities, towns, fortresses, districts, individual buildings, the floors within those buildings, and so forth. Although these smaller examples are arguably not quite the creation of worlds (unless the building were some truly towering megastructure of the sort found in *Halo* or *Dark Souls*), all these are still concerned with the creation of unique spaces for the player to experience, and it is the grander ends of this spectrum of practice we'll look at here.

This chapter closely examines three elements of procedural world generation. First, it offers a brief history of world generation with a range of examples, and we'll seek to identify a timeline of sorts and some of the commonalities of world generation up to the present day. Second, it delves deeper into the design rationales behind the development of world generation and the desired gameplay such algorithmic realities are intended to foster. Lastly, in looking to the future, the chapter explores in depth my fairly unusual work in this area, in which I have been broadly unconcerned by the creation of physical and spatial "world" characteristics of the sort outlined above, but instead with the development of what I have termed "qualitative procedural generation" and its implementation and deployment in a world-building context. By this, I mean the procedural creation of cultural practices, social norms, religious beliefs, ways of speaking and behaving, and the like, and their physical instantiations and reproductions within a game world, intended here as a contrast to previous world generation focuses upon the genesis, variation, and delineation of procedural in-game spaces and places. In doing so, the chapter gives an outline of the past, present, and future of procedural world generation; brings our attention to some of the core philosophies behind these practices; and examines what exactly it is that makes exploring a procedural world such a distinctive pleasure.

BRIEF HISTORY OF WORLD GENERATION

It is difficult to establish the moment of the first generated "world," due primarily to the vagueness of that five-letter word and the attendant difficulty in drawing the line between a world and a "very large generated space." However, some obvious early iterations of the idea, or the sorts of game spaces that would later become indicative of generated worlds, can easily be identified. *Akalabeth* (1980) generated worlds from seed numbers the player could offer; *Elite* (1984) was originally planned to include trillions of galaxies, although its final version contained only a tiny fraction of that; and then *Civilization* (1991) generated Earth-like worlds according to assorted variables (land mass, temperature, climate, and age) upon which real-world civilizations battled for supremacy, becoming perhaps the first major mainstream game to offer the player an endless volume of planets to explore. Even the game *River Raid* (1982), which offered endlessly scrolling procedural terrain, could be understood as the gradual generation of a world, albeit one that takes some time to appear and can never be viewed in its entirety. In more recent years, the most noteworthy examples are perhaps the distant alien planets of *Alpha Centauri* (1999), the intricately modeled high-fantasy worlds of *Dwarf Fortress* (2006), the sprawling cuboid terrain of *Minecraft* (2009), the postapocalyptic wastelands of *Cataclysm: Dark Days Ahead* (2013), and the uncountable planets and systems of *No Man's Sky* (2016).

In briefly considering the rise of more-than-world generators, such as those concerned with creating solar systems or portions of a galaxy, we actually see something of a shift in the spatial topographies of these games. Due to the nature of space as being composed of fleeting points of interest—stars, planets, etc.—in a void of irrelevant nothingness, these games generally abandon the square or hexagonal grids that are more traditional in procedural worlds, and instead the systems or galaxies in other procedurally generated space games like *Faster Than Light*, *Stellaris*, and *Aurora 4X* are node-based networks between which spacecraft travel. Procedural "worlds" are therefore not just limited to standard global geography, but can extend into both grander spaces of play and other forms of spatial representation.

Taking stock of all these examples, we can perceive two different models of procedural generation. One of these is absolutely exemplified in *Civilization*, while the other is exemplified in *Dwarf Fortress*: these are the creation of procedural worlds as a space for the player to act upon, and the creation of procedural worlds as a system for the player to act within. Let us first consider the generating of worlds as a game space for the players to affect through their in-game actions.

Games that employ this model create a world that is effectively completely empty when the game begins, although *Civilization* sometimes places "Natural Wonders" or other equivalent points of interest, depending on the version, and newer versions of *Minecraft* can generate worlds that contain existing structures of various sorts. In the case of *Civilization*, each civilization starts off with just a single Settler unit about to found a single city, and the majority of the map will be unexplored and uncontrolled by any of the game's civilizations for a substantial amount of the gameplay—in later versions of *Civilization*, where the player is given more options, generating a world that is especially large and then populating it with the smallest possible number of civilizations will lead to a situation where, even at the end of the game in the present day, parts of the world will still be untouched by player or artificial intelligence (AI) action. The map is therefore a blank space upon which the game plays out.

In *Minecraft*, meanwhile, the player's "goal" is to construct structures of whatever sort they desire on this generated world, ranging from functional buildings of the sort seen in the real world to grand artistic projects. In some extreme cases, the world is truly little more than a backdrop for action, as it is possible to play *Minecraft* with an entirely blank map, rather than a generated world, and to then enact one's creative will on that world instead. The generation of worlds as a "space" therefore holds to quite a "sandbox" conception of the purpose of generating procedural worlds—these sorts of games leave a tremendous amount to the player, and are concerned only with making an interesting space for the player to explore and play with.

The other form of massive generated space we can identify is that of the procedurally generated system of the world, designed as a complex backdrop for the player to act within. By this, I mean games that are focused on giving the player a range of interlocking mechanics dispersed around the in-game world, such as the thousands of planets and factions in the *Elite* games; the towns, villages, peoples, and still-being-written mythologies of *Dwarf Fortress*; the Iron Age expanses of *UnReal World* with its detailed weather, flora, and fauna simulations; the feuding medieval factions of *Europa Universalis* or *Crusader Kings*; and the highly distinctive but globally intermeshed cultures and societies of my own *Ultima Ratio Regum*.

These generated worlds are designed less with their terrain and topographies in mind, although these of course matter and will always affect other aspects of the game's generation, but a world is here instead seen as something already present into which the player slots, rather than a blank canvas upon which the player builds. In these "system" worlds, we also see something of a precursor to my own qualitative procedural generation work to be explored later in the chapter—a concern with a massive range of interlocking elements, generally nonphysical (for terrains and biospheres and tectonic plates tend to move a tad slower than social and political life) but sometimes including shorter-term physical processes, and on a range of scales from the grand and abstracted worlds of geopolitics and economies to the microsocial elements of individuals and conversations, or animal tracking and plant gathering. Players are then actively invited to engage themselves in these systems and experiment with the extent to which they can be adjusted, interfered with, turned to one's advantage, and made the center of intriguing emergent phenomena whereby the player alters one system and sees a knock-on effect in another. These two rationales therefore produce very different worlds, require very different forms of procedural generation, and result in games with very different design objectives.

WHY MAKE WORLDS?

What kinds of feelings and experiences are procedural worlds intended to foster in the player, and how do they differ from offering large worlds that have been uniquely designed and packaged with a game?

There are three main reasons to generate rather than handmake a world: the use of exploration as game mechanics; the use of procedural generation as a method for creating worlds that are simply too large or too complex, or both, to ever be handmade; and the use of procedural world generation as a way to "enforce" gameplay variation through providing different affordances to players each time they start the game.

Exploration

In a nonprocedural game, exploration as game mechanics can only ever be truly and fully present on the first-ever playthrough of a game when the player has no prior knowledge of the single fixed game world. Although games do mitigate this in various ways, such as the difficulty of progression and the narrative obtuseness of the *Souls* series, it is only in procedural worlds where exploration can be consistently fresh game mechanics. This takes many forms. In strategy games, exploration is essential for the player who needs to discover the location and disposition of enemy positions and forces, the distribution of land and ocean and therefore what units and technologies should be pursued, the location of particularly valuable resources, and so forth.

In games like *Minecraft*, and even more so in "pure exploration" games like *Proteus*, exploration for its own purpose is a central game mechanic and a focus of the play experience, centered around the discovery of interesting sites and varied in-game regions, although in *Minecraft* concerns of resources and the like are nevertheless also present. In more systemic procedural game worlds, exploration is crucial to uncovering the best trade routes, the most important clues (as in *Ultima Ratio Regum*), or locations that might merit exploring for loot or story information. Procedural world generation therefore ensures that exploration remains a game mechanic that can deliver gameplay experiences on every playthrough, rather than just the first, by keeping every world unknown until the player actually sets foot within it.

Expansive or Complex Worlds

Procedural world generation can produce in-game worlds of a scale and complexity that handmade worlds could never hope to match, given the time and effort required by a developer to place every little part of that world. This is apparent for some of the most complex generated planets in games in the present day, such as *Dwarf Fortress* and *Ultima Ratio Regum*, but becomes even more apparent when we consider the generation of entire galaxies, as in *No Man's Sky*—one suspects that there are few game designers on the planet with the time or motivation to handmake millions of worlds.

By contrast, a sufficiently robust procedural generation system can create worlds that could never be produced by hand, and ensure that all areas of that world can be potentially extremely complex. The largest handmade game worlds, such as those of the *Elder Scrolls* or *Mass Effect* series, for example, contain only a tiny fraction of in-game areas that can be explored and interacted with compared with the games listed above.

Of course, not everything generated in a procedural world is of the same gameplay interest or gameplay value as elements handmade in another game world, as generating elements with meaning and interest is a challenge in its own right. However, speaking in purely spatial and volumetric terms, there is no way for procedural generation to be trumped. This makes such worlds particularly intriguing to explore for players of a particular mindset who are comfortable with potentially never seeing everything in a game world, and who understand that some areas will be of less interest than others purely due to the whims of the underlying algorithm and the lack of a game designer directly overseeing the process, but instead want the closest possible experience a game can offer to the true size and complexity of the real world.

Gameplay Variation

Procedural worlds push increased gameplay variation on the player. This point is somewhat related to the first in this list, but is distinct—generating a new world each time a game is played does add replay value, but it also has the intriguing side effect of forcing gameplay variation and encouraging players toward new forms of play.

If a game of the sort procedural world generation is often used in (strategy, exploration, roguelike, etc.) was only ever played on a single map, it would quickly become comparatively simple to divine the strongest strategies and omit any aspect of the game's design that didn't fit into that strategy.

By contrast, using procedural world generation forces players to sometimes experiment with parts of a game's design they might ordinarily not use. A player might be planning to execute a particular strategy in *Civilization*, for example, but then finds the generated world is covered with oceans and therefore necessitates the construction of a strong navy for any chance of victory, encouraging the player toward playing with naval units and naval strategies he had perhaps never previously employed. A world might be devoid of a particularly crucial resource in a playthrough of *Dwarf Fortress*, which means certain structures or weapons can no longer be produced (or can no longer be produced in any kind of quantity), encouraging the players to think outside their traditional in-game routines and patterns to find new ways to achieve their goals.

Generating in-game worlds of sufficiently high variety is therefore a way to gently nudge players toward exploring the full scope of a game's possibility space, instead of falling back on well-tried and well-tested tactics and strategies every time the game is played. The combination of these three elements—the use of exploration as a central game mechanic, the size and complexity of procedural worlds, and the ability for procedural worlds to encourage players out of their comfort zones and into the creation of new choices and decisions—makes playing in procedural worlds a very distinctive experience, and one that cannot ordinarily be offered (more than once, anyway) by their handmade cousins.

QUALITATIVE PROCEDURAL GENERATION

With the different kinds of generated worlds established, and some of the player experiences of actually playing through such worlds, at the end of this chapter I focus in on a case study of my own work in *Ultima Ratio Regum*, specifically in developing what I've termed "qualitative procedural generation" as a method for creating complex systemic game worlds.

Instead of focusing on terrain and environmental modeling (although these are present and lay the geographical backdrop onto which all the other elements are added), I've instead chosen to really push the possibility of generating aspects of "worlds" that we experience far more frequently and far more intimately than any relationship with the physical landscape upon which we live: that of societies, cultures, politics, religions, institutions, social norms, aesthetics, and the like (Figure 10.1). Although a few games have touched on generating these sorts of elements, most portrayals tend to omit the nuance and incredible detail of real-world social interactions, whether in the explicit interactions of conversations and the meetings of cultures, or the microinteractions of how people move around a space or how they present themselves to others.

I'm therefore trying to move away from these quite "mechanistic" models of culture, and toward a deeper portrayal of individual cultures in the actions and deeds of their peoples, in shared aesthetic styles and the embodiment of practices and beliefs, in order to lend a depth, believability, and most importantly meaning to generated worlds, which are so often lacking.

This task therefore extends from the system rather than the space approach, as outlined above. Many procedural generation games have complex systems for aspects of social life, like trade or political relationships. However, instead of abstracting out high-level "relationships" between

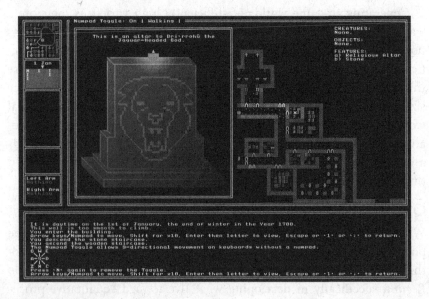

FIGURE 10.1 Generated religious object.

nations into numerical values of the sort that the *Civilization* series does, perhaps allow the player to walk between cities of two nations. The player would see how the artifacts of one culture bleed into the other (and vice versa), or how much linguistic and cultural exchange there is between the two, how well-patrolled the border is, and how people from each land talk about those from the other. This is a classic "show, don't tell" approach, and one that can only really take place at a particular scale—when dealing with a world-level strategy game, of course individual cities cannot be explored and depicted, as that would take away from the main focus of the game.

When controlling a single-player character walking through a generated world, however, the possibilities open up for portraying a complex sociological and cultural system in everything the player sees and discovers, rather than just offering a little textual description or numerical value to this effect instead.

Key to this system is the intersection between all the different elements the game generates. A particular religious belief about the nature of the afterlife may affect the colors on book covers; a particularly powerful house might influence the design of all the weapons and armor manufactured in a nation; the flora and fauna of a particular region might influence the designs of the sigils of important families; a past war, ancient but not forgotten, may influence how people from one culture respond to the player who happens to be from that long-resented foe; the geographical location of a city might affect the religious beliefs that spring up there, connected perhaps to the seas or the mountains nearby; and so forth.

Systemic procedural worlds hinge in part upon the interactions between large numbers of complex systems that have to be uncovered by the player, but these systems need not be entirely quantitative and reflect only the flow of trade or battle or some abstracted notion of culture—instead, these systems can be qualitative in nature and reflect the beliefs and practices of procedurally generated peoples, and lose none of that desired complexity in the process. Indeed, if anything, quite the opposite is the case—so many players of procedural games find their complexity to be one of the most important selling points (the popularity of *Dwarf Fortress* and *Aurora 4X* is a testament to this), and these layers of sociocultural detail only add to the granularity and detail of the player's world-exploring experience.

At this point, one might ask, what is the value of such systems? Generating spaces offers an area for play, and many games with complex generated systemic worlds already have a massive wealth of interactions for the player to engage in. What value does this kind of qualitative procedural generation bring to the procedural generation of entire worlds?

As above, part of the enjoyment of exploring procedural worlds lies in uncovering their complexity, and yet the forms this complexity has taken to date are only the smallest fraction of forms that real-world complexity adopts. Incredible detail and nuance can be added to procedural worlds through these sorts of techniques, especially when the overwhelming majority of procedurally generated worlds, regardless of their size, are beset by remarkably large numbers of AI actors speaking the same language, building similar buildings, or having few differences beyond the flags they wave and the procedural histories they share.

The second answer lies in the use of these systems for gameplay—it is obvious how a complex trade system can be used for gameplay, but what about a complex cultural system? A complex cultural system allows for the player to explore the world through means other than walking around it. It allows for a game to be based around the discovery of in-game cultures and to develop "cultural knowledge" as a crucial skill for a player to be successful; it allows for the player to attempt to fake their cultural or religious origin as a form of covert or espionage gameplay; it allows for the player to make informed judgments about their travels in the world, based on their knowledge of allied and feuding countries. Similarly, it allows the player to make judgments about what options should be selected in what conversations, based on their acquired knowledge (acquired through investigation and learning, not through direct exposition) of the dispositions of the world's various peoples.

Qualitative procedural generation is a major future step in the generation of procedural worlds, both for the sake of the complexity and for the sake of innovative gameplay.

CHAPTER 11

Puzzles

Danny Day

QCF Design

*D*ESKTOP *D*UNGEONS IS A puzzle roguelike that gives you a disposable adventurer to guide through randomly generated, single-screen dungeons. Your goal is to defeat the dungeon boss(es), leveling up through combat with less terrifying enemies along the way, and then escape to pawn boss heads in a kingdom whose economic progress is worryingly tied to exotic taxidermy. *Desktop Dungeons* won an Independent Games Festival (IGF) Excellence in Design Award in 2011; it was released in 2013 and extensively updated in 2015.

This chapter explains how we built the random puzzle generation system that powers *Desktop Dungeons'* replayability and the issues that made that a unique problem.

PROCEDURALLY GENERATING PUZZLES

For the purposes of discussion, I'll assume that puzzles have a determined starting state and an end or goal state, and that players perform atomic actions on the puzzle to move it from one to the other (note that puzzle games may hide or only partially display the game's current state for the player, but the assumption is that the entire state is known internally). Given that, we can start to consider the kinds of puzzles that can be usefully procedurally generated and what the outputs of such a system should be.

Puzzle-Spaces

Algorithms are great at churning out puzzles that are variations on a theme, puzzles that come from a large and reasonably uniform puzzle-space. If a puzzle-space is the abstract space populated by every single puzzle that could emerge out of a set of gameplay rules, then a puzzle-space can be

- *Large* if it contains many puzzles with distinct start and goal states

- *Small* if the number of distinct start and goal states is few

- *Shallow* if each distinct start state has exactly one corresponding goal state

- *Deep* if a single start state has multiple viable goal states, or vice versa

Puzzles can be defined in terms of the puzzle-spaces they come from. Human designers are great at producing puzzles at extreme ends of the puzzle-space spectrum. One-shot puzzles that are enjoyable due to a novel twist, setting, or presentation require a human in the loop to make them feel impactful and make poor targets for procedural generation. Puzzles from a vast or extremely deep puzzle-space generally require a human to cherry-pick goal states that have some kind of value that makes them stand out (e.g., humor or carefully selecting for novelty); procedurally generating within such a puzzle-space produces boring puzzles that feel too similar.

Desired Outputs

Often, the primary role of a procedural puzzle generator is trimming down a larger puzzle-space into a subset of possible puzzles that differ along axes that can be easily randomized. A functioning game usually requires several different types of puzzle to give players a complete experience. It's common to find that you'll either have multiple generators that operate on different "areas" within the puzzle-space, or parameters that move their sampling around within the puzzle-space itself.

One of the most important things a generator needs to do is ensure that it produces puzzles that are actually solvable! It does nobody any good to produce a sea of starting states with no guarantee of at least one corresponding goal state for players to reach. Without a goal, you're not generating puzzles and you're certainly not respecting the player's time. Thus, our first generation requirement is *solvability*.

After that comes the requirement for a continuous solution. A puzzle is continuous if players can progress from the starting state to a goal state by following the rules of the game. Applying the atomic actions available to them should drive the player toward a goal. It's surprisingly easy to generate puzzles that technically do have goal states but don't have continuous paths to those states: if a procedural generation system produced a puzzle as nonsensical as the infamous *Gabriel Knight* cat–hair–mustache puzzle, we'd consider it discontinuous. Sudoku-type puzzles are considered discontinuous when they have multiple solutions, because at some point the player has to arbitrarily choose between values for cells instead of following the deductive rules of the puzzle.

Continuity doesn't rule out deep puzzle-spaces. It's perfectly possible to arbitrarily remove walls in a single-path maze to create multiple viable paths; this would still be a continuous maze puzzle. In order to make a maze discontinuous, you'd have to remove a reasonable number of adjacent paths and walls, rendering maze traversal actions meaningless when they encountered the lack.

Finally, a *deterministic* generator can be very useful. This isn't a hard requirement to produce viable puzzles, but it can speed debugging and allow players to return to the same puzzle more than once (should you want to allow them to)—it's also a key component of shared "daily" puzzles. Chapter 12 outlines this in detail.

PUZZLE GENERATION APPROACHES

Exactly how you go about structuring a puzzle generator depends massively on the rules of your game and the kinds of puzzle you're trying to produce, but there are some broad categories of approaches that we can identify. Examining them each via their puzzle-space and desired output should help you narrow down good approaches for whatever game you have in mind.

Random Start State

Generating a novel starting state for a puzzle is often a nontrivial problem, but provided you can create a random initial state, sometimes that's enough. Usually, this is great for puzzles that are about progressively revealing (or discovering) information, which makes your generation step a simple rearranging of known data. Of course, this requires that your game's rules guarantee that starting states generated this way are automatically solvable and continuous. This is easier to achieve with deeper puzzle-spaces that only have one or two axes of differentiation between puzzles.

Minesweeper is a good example of this sort of generation: to generate a minesweeper puzzle, simply place a number of mines at random positions in a grid. Players are able to theoretically solve any puzzle generated this way, as the rules are simply about deducing the placement of the mines. Any minesweeper puzzle is generally continuous after the first move as well, even though players may make a mistake and click on a mine, they're only forced to guess when the visible information describes only the currently revealed tiles. This happens at the beginning of the game when no squares are revealed, as well as when enclosed "pockets" of nonmine squares are surrounded completely by mines.

It's worth noting that random start-state generation can be a great source of designer inspiration for games with extremely broad puzzle-spaces. The randomly generated states don't even need to be playable, because all they're doing is providing serendipitous new arrangements of elements that a designer then steals and places into more polished, hand-tweaked puzzles.

Backward from Goal State

One way to guarantee solvability and continuity is to start from a specific randomly generated goal state and repeatedly undo atomic player actions at random until you reach a state of desired complexity. This then becomes a generated starting state. Backward generation can only produce single-path solutions; players must exactly replicate the moves the generator undid in order to reach the goal. This works well for games with shallow puzzle-spaces and high information transparency in which players won't get lost or discouraged while looking for a single-path solution.

For this approach to work, your player actions need to be bidirectional: player moves shouldn't introduce new information to the game state during regular play. It's also always a good idea to keep track of previous states along the generation path so that moves that create identical states (and thus possible loops or shortcuts) can be avoided or rolled back.

Examples of backward generation include math and word puzzles. Word search puzzles don't start with random jumbles of letters! They start with the words players are going to find before arranging them in a sea of randomness.

Heuristics

All the above-mentioned generation paradigms stand to benefit from specific game-relevant rules: heuristics. We can certainly generate viable puzzles purely mathematically, but it's possible to generate richer and more interesting puzzles, faster, with clever heuristic choices. Often, heuristics take the form of puzzle disqualification states that force the generator to start again or redo a particular generation step if they're triggered.

It's possible to solve the discontinuity problems in *Minesweeper* with relatively simple heuristics based on how players play the game; for example,

- You could detect a pattern of where players click first when playing and make sure those squares are guaranteed clear of mines for the next X puzzles.

- You could offer to suggest the player's first move as a guaranteed safe move, or even perform the least information-revealing move for them at game start.

- You could simply replace any mines discovered when you detect the game state to be discontinuous, repositioning the mine in a way that won't invalidate any of the revealed game information.

In *Sudoku* puzzle generation, solvers are often used to calculate the difficulty of the resulting puzzles based on heuristics that provide a difficulty rating for specific solving techniques. It's worth noting that this heuristic is a postgeneration calculation; if you want a specific difficulty *Sudoku* puzzle, you'd keep generating puzzles until one was produced (presumably keeping the discarded puzzles in buffers for their relevant difficulties to prevent needless duplication later).

Extra Bonus: Permutations

Depending on your puzzle rules, it may be possible to transpose elements of an existing valid puzzle starting state while maintaining solvability and continuity, essentially generating an entirely new puzzle. While this approach can broaden the size of your puzzle pool, it cannot help generate new puzzles from scratch because it always requires a valid puzzle to start from.

Permutations can be a viable strategy to add variety to your puzzle-space coverage as a whole, but a reasonable sample size of starting puzzles is necessary in order to prevent the results from feeling formulaic as players learn the permutation rules through inspection.

DESKTOP DUNGEONS, THE PUZZLE ROGUELIKE

Desktop Dungeons started as a 48-hour prototype when its designer, Rodain Joubert, wondered how you could make a roguelike that only took 10 minutes to play. The result quickly gained traction, turned into a freely available "alpha," and was fully rebuilt from the ground up for release once we understood the game better. That means it underwent open development twice, most importantly during a year-long beta that saw us putting out weekly updates. This gave us massive amounts of player feedback to work with, much of it relating to dungeon generation in some way.

More Puzzle than Roguelike?

Desktop Dungeons is primarily composed of randomly generated single-screen dungeons, each 20 × 20 tiles. Most roguelikes are sprawling exploration affairs with multiple levels that players traverse as they get more powerful. These small maps are populated by immobile enemies that, unlike roguelikes, where monsters take turns moving and attacking when you do, will only attack if you attack then first. The game also has very little randomness (outside of the initial dungeon generation); almost everything is deterministic—the game even goes as far as to show you 100% accurate results of projected attacks so that you can plan better. All the resources are designed to be granular, and where math became a problem in player feedback, the game's user interface (UI) was progressively changed to make calculated truths instinctively graspable instead.

The core element that makes *Desktop Dungeons* a puzzle experience is how regeneration works. In most roguelikes, players heal over time (turns) based on some sort of food or rest value. *Desktop Dungeons* focuses on using the condensed nature of its maps and turns unexplored terrain into a resource: you regenerate health and mana when you uncover new terrain (maps start covered by a fog of war; pushing this back regenerates any damaged enemies as well). Exploration in roguelikes is traditionally a boring affair; some even automate exploration until something happens. *Desktop Dungeons* turns this on its head and focuses on making every player action meaningful, including choosing when, where, and how to explore.

More Roguelike than Puzzle?

You don't get many puzzles with permadeath: the idea of only being able to try a puzzle only once, and too bad if you mess it up? That's usually not a great thing for puzzle gameplay, but it's great for the tension and desperation that drives players to tell stories of their exploits in roguelikes. The design goal of *Desktop Dungeons* was to condense those moments down into short, but intense sessions. It achieves this by riding that desperation line really hard—it constantly feels like you're not going to succeed in any given run. Until suddenly you do, and it feels great!

Desktop Dungeons is, like most roguelikes, a resource management sim at its core. The resource model in the game is all about trading off differently earned currencies against each other to keep ratcheting up the power level of your character (which is basically shorthand for the amount of resources you can bring to bear at any one moment). Playing the game is an exercise in spending health and mana to earn experience, which increases your health and mana pool. Except you're also spending black space (unexplored regions of the level) to regain health and mana. But then you need to hunt for enemies in the black space; maybe there's a better target just around the corner? And that's completely ignoring other complexities, like gold, items, the gods, piety, conversion points, and inventory space.

Everything trades off against everything else, often in ways that aren't atomic actions (and have multiple side effects)—you have to feel the resource economy on an intuitive level rather than strictly plan your gameplay responses. It's that sort of responsive play that makes *Desktop Dungeons* a roguelike.

PLAYER HOPE AS A RESOURCE

If your players feel like they're constantly walking on a knife-edge, one wrong move away from failing completely, the risk is always there that they'll assume they've made a fatal mistake when they haven't. In fact, players are generally completely wrong when they diagnose an early defeat: *Desktop Dungeons* is a game about gradually uncovering efficiencies in the resource economy of a dungeon run; thus, players who don't know those efficiencies are going to be wrong when they judge their chances.

The game is balanced to be constantly pushing at the boundaries of what players are capable of handling. Difficulty is a function of how forgiving a given dungeon's resource-spending values are. Players are also constantly increasing in skill: a veteran player can absolutely destroy a dungeon early in the game's progression, but it takes desperate situations to make players see themselves becoming veterans.

We attempt to train players to keep trying, even if they feel they might have already lost—in practical terms, the puzzle-space is generally so deep that there's a large buffer for nonoptimal actions in large numbers of potential solution paths for any given generated dungeon. But this carefully herded optimism is completely shut down if the player gets stuck in a dungeon that's actually unsolvable. When a player dies in a run, they need to feel that they could have done better, not that their attempt was pointless from the start.

Guaranteeing Solvability

During *Desktop Dungeons'* long alpha, it became clearly important that any run is solvable. But, given how the game was generating levels, we couldn't guarantee solvability in any of the usual ways:

- The hidden information lurking in a dungeon's black space meant players were constantly making irreversible decisions in discontinuous puzzle states, so the game rules couldn't guarantee solvability.

- Generating backward from a goal state was possible but didn't lead to good results; the odds of players finding or deducing the correct single solution path were far too small, given the massive number of potential actions available to players at every step.

- Building a solver that played the game to prove a generated dungeon had a solution ran into two problems: First, how many solutions were "good enough" for the generator, and how would we make our searches different enough to not simply find a single major solution path with a couple of actions switched around every time? And second, it's a damn hard game to play already; writing an artificial intelligence (AI) that can play *Desktop Dungeons* was beyond both our budget and time frame.

We had to come up with a different solution.

Because *Desktop Dungeons* emerged as a 48-hour prototype, it used the quickest and dirtiest generation strategies possible just to ensure that something possibly playable was ready to go when you entered a new dungeon. The game would first generate a map by clearing out lines of walls until a guaranteed amount of walkable contiguous space was made available. Then monsters would be randomly placed around the map (up to 40 of them for a single dungeon, including bosses). After that, we'd add pickups and interactive items in empty spaces. Finally, we'd add the player starting point and clear walls in a 3 × 3 space around that. Then it was go time. Good luck!

That worked surprisingly well, but it could (and did) generate completely impossible dungeon layouts by "blocking the player in" with enemies that were too high level to kill. In the resource parlance of the game, player progression was blocked by experience having health and mana costs too high for a low-level player to pay. It didn't happen as often as players assumed it did, but the sheer fact that impossible layouts could happen lent credence to players' feelings of unfairness when faced with a difficult but possible dungeon.

Generating Hope

In the end, we didn't change away from random start-state generation. Adding layers of heuristics to the generation systems produced encouraging results. We also added more terrain generation methods that produced different overall dungeon layouts for variety.

The first heuristic attempted to keep the available resource costs near player starting positions within acceptable bounds by introducing a minimum distance threshold to enemy spawns. Higher-level enemies that spawned too close to the player start location kept rerolling their positions until they were far enough away. Note that we didn't also apply maximum distances, so lower-level enemies could still spawn far from the player's starting position. Our focus wasn't on making sure "easy" enemies didn't cost a lot of exploration; rather, we wanted to make sure players were free to spend exploration if they needed to. This had the predictable effect of slightly depopulating the area near the player starting location overall, but this meant that helpful pickups were more likely to spawn in easy-to-reach locations, so we didn't try to correct that.

Minimum spawn distances for enemies definitely helped address the issue of experience blocking, but we found that player win rates actually went down during the *Desktop Dungeons* beta after the change. It turned out that the sparse enemy numbers around player starting locations meant that players were running right past low-level enemies in search of more pickups, wastefully spending exploration that could have replenished their health and mana after fights. The optimism for exploration was something we wanted to encourage, but we needed players to at least have a couple of lower-level fights to encourage good usage of exploration regeneration.

Our second successful heuristic made lower-level enemies look near their random spawn locations for nearby positions that would block off player movement. This clustering mechanic resulted in layouts similar to those of the original impossible dungeons, except instead of a level 1 player being blocked by level 5+ enemies, the player would only have to fight a level 1 or 2 in order to proceed down a passage. Enemy clustering logic also helped enemies "cooperatively block" wider areas.

Finally, we made specific glyphs (spells that players could use to spend mana to affect the world) that could have smaller but still useful impacts at lower player levels bias themselves closer to the player start location in the opposite way of high-level monsters. This helped players have mana spending options at lower levels and often resulted in providing them with an extra method to deal with potential blockages.

We tried a number of other generation heuristics during the *Desktop Dungeons* beta, but these were the ones that had the best impacts without drastically changing the gameplay. That's not to say we didn't add to the gameplay as well! The final version of the game had an entire metagame element that allowed players to bring certain items with them into a dungeon run (at a cost). These "preparations" would help increase player resource efficiency, as well as often having side effects that allowed players to handle potential blockages.

It is unfortunately hard to prove that these changes eliminated impossible dungeon layouts altogether, seeing as we still don't do any solvability checking in *Desktop Dungeons*. It's completely possible that these statistical approaches only make unfair starting states less likely.

However, there's an exception that helps prove their efficacy: one of the dungeons in the game, Doubledoom, doesn't use any of our monster positioning heuristics. It's a callout to the alpha and even warns players that it might be impossible. Before adding the positioning heuristics, we used to get regular reports and complaints on our beta forum about unfair dungeons. These days, the only complaints we get are about Doubledoom. In fact, it's now standard practice for our veteran players to ask people complaining about unfair starts if they were playing Doubledoom or not. So far, the answer has always been yes.

We can also look at *Desktop Dungeons*' seeded daily dungeon challenge as another sampling point. In the 500 daily dungeons shared by players since the feature launched, every single one has been beaten by at least 32 players. There have been some truly diabolically difficult ones, granted (hence the 32-player stipulation), but so far the game hasn't provided any truly impossible dailies. That's a success rate I'm more than happy with! Players seem more hopeful about the game as well; reviews of the full game don't mention unfair dungeons when that was a regular feature in writing about the alpha.

CONCLUSION

Procedurally generating puzzles can both produce endless possibilities for your players and create novel arrangements that inspire hand-designed puzzles. Generating puzzles successfully requires a pronounced understanding of the puzzle-space you're exploring.

Defining your generation needs via a deep or shallow puzzle-space, how many viable solution paths you require, whether solvability needs to be guaranteed, and whether your puzzles are continuous is extremely helpful at a conceptual level. The final generation approach you take depends very much on the interaction between player actions and the information your game presents.

It's usually best to start with a naïve approach: learning what makes a bad puzzle is just as important as producing good ones while you're starting to explore a new puzzle-space. You can always layer on heuristic complexity later as you understand your game's requirements and player limitations better.

A system that covers more of your puzzle-space is always preferable to one that is incredibly specific: it's easier to prune out undesirable puzzles than it is to coax an overly specific algorithm to produce variety.

CHAPTER 12

Procedural Logic

Ben Kane

Independent

PROCEDURAL GENERATION PLAYS A vital, and largely unseen, role in *Keep Talking and Nobody Explodes*. The content we generate is not the models or the environment or even the game state (though we do that too!), but rather the game logic itself. Throughout development, we relied on the generation of data to rigorously enforce the rules of the game while blurring the line between code and data.

This chapter is presented as a case study for *Keep Talking and Nobody Explodes*, so it will be a deep look at the design of the game and what considerations needed to be made in our approach to procedural generation. It's unlikely that this will be an appropriate solution for your game, because your game will inherently be facing different design problems. Instead, read about how our design goals were used to shape our application of procedural generation and consider how your own goals should influence your approach.

BACKGROUND

First, a few words about *Keep Talking and Nobody Explodes*, because it's a weird game with some weird restrictions. It's a cooperative game about defusing a bomb, but the twist is that only one player, known as the Defuser, is actually playing a video game. The Defuser sees a randomly generated bomb, with wires, buttons, symbols, lights, labels, and even a serial number. To defuse it, he or she must solve a series of puzzles and cut the correct wire, enter the right sequence, push the button at the right time, and so on.

The Defuser, however, has no idea what the correct solution is. For that, he or she needs the help of other players, called the Experts.

The Experts have access to the manual, which is a document featuring instructions on how to solve all possible cases for these puzzles. The manual is a static document, available for free at www.bombmanual.com. It's up to the Experts to obtain a copy of this manual, by either printing it out or viewing it on something like a computer, phone, or tablet.

The gameplay hinges on player communication, with the Defuser relaying information about what he or she sees, while the Experts sift through the manual and figure out the solution based on the details that have been described to them. Once they find the answer, they relay it to the Defuser, who cuts the wire and saves the day—or explodes.

The communication is where the fun lives, and all of our design decisions are made in favor of fostering interesting communication. Players should be placed into situations where they need to talk with each other, trip on their words, get confused, and make mistakes. We use this singular focus to evaluate design throughout the rest of this chapter.

USUAL APPROACH TO PROCEDURAL GENERATION

Procedural generation is used in several traditional ways. The states of the puzzles on a bomb are randomized so that there is variance in properties like the number of wires, their colors, the symbols on buttons, the state of lights, the presence of batteries, and more. This is what keeps the game replayable, because each round has a bomb that looks different, and the solutions to the puzzles, which are dependent on these properties, are accordingly different too.

At a higher level, the "missions" of the game also rely on procedural generation. A mission is essentially a level or scenario where the puzzles chosen for the bomb are restricted to an authored subset of the possible puzzle types. This is because each of the 14 types of puzzles plays differently, and some will inherently take longer to solve or are more difficult than others. We therefore create a set of broad parameters according to the difficulty or style of gameplay we're aiming to achieve.

For example, an easy mission might entail a bomb with just three puzzles from a small subset of the simplest puzzle types. More complicated missions can be authored that result in bombs with puzzle types that are difficult in combination with one another, such as a puzzle that requires remembering small bits of information over a long period of time combined with a puzzle that demands immediate attention, making for challenging time management. Without tailored missions, a truly random collection of puzzles on a bomb could vary widely in its difficulty and players might never experience certain challenging or interesting combinations. Procedural generation allows us to create missions that have some degree of variance and are therefore replayable, while still satisfying our need to have a controlled difficulty curve.

These are forms of procedural generation that are very visible to the player. They will notice that each bomb is different. They can see that replaying a mission will result in similar selections of puzzles with roughly consistent difficulty (or if not, they will at least be aware that later missions are harder than earlier ones, even if they can't describe why).

What won't be obvious is that the logic of the game is also built on procedural generation.

A DIFFERENT APPLICATION: PROCEDURAL LOGIC

The rules of *Keep Talking and Nobody Explodes* are the meat of the game. The rules make up the manual that the Experts read, and they are the logic that the game executes to determine whether the bomb explodes. They are what force players to communicate back and forth in interesting ways.

The rules are also procedurally generated, which may seem a bit confusing. After all, the manual is available on our website and can be printed out by players. It has no actual connection to the digital game, yet it absolutely must contain the same logic that the game executes. If the two were ever to deviate—for instance, if the game was executing a new, different set of rules—then the whole concept would fall apart. This is a core design constraint behind our rule generation process.

To make this work, the game shipped with a fixed random seed. That is, the game procedurally generates its rules, but always does so in the same way, thus ensuring it matches the manual that players may have already printed out. This is similar in concept to a game where a large landscape is generated during development to aid in content creation, but is later locked down and made permanent before the game's release.

Why use procedural generation at all then? The first reason is for future-proofing. Although our manual is dense with information, it is not impossible for dedicated players to memorize portions of it. We developed the manual with procedural generation in mind from the beginning so that we could refresh its contents on a periodic basis if it seemed necessary. Going forward, we can add additional manual variants for players who wish to swap out the rules while still supporting previously published rules.

The main motivation to generate the rules, however, was to ensure our manual and the game itself would stay in sync. We discovered early on that creating a manual, well, manually is an extremely error-prone process, and the results are difficult to verify. Since a large part of our game involves players attempting to learn the rules, misinterpreting those rules, and making mistakes, we had to be absolutely sure that the manual was correct and accurately reflected the logic of the game's code. This was vital during development when the game was both undergoing frequent changes and being exhibited at conferences in order to get player feedback.

To enforce the desired synchronization, we took a data-driven approach. The rules could be expressed and stored as data, which could then be used to generate a manual from templates and would be executed by the game's logic. The key here is that both the manual and the game would be working from the same data, and thus we could have some assurances that the two would be in sync (Figure 12.1).

HOW THE RULE LOGIC IS GENERATED

The puzzles and their rules are quite varied, so the method of generating rule data differs from puzzle to puzzle. In the simplest case, we need only scramble a list of possibilities. On the other end of the spectrum, more complicated puzzles require generating logical queries, as well as corresponding solutions.

Trivial Case

In the Morse code puzzle, the Defuser must observe a blinking light and describe the dots and dashes to the Experts. The Experts then use actual Morse code to determine which letters the dots and dashes correspond to. They then look up the word spelled out in a table and finally relay the associated frequency back to the Defuser. It's a tricky puzzle for players to

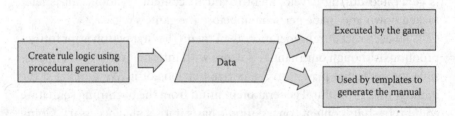

FIGURE 12.1 Diagram of how generated data is used by both the manual and the game.

If the word is :	Respond at frequency:
Shell	3.505 MHz
Halls	3.515 MHz
Slick	3.522 MHz
(...)	(...)

FIGURE 12.2 Example of Morse code puzzle rules used by Experts.

execute, but generating the rules is straightforward. The rules are simply the mapping of code words to frequencies (Figure 12.2).

To generate these rules, we just need to construct this mapping. We first author a list of possible four- or five-letter words to be used. Then we randomly associate each word with one of the response frequencies. And that's all there is to it!

It's worth noting that we could have overdesigned the solution here and tried to take into account how similar the Morse code representations of words would be in order to cause more difficulty. In practice, we found that players had ample difficulty communicating already, and our design goals would not be better served by increasing complexity.

Countable Problems

Puzzles have properties, such as color of wires, that vary from bomb to bomb, which keeps the game replayable. For some puzzles, the possible varieties are limited, and thus are easily enumerated. The Complicated Wires puzzle is one such case, but the rules are presented as a set-set Venn diagram, and the challenge is interpreting the diagram quickly (Figure 12.3). The four-set Venn diagram means there are four different properties that must be examined in order to determine whether to cut a given wire. This is a small set of possibilities: each property can be either true or false, so there are $2^4 = 16$ states. Creating the rules is a matter of randomly assigning a "cut" or "don't cut" solution to each of the states.

Of course, that would make for a fairly trivial puzzle. Our design goal is to foster interesting communication between the Expert and the Defuser, so instead we add a bit more depth by making the solution require some additional information. For instance, a solution could be "cut if the bomb has more than two batteries on it." Despite being a fixed instruction (i.e., something that can be printed in a manual), it will result in dynamic

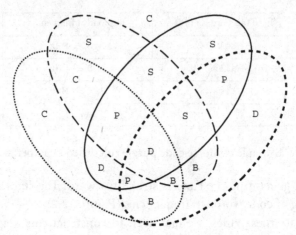

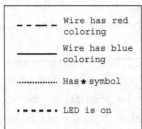

	Letter	Instruction
Wire has red coloring	C	Cut the wire
Wire has blue coloring	D	Do not cut the wire
Has ★ symbol	S	Cut the wire if the last digit of the serial number is even
LED is on	P	Cut the wire if the bomb has a parallel port
	B	Cut the wire if the bomb has two or more batteries

FIGURE 12.3   Four-set Venn diagram.

player behavior based on the particular properties of the randomly generated bomb.

There are a pool of such solutions, both simple ("cut") and involved ("cut if the bomb has a parallel port"). When selecting a solution, we weight the possibilities to make repetitions less likely and to encourage the appearance of the more complicated solutions. By authoring solutions like this, our procedurally generated rules can help force players to share more information, supporting our goals.

Not So Trivial: Procedural Logic

Other puzzles have states that don't lend themselves to being so easily enumerated. Consider our Wires puzzle: it's a series of three to six wires, each with five possible colors. That's already tens of thousands of possible combinations and would make for a very thick printout if we tried to describe states exhaustively. It also probably wouldn't be much fun if the entire game was just a lookup table.

- If there is more than one red wire and the last digit of the serial number is odd, cut the last red wire.
- Otherwise, if the last wire is yellow and there are no red wires, cut the first wire.
- Otherwise, if there is exactly one blue wire, cut the first wire.
- Otherwise, if there is more than one yellow wire, cut the last wire.
- Otherwise, cut the second wire.

FIGURE 12.4   Part of the manual for the Wires puzzle.

Instead, we wanted a more logical approach that used natural language. We ended up with a series of rules like those shown in Figure 12.4.

We call each of these statements a *rule*. It's a logical predicate (a *query* of the puzzle's properties) paired with an actionable *solution*. It covers a small part of the possibility space that wire puzzles can occupy, and so this particular rule will be true for some randomly generated puzzles, but not all of them. With multiple rules put together, we can cover all possible puzzle states.

Generating Rules

To generate sets of rules for a puzzle, we author various types of queries and solutions, and then combine them procedurally. The result is a surprisingly expressive system that can create rules, such as those shown in Figure 12.5.

Generating rules is more involved than simply randomly drawing from a pool of possibilities, however. Since the rules make up the logic of the game, and inherently impact how players will need to communicate, we needed to keep our design goals in mind when creating our generation algorithms. Let's take a closer look at how a rule is made.

Queries: Asking Questions

A query is designed to ask a yes or no question: Is the wire red? Are there four wires? Does the serial number start with a letter? A query is based on a property of either the puzzle or the bomb itself, and evaluates to either

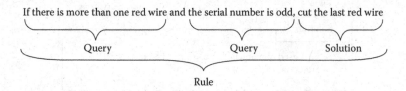

FIGURE 12.5   Diagram of how a rule is composed of queries and a solution.

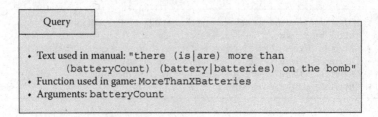

FIGURE 12.6   Simplified example of the structure of a query.

true or false for a given puzzle during gameplay. The query has a textual representation that can be used within the generated manual and is also tied to logic in the game that evaluates the question.

Figure 12.6 is a simplified example of a query template that asks a question about how many batteries are on the bomb itself.

Note that this template can be used with different values for "battery-Count," so we can easily generate several queries from this single template. The manual will be populated with the text in the query, substituting in the appropriate values within a range we define. The game will execute the function called "MoreThanXBatteries," using the chosen "batteryCount" (say, 1, 2, or 5) to evaluate the answer. And because both the manual and the game will use the same generated data, we can achieve our goal of keeping the two in sync.

Solutions: Taking Action

When queries are satisfied, the player must perform an action to solve the puzzle: cut a wire, push a button, or do some other sort of interaction. Much like a query, the solution encapsulates this action in a way that can be used both in the manual and during game execution. Figure 12.7 shows an example.

Solutions are specific to a particular puzzle type, so a pool of possible solutions is authored for each of them. As rules are generated, solutions are drawn from the appropriate pool.

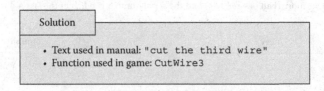

FIGURE 12.7   Simplified example of the structure of a solution.

IMPROVING THE PROCESS

With the concept of a query and solution, it's possible to generate a basic playable set of rules for the game. Throughout development, we listened to how players communicated with each other and modified the rule generation process to create better rules. For our game, "better" generation would mean creating rules that are more varied, require more back and forth communication, are less unintentionally confusing, and toughest of all, "feel" better.

Better Queries

Queries are the building blocks of the game's logic, and they represent questions that players will need to ask one another during gameplay. Since fostering interesting communication is the primary design goal, creating interesting queries is a vital part of the design process. The next sections are a few additions we made to the query generation process.

Compound Queries

Rules can have several queries associated with them, creating more specific questions that are less likely to all be true. Complex queries take longer for players to resolve and are more likely to cause confusion and mistakes during communication, both of which are desired outcomes for us as designers. A compound query can look like this:

> If there are more than two red wires and the bomb has a parallel port ...

Compound queries cover a smaller subset of the possibility space and thus are less likely to evaluate to true. For this reason, we opt to have a variety of compound and simple queries, so that players aren't always answering no to the majority of questions, as this proved tiresome and unsatisfying in testing. Our goal is to have interesting communication and not just more communication, so the rule generation follows accordingly.

Query Contexts

Some queries reference the bomb itself, asking questions about its serial number or how many batteries are attached to it. These have gameplay ramifications, as the Defuser must search around the bomb to determine the answer. However, the answer applies to the bomb itself, and thus any other rules that make a similar query are going to be less effective, as the

Defuser will be able to recall the answer rather than searching for it. For this reason, we make sure that our queries are never based solely on properties of the bomb itself, but rather involve at least one query that is specific to a given puzzle module. Otherwise, the solutions to multiple puzzles on a bomb could degenerate into a single bomb-level query, which is neither difficult nor satisfying for players.

In practice, this entails adding some information when authoring a query so that we can classify it as being "puzzle specific" or "bomb specific." The rule generator in turn can take this information into consideration and generate rules that better support our desired gameplay. Like many improvements, this is not without cost. A more complex rules generator takes longer to implement and maintain, so any such addition should be weighed carefully.

Better Solutions

For players, figuring out which solution applies to a puzzle is the challenging part of the game. Executing the solution is meant to be straightforward. After all, this is a game about teamwork and communication, so that's where the challenge should lie. For this reason, a solution directs a player to take a single action, like cutting a wire. However, in a puzzle with six wires, that amounts to just six solutions. We needed a way to introduce more variety.

Our compromise was to introduce a bit of logic into the solutions themselves. As long as a solution unequivocally corresponds to one and only one action, it will work within our rule framework. That means that instead of just saying "cut the last wire," we can do things like "cut the last red wire." It's a subtle difference, but in practice, it successfully results in more communication and opportunities for errors.

In order to do this, however, we need to make sure that there is a red wire to cut. This is where the query comes back into play. Recall that a query is essentially predicate logic, and so when authoring a query, we can recognize that the query being "true" gives us information about the puzzle itself. For instance, consider this query:

If there are more than two red wires ...

If this query is true, then we can be assured that there is a red wire to cut. The rule generator is informed of extra bits of information like this from the query and uses it to expand the pool of possible solutions. This added complexity to rule generation is worth the extra variety that it provides, not to mention it makes rules that feel more cohesive as the query directly relates to the solution.

RIGGING THE DECK: RANDOM THAT FEELS GOOD

In practice, randomly drawing queries and solutions from a pool of possibilities doesn't always result in rules that feel good. Playtest observations revealed cases where rules sounded repetitive or ended up being easier to answer than intended. We realized that truly random rules were undesirable. Instead, we found we got better results by weighting our selections. Each time a particular query (or even one from a group of related queries) is chosen, the rule generator adjusts that query's weight to make it less probable that it is chosen again in subsequent rules. This results in more variety, and the distribution of types of queries feels more balanced.

In general, we use this weighted selection approach to make less desirable selections less likely. We could opt to simply remove the option from the pool altogether and prevent any sort of repetition, but we found that having rare exceptions was actually beneficial. It leads to players making incorrect assumptions and taking shortcuts, only to have their assumptions sharply corrected as they realize they have gotten too comfortable and made a mistake.

Weighting is also used to tune generation toward more desirable options, which is an approach we employ to emphasize the challenge in some puzzle types. For instance, a puzzle based on remembering your input from previous stages is weighted so that rules in the later stages are more likely to reference actions in the earliest stages. Again, though, we choose to weight these choices to be more likely rather than outright enforcing them in order to keep things varied and prevent players from making too many assumptions.

Dealing with Degenerates

Random rule generation can occasionally result in rules that are degenerate cases of what is intended. In one puzzle, players are tasked with finding the first matching word in a list. By simply scrambling the list, the desired word can end up anywhere—even in the very first position! This makes for a rather trivial search. We could modify our generation logic to ensure the word only appears midway down the list, or even right near the end. But players will catch on to such things and will realize that they can ignore the earlier portions of the list. Procedural generation alone won't be enough to solve this design problem.

Instead, the puzzle design makes use of many such lists, and the scenario where one or two are degenerate search cases is not a problem. Players are quick to identify these and feel a degree of mastery in their knowledge. If we were to try to "fix" this problem with a more involved procedural generation algorithm, we would actually be working against our own design goals. It's important to keep in mind that more sophisticated procedural generation is not the solution to every problem.

Avoiding the Impossible

As the complexity of rule generation increases, it becomes possible to generate invalid rules. For instance, consider what may happen if any combination of queries and solutions were to be permitted:

> If there is more than one blue wire and there are no blue wires, cut the blue wire.

This is not an acceptable rule. Logic purists may argue that it's simply a rule that can never be satisfied, but in practice, most players will be confused in a way that is undesirable. Rule validation is one approach that could be taken to address this situation: generate a rule, check if it makes sense, and keep generating rules until you get one that does. Inefficiency aside, it's not a trivial task to verify whether a rule makes sense. Bombs, and their puzzles, have randomly generated states with billions of possible combinations, so exhaustive testing is intractable. We would require a better understanding of what is valid and what isn't in order to prove whether a rule is acceptable.

Instead, we recognize which combinations have the potential to be invalid and remove them from the possible query or solution pools. The general reasoning is that we wish to avoid compound queries that ask different questions about a single aspect. In the example above, there are two queries that both relate to how many blue wires are present. To prevent the situation from ever occurring, we simply remove all "blue wire" queries from the query pool as soon as we select one of them.

The keen reader may notice that this approach will also remove some valid combinations. For instance, you can no longer generate valid compound queries such as

> If there is more than one blue wire and less than five blue wires ...

We could devise yet more sophisticated generation algorithms to prune invalid combinations more closely, but first consider if the results are worth the investment and complexity. In our case, the design goals of our game could be met with greater query diversity rather than trying to ensure that every last valid combination could be included. It was much more practical, and manageable, to simply create additional types of queries.

PUTTING IT ALL TOGETHER

Rules deliberately cover just a small part of the possibility space for a puzzle. Players are expected to evaluate several rules by asking questions back and forth, eventually finding the one that applies to the bomb that was generated for them. No matter what combination of wires and colors a bomb is generated with, one of the rules will apply and there will be a single correct solution.

There are two small considerations that may not be immediately apparent but are vital to guaranteeing one and only one solution. The first is that the list has a defined precedence order. There may very well be several rules that are satisfied within the rules list for a given wire puzzle, but only the first satisfied rule is deemed to be the correct one. The second consideration is that we always include an "otherwise" case with no associated query as our final rule. This is a simple way of guaranteeing our rules list will contain an applicable solution regardless of the properties the bomb is generated with.

The otherwise rule is a necessary addition to keep our rules list from ballooning in size to cover the possibility space. Initially, we were concerned that it would be difficult to ensure that the rules weren't too specific, covering too little of the possibility space and leaving the majority of playthroughs simply degenerating to the otherwise case. In practice, this actually proved to have some gameplay benefits when used in moderation. Players would become complacent and make assumptions based on their experience with the likelihood of particular solutions. It made the rare exceptions that much more noticeable when their assumptions failed them and suddenly the tamest puzzle had caused them grief.

As an improvement to gameplay, we also sort the precedence list from most specific (i.e., the greatest number of queries) to least specific. This makes it more probable that players will need to check several rules before finding one that is satisfied. It's desirable to have this gradient of rule specificity because just having a lot of very specific (and thus very rarely satisfied) rules ends up feeling repetitive, as the solution will almost always just be the otherwise catchall case.

CONCLUSION

Procedural generation can be a valuable tool during development for content creation, even if that variety isn't exposed to the end user. The content you create is limited only by your ability to model the data, so even things like logic can be generated if you have reason to do so.

We tried to keep our core design goal of fostering interesting communication in mind throughout our project. That pushed us to expand our procedural generation logic in cases where it would support our design, such as creating more sophisticated queries and solutions. Perhaps more importantly, it kept us from getting carried away with overengineering the generation algorithm to squeeze out every last valid combination when a simpler culling approach worked just fine.

Procedural generation is fun, but shipping a game is more fun. Always keep sight of your design goals and ensure that your procedural generation is in service of those goals.

CHAPTER 13

Artificial Intelligence

Dr. Mark R. Johnson

Independent

NOT ALL PROCEDURAL GENERATION (PCG) games need artificial intelligence (AI). Some games have no other actors within the game world beyond the player—games like *Proteus* and *In Ruins* are focused on the feeling of exploration of an unpredictable space, specifically designed to present enough interest to the player to make this process engaging in its own right. Such games are concerned primarily by the experience of discovering the algorithmic world rather than anything else, and such exploration forms the only form of gameplay they offer. However, when used, PCG AI brings with it a particular set of design necessities and possibilities.

AI in procedural games must instead be able to cope intelligently (or at least with the resemblance of intelligence) with near-infinite varieties of spaces, other actors, and gameplay scenarios. AI in handmade games needs to deal with unpredictable situations, but it is only in games with a strong PCG component that AI might be forced to navigate entirely unknown and unforeseen terrain, deal with orientations of gameplay elements that were potentially not even understood by a game's designers as being within that game's possibility space, and still present whatever level of AI challenge and complexity was intended.

This chapter focuses on player experiences of AI and designer intentions of AI, common requirements for AI in games with PCG, and new and innovative AI development methods that offer potential for the subfield's future.

UNPREDICTABILITY AND ARTIFICIAL INTELLIGENCE

AI often contains elements of unpredictability, as governed by some form of random number generation system that is hidden from the player. There are several reasons for this:

1. *Challenge*: By making players respond rapidly, increasing replay-ability, opening the possibility of emergent phenomena through the unseen interactions of disparate in-game elements, and so forth. Unpredictable AI can boost the range of gameplay possibilities over a more deterministic equivalent.

2. *Exploit resistant*: Opponents who behave predictably can often be exploited. I'm sure most readers will recall playing older games whose AI characters followed quite simple processes that could easily be taken advantage of to subvert design intent. An AI designed to always dodge a grenade is prone to players using grenades to "force" the AI to dodge in a particular direction; an AI designed to pursue a player can be lured into traps. Deeply unpredictable AI reduces this possibility.

3. *Balance*: The technical development of an effective AI that succeeds well at the mathematical and game-theoretic challenges of a game is vastly simpler than designing an AI in such a way that players actually want to play against it. A "fun" opponent includes elements of game design, psychology, sociology, and even interface design, whereas the former is concerned only with computer science and game theory.

It's generally simpler to design a strong or even game-theory-optimal AI than an AI that can appropriately and competently weigh up metrics of challenge and fun. The latter requires selecting an action that perfectly matches up the player's current gameplay condition and psychological condition. AI systems like the AI Director in the *Left 4 Dead* games attempt to do precisely this, but it is relatively uncommon.

One of the most active current areas in game AI design is the concept of designing for fun as a counterpoint to designing for challenge, but such a concept is far harder to write into code than a mathematical decision of the best in-game move. Otherwise strong AIs can simply be weakened a little in order to produce an effect that, on the surface, is quite similar. In the roguelike game *Dungeon Crawl Stone Soup*, for example, many bosses and high-end enemies are given a selection of "spells," from which (in some versions of the game) they choose randomly each turn. This is designed to provide unpredictable challenge, but also to balance the game's more difficult enemies through giving them a selection of stronger and weaker spells. This allows bosses to deploy deadly attacks without being game-theory optimal and using their strongest attack on every turn, which would result in enemies that were far more challenging (although also far more predictable) and far less interesting.

Players can also assign spurious intention and agency to simple and semiunpredictable AI patterns. In early roguelike games, monster AI was rarely more complex than "wander around, and then when the player is sighted, pursue them by the most efficient path possible." Players, however, often thought that a far more complex monster AI was at work, and that monsters would deliberately show up at the worst possible time for the player. What was happening, of course, was that monsters that appeared (whether through random movement or active pursuit) at moments where the player character was safe, well rested, and at full health were rarely remembered, since those resulted in trivial fights.

By contrast, if the player had just fought a brutal battle and was at death's door, and then two other monsters come around the corner, that becomes an event the player will remember for a long time and may subconsciously blame on the monster's decision making, instead of the unlucky vicissitudes of fate or the eventual outcome of a tremendously simple follow-the-player AI routine.

The unpredictability and predictability of AI can therefore readily become interwoven and confused even without the role of PCG. PCG's inclusion in the design processes leads beyond these concerns of player-side understanding of AI actions toward a range of designer-side questions, focused on how AI should be programmed to respond well in procedurally generated spaces and settings, and how the player will engage with such AIs.

MOVEMENT AND COMBAT

AI in the overwhelming majority of games tends to be heavily focused on two related but distinct elements—movement and combat. This is as true of PCG games as it is of their handmade cousins, but PCG games bring with them a distinctive set of design challenges.

In the majority of cases, AI actors will be expected to move over terrain with likely millions of possible permutations, preventing game designers from programming in methods for handling specific regions, and instead resulting in a focus on the handling of more general case and scenarios, which requires the accurate prediction of all possible categories of movement scenarios.

If an AI actor is expected to move around a city, then code must be put in place to ensure they can traverse wide alleys and narrow alleys; get around other individuals; and handle bridges, rivers, other traffic, and whatever else might be present within that particular world. This uncertainty over the tasks that AI in PCG games will be asked to perform is further complicated by different kinds of terrain, from standard ground to ice, water, lava, temporary hazards, oceans, mountains, deserts, alien terrain, and so forth.

Such extra layers cannot be specifically predicted, and therefore the ability to navigate them cannot just be coded into a limited number of creatures who will potentially need to pathfind through such situations, but instead all creatures need these abilities. This leads to particular kinds of monster design architectures that are easily modifiable, easily influenced by the particular affordances of a specific creature (cannot traverse lava, can traverse water, etc.), and applicable to any creature so long as it has the appropriate information relating to its abilities and restrictions.

All possible permutations must be accounted for—even if a city with an enclosure of buildings is a one-in-a-million possibility, if an AI starts within that enclosure, it must be able to figure out how to enter one of the buildings and then leave on the other side beyond the enclosed space. If designers do not anticipate the possibility of that enclosure, then it is unlikely the AI will be able to respond to it, resulting in the game's PCG upsetting the intended behavior of the game's AI.

Combat, meanwhile, is a staple of computer games generally, including those with PCG. The design requirements for combat in PCG games is broadly comparable to the concerns over movement outlined above, which is to say that strong PCG AI needs to be programmed not to handle specific forms of combat in specific known-beforehand contexts, but rather to respond to any possible scenario. In roguelikes, this normally means intelligent decision making with regard to various weapons and various ranges of combat, and more advanced strategies, such as retreating, flanking, or calling for assistance, and an AI needs to be able to assess these without any prior notion of the combat scenario it will find itself in.

Once again, there is the question of the extent to which all combat scenarios can be predicted, and therefore factored into the AI design process. Movement and combat thus both pose comparable design questions centered around the extent to which designers can predict all possible PCG scenarios—or rather, the elements of all scenarios, which the AI then identifies—and the extent to which the game's PCG and AI systems can thereby become closely integrated. If this integration is low, unusual outcomes will leave the AI unable to make a sensible choice about its actions, resulting in the AI either freezing, defaulting to a simplistic option, or selecting a bizarre option for the current scenario; however, if this integration is high, players will see procedurally placed AI characters behaving well in procedurally generated spaces, irrespective of the nature of the space and the condition of the character, and thereby behaving comparably to convincing AI in an equivalent handmade game.

AMBIENT BEHAVIOR

Ambient behavior refers to AI that carries out certain actions even when the player is not nearby or engaged with the AI actor. Perhaps the current and most fascinating exemplar of ambient behavior is the science fiction roguelike game *Cogmind*, in which the player is placed in a world containing large numbers of robotic "species," many of which ordinarily ignore the player and go about their business without being concerned by the player's actions, unless the player attacks them, interrupts their routines, and so forth. This poses a challenge for designers because the AIs must be able to "go about their day" on any possible map, necessitating the development of a system that can identify points of interest for each AI actor when the map is generated, and build up a completely unique spatial and temporal schedule for that actor each time a level is generated. Equally, however, it affords opportunities for creating game spaces that feel deeply alive and lived in, even if they had only actually been generated a split-second prior, and therefore performing a kind of visual trick on the player ordinarily only possible in handmade games with AI actors who have been given meticulously thought-through handmade schedules for their days.

EMERGENT PHENOMENA

Emergent phenomena refers to situations where sets of simple behaviors lead to often unanticipated sets of more complex behaviors. The classic roguelike *NetHack* perhaps contains the most illustrative examples of emergent phenomena. *NetHack* contains a range of in-game systems and AI behaviors that can readily be overlooked by players—the game is technically winnable without ever truly engaging with or understanding some of these systems and AI behaviors.

For example, if reading a scroll of "genocide" would normally wipe out an entire species of monster, a cursed version of this item could result instead in the creation of those monsters around the player. Deliberately reading a cursed scroll of genocide and attempting to wipe out the "nurse" creature will spawn a ring of "nurses" around the player, whose "attacks" in fact heal the player and can even boost the player's maximum health. This means that a desirable item used to destroy monsters was cursed to become "bad," but some uses may still result in a "good" outcome, through the interaction between the behavior of those AI monsters and other in-game elements. In this and many other emergent phenomena, AI and monster behaviors are integral to these processes, and although they are almost certainly both entirely unintended uses of the AI, these kinds of emergent phenomena are compelling aspects of AI behaviors in procedurally generated games.

CONVERSATIONS

One of the most interesting aspects of AI in PCG games is the generation of speech and conversations appropriate to a procedural world. *Ultima Ratio Regum* (*URR*) development is focused on a complex conversational AI rather than a complex combat, movement, or ambient AI, as conversations are fundamental to how players of *URR* engage with the game's AI.

We can reasonably split generated conversation elements into two categories—the PCG of the actual words that the AI actors speak, and the conversation system itself.

The procedural sentences spoken by *URR*'s AI characters consist of a range of elements, which draw on procedurally generated dialects, and also the specific opinions and current mood of the person doing the speaking. World generation in *URR* includes creating a unique dialect for every in-game culture, of which there are ordinarily roughly 40, consisting of large feudal nations, smaller tribal nations, nomadic nations, and perhaps someday independent city-states (Figure 13.1).

Dialects

Generated dialects consist of several components.

First, the game selects a group of consonants, vowels, and syllables, from which all "invented" words for that dialect (such as the names of places and people) will be constructed—this is a reasonably standard technique for

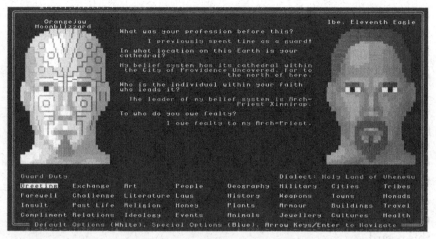

FIGURE 13.1   Conversation in *URR*.

generators that produce words meant to be indicative of a shared language, and results in groups of words like *Xonatov, Vonnerto, Toravert,* or *Kaeltram, Malatrakel, Altrakem*. Different languages and dialects are distinctive and identifiable by an observant player as belonging to one culture or another.

Second, dialects include generated "references," which are cultural, historical, political, and religious elements used by all speakers within a certain culture. These might include nearby terrain; the dominant religion within a nation; recent history, political ideologies, or diplomatic relations; or artistic and aesthetic preferences. These are then present in all conversations from individuals in a particular culture, strengthening the similarity within one culture, and the differences between many.

At this point, also, we begin to see the development of a conversation AI that is rather more complex than that in most games, where characters from different cultures are either handwritten to be different or produce the same set of identical or almost-identical statements regardless of cultural backgrounds. The "rumor" options in conversations with *Elder Scrolls* characters provide a particularly striking example of culture-agnostic character speech.

The third element of generated dialect is the generation of greetings, insults, farewells, and threats. This does not directly alter AI behavior, but it does continue to develop nonplayer character (NPC) actors who, when they speak, sound extremely distinctive as a result of the procedurally generated origins of their procedurally generated character.

The fifth and final element of generated dialect is what I've termed sentence complexity, which affects how much an individual says. This is the difference between introducing yourself in a few words and including a short list of the great achievements of your nation in your introduction. More loquacious AI actors therefore offer far more information to the player than their more taciturn comrades.

The design goal here was to create interesting, procedurally generated, culturally distinctive AI actors who would speak in unique ways dependent on their origins. As an element of game design, this is almost entirely overlooked in even handmade games, let alone procedural games. Conversant game characters tend to lack any real differences based on their origins, although a rare few games, such as the *Mass Effect* series, are exceptions. Equally, as above, PCG rarely affects AI speech and conversations, *Dwarf Fortress* being the obvious other current standout project in this regard.

Conversation System

In addition to the dialect and subsequent sentence generation system outlined above, *URR* also deploys a particular kind of conversation system. The player chooses from dozens of topics—artworks, history, ideologies, religions, monasteries, travel, animals, and books—and the list of potential questions in each topic grows as the player learns more about those topics.

Upon learning about a new artistic movement in poetry, any NPC can be asked about that movement; upon learning about a particularly bloody war fought 80 years ago, any NPC can be asked about that war; or upon learning about a reclusive hermit who might hold a crucial clue to the player's victory, any NPC can be asked about the location and disposition of that hermit. Crucially, of course, none of these elements were fixed in world generation—all these conversation options have emerged through the game's PCG.

The conversation system is therefore designed specifically to take advantage of the fact that these are AI actors within a procedurally generated game. *URR* adapts immediately to whatever new output of the procedural generators has been created and identified by the player, whether it's a painting, a person, or a piece of history, and allows the player to start a conversation about an effectively infinite number of topics.

Similarly, while sentences are constructed from many elements, an AI actor is always able to put together an appropriate reply to any topic asked. This yields a PCG response to a PCG question, even if that response is only to express a lack of interest because you are asking them about a piece of artwork they've never heard of, a moment of history from a thousand years ago and half a world away, and so forth.

Conversations with AI actors are core to the gameplay of *URR*, even though everything to do with conversations—from sentences and dialects to questions and replies—is procedurally generated from scratch each time the game is run. This represents an intriguing fusion of PCG and AI behavior, and one I plan to develop further in the coming months and years.

CONCLUSION

Whether your actor navigates terrain, attacks, or sociopolitical debates, their ability to detect and adapt to changing circumstances is key to their satisfying performance in a procedurally generated game. The question is often not how many verbs the AI needs, but rather what types and combinations of input it can react to, and what elements of its reaction can be generated and will yield interesting outcomes. When trying to make a world that feels alive and unique, PCG developers must consider the values they want their world to express, and move from this into developing their characters' strategies, speech, and desires.

CHAPTER 14

Procedural Enemy Waves

Wyatt Cheng

Blizzard Entertainment

A COMMON PRACTICE IN PLAYER versus environment (PvE) games is to have situations where many enemies are set up to attack the player as the fight progresses. Sometimes, there are large waves that are distinct and obvious. Other times, enemies come more in the form of "adds"—individual additional enemies who join a battle in progress. Sometimes this will be a triggered event; sometimes entire levels are created based on the notion of fighting multiple waves.

Examples of procedural wave spawning in Blizzard games include

- *Starcraft 2: Wings of Liberty*: In the mission "Mar Sara 3: Zero Hour," you must survive for 20 minutes against incoming attacks. Missions where you have to survive for a minimum amount of time are called "holdout" missions.

- *World of Warcraft*: Many bosses will spawn monsters in waves. Gluth, one of the bosses in Naxxramas, spawns zombies every 10 seconds.

- *Diablo III*: There are events called "Cursed Chests." Cursed Chest events always last exactly one minute. Monsters spawn continuously, and the faster you kill the monsters, the faster they spawn. If you kill at least 100 monsters, then you are granted additional reward.

As you can see, spawning waves can be used in a variety of contexts. Here I'll cover four different methods that have different advantages and disadvantages. You can adapt these methods to suit your needs.

METHOD 1: SPAWN BY TIMER

When using Spawn by Timer, the enemies are spawned based on elapsed time, regardless of the situation and player state. A single enemy can spawn at a fixed time, or you can spawn many waves (multiple enemies who all appear at the same time).

Spawn by Timer Pseudocode

```
// Waves is sets of data pairs that represent the
// time into the mission to spawn a wave
// and the data required to spawn that wave.
Waves = {
        {time=15, spawndata=SpawnData1},
        {time=30, spawndata=SpawnData2},
        {time=45, spawndata=SpawnData3},
        {time=60, spawndata=SpawnData4}
}

// A function that is assumed to run every
// game tick (for example, every 60th of a second)
Global currentWave = 0;
Function UpdateTick()
{
    // If we are ready to spawn the next wave
    If (Waves[currentWave].time <
GetCurrentGameTime())
        {
            // Spawn the next wave
            SpawnWave(Waves[currentWave].spawndata);
            currentWave = currentWave + 1;
        }
}
```

Commentary

Spawn by Timer is a good spawn technique when you want to test the player's skill, aptitude, or general power level. The enemies appear whether the player is ready or not, making this a good technique to use when the approximate power level of the player is fixed and relatively the same for everyone. Factors such as level-ups, gear, or player skill can cause the effectiveness of the player to vary considerably, making Spawn by Timer quickly lose its appeal.

Levels that use Spawn by Timer are often crafted for a specific difficulty by a designer—if the player is a bit stronger, each wave becomes too easy and the player can be left bored. If the player is a bit weaker than the designer anticipated, then the player quickly becomes overwhelmed.

This latter problem is extremely common when using Spawn by Timer. Suppose you have waves of five monsters. Based on the designer's playtesting, it takes 15 seconds to defeat a wave, so the waves are set to be 15 seconds apart. If the player is even 20% weaker than the designer anticipated, then each wave might take 18–19 seconds to defeat. Just 15 seconds into the fight the player might still have one enemy at full health when wave two spawns. This combination of enemies might be so challenging to the player that they have three monsters alive when wave three spawns. This effect can "snowball," causing the player to become farther and farther behind the intended difficulty until completely overwhelmed.

Whether this snowball effect and sensitivity to player power can be beneficial or detrimental depends on the design goals of the level. If the strength of the player character is well known and it is the designer's intent to test whether the player has reached a certain level of mechanical proficiency with the game's controls and strategy, then a Spawn by Timer event would be very appropriate. On the other hand, if the goal is to provide a cool experience for the player regardless of their gear or skill level, then the snowball effect is inappropriate and a different spawning technique should be used instead.

The *Starcraft* holdout missions are a good example of Spawn by Timer. On a typical *Starcraft* level, the power of the player is relatively well known and the goal is to test the player's ability to play strategically in order to win or lose.

Some players may be so quick and adept at killing the enemies of each wave that there is a possibility they clear a wave before the next wave is ready to activate. In this situation, the designer has two choices:

1. Delay until the timer elapses, allowing the player a breather. This approach not only is simpler to implement but also rewards the player for finishing early. However, this approach also risks disturbing the pacing or boring the player, as they will have no enemies to fight until the next wave is spawned.

2. Set up your level so that the next wave triggers on a timer, but should the player clear the wave early, then the next wave triggers

immediately. This becomes a blend of this method with Spawn on Completion, which we'll discuss next. In this latter case, you should be cognizant of any player advantages to dragging out the fight (such as health and resource regeneration or cooldown activation).

Key Characteristics

- Good if you want to test whether the player has mastered certain game mechanics

- Sensitive to the player's current power level

- Can lead to snowballing

- Allows precisely designed pacing

METHOD 2: SPAWN ON COMPLETION

Spawn on Completion is a spawn technique that involves spawning waves of enemies where each wave is triggered by the previous wave dying.

Spawn on Completion Pseudocode

```
// Waves is simple data that contains the
// information required to spawn each wave.
Waves = {
     {spawndata=SpawnData1},
     {spawndata=SpawnData2},
     {spawndata=SpawnData3},
     {spawndata=SpawnData4}
}


// A function that is assumed to run every
// game tick (for example, every 60th of a second)
Global currentWave = 0;
Function UpdateTick()
{
     // If we are ready to spawn the next wave
     If (NoEnemiesAreAlive())
     {
          // Spawn the next wave
          SpawnWave(Waves[currentWave].spawndata);
          currentWave = currentWave + 1;
     }
}
```

Commentary

Spawn on Completion presents some amount of challenge to the player, but with some flexibility to adapt to how well the player is doing. The difficulty of each wave can be calibrated by the designer without the difficulty of one wave affecting the others. Unlike Spawn by Timer, if the player struggles with one of the waves (but manages to complete it), it won't have a disproportionately adverse effect on subsequent waves.

Spawn on Completion is used in the *World of Warcraft* raid zone "The Battle for Mount Hyjal," in which players repeatedly confront 10 waves followed by a boss fight. The approach allows a mix between testing players for a minimum gear or skill level and still keeping players engaged the entire time.

Since the difficulty of each wave does not directly affect the challenge of other waves, Spawn on Completion can also be a way to test the power of the player when there are multiple vectors on which to measure player power. For example, if a spaceship game allows players to excel with missiles, laser beams, and shields, then three different waves might test the player's abilities along these three different vectors. If the player is strong or weak against one vector, then the player will find that wave to be particularly difficult or easy; however, the player still needs to demonstrate sufficient proficiency along each vector to complete the level as a whole.

One cautionary note: Waiting for the previous wave to be completed before the next wave spawns can sometimes lead to a behavior in which the player deliberately avoids killing the last monster to "drag it out" and allow health, resources, and cooldowns to recover. This can be mitigated somewhat (but not entirely) by combining this spawn technique with a Spawn by Timer and allowing either condition to cause the next wave to spawn. Doing so introduces the risk of introducing the snowball effect that Spawn by Timer is susceptible to, but the two techniques are very often combined successfully.

One often desirable characteristic of Spawn on Completion is that it is readily apparent to the player that the enemies are coming in waves. This can be very exciting, as it allows alternating periods of tension and release as the waves come in.

Key Characteristics

- Good if you want to be somewhat adaptive to how powerful the player is but still want to have minimum performance requirements

- Can be exciting to alternate tension and release

- Good for testing along multiple vectors

METHOD 3: CONTINUOUSLY ESCALATING TOTAL

With a Continuously Escalating Total spawning scheme, the number of enemies active at a time is always increasing. As enemies are killed by the player, new enemies spawn to maintain a minimum count of active enemies.

Continuously Escalating Total Pseudocode

```
// Waves is a set of data pairs that represent the
// time into the mission and the number of enemies
// that should be onscreen at that time
Waves = {
      {time=15, minimumEnemyCount=5},
      {time=30, minimumEnemyCount=10},
      {time=45, minimumEnemyCount=15},
      {time=60, minimumEnemyCount=20}
}


// A function that is assumed to run every
// game tick (for example, every 60th of a second)
Global currentWave = 0;
Function UpdateTick()
{
      int minEnemyCount;
      For each (wave in Waves)
      {
            If (wave.time > GetCurrentGameTime())
            {
                  minEnemyCount = wave.
                  minimumEnemyCount;
            }
      }

      While (NumberOfEnemiesAlive() < minEnemyCount)
      {
            SpawnAnEnemy();
      }
}
```

Commentary

Continuously Escalating Total is a good technique to use when a dramatic arc is desired. Because enemies are continuously replacing themselves, the fight needs to end based on a criterion other than "defeating all the enemies." The most common is reaching a kill total or a time limit.

With aggressive tuning values, Continuously Escalating Total can be a fun spawning technique to use for a bonus level or other minievent. Since the number of active enemies is continuously increasing, the player never truly "beats" the event. In this context, the event instead becomes a test to measure how far the player can get.

In many games, gauging the player's power level is difficult due to the number of factors that contribute to player success. This makes Continuously Escalating Total a good spawning technique to use when the player's power level may vary widely due to either play skill or character progression. Early on, the player might play a Continuously Escalating Total level and find they could survive 30 seconds, and then later in the game, when they have grown in skill or character progression, they are able to play the same level but survive for two minutes. This provides a tangible benchmark of how far they have come.

A variant of Continuously Escalating Total is used in *Diablo III* for the Cursed Chest events. The goal of the Cursed Chest events is not for the player to either defeat the enemies or die trying. Rather, the design intent is for the player to always kill enemies, but for the event to be a test of how many enemies the player can defeat. The player has exactly one minute to kill as many enemies as possible, and the faster the player can kill the enemies, the faster they spawn.

A cautionary note: Depending on the exact mechanics of the game and the presentation of the results, overreliance on Continuously Escalating Total can become exhausting for the player. Constantly growing in intensity until you are ultimately overwhelmed can be exciting, but as designers, we should be cautious when we require players to maintain this excitement cycle for extended play periods.

An interesting property of Continuously Escalating Total is the relationship between player power and how long the event takes based on the completion criteria:

- If the event is timed, more powerful players cannot complete the level faster.

- If the event is based on "kill X enemies to complete," then the level will complete faster as the player becomes more powerful.

- If the event is based on "how far can you get," then the level actually takes longer to complete as you improve in gear.

Choosing the right completion criteria based on the needs of your game is an important decision for effective use of this spawning technique.

Key Characteristics

- Adapts to being fun and challenging for both low-end and high-end players

- Good at allowing players to measure themselves along a continuous spectrum of progression rather than being a binary pass–fail check

- Can be mentally exhausting to do for a long period of time

METHOD 4: HITPOINT PROGRESSION

With Hitpoint Progression, additional waves are spawned when damage equal to a specific percentage of maximum health has been done to the enemies spawned in the previous wave calculated against the sum total of health. This means that if the player is less powerful, then spawning will happen slower, and if the player is more powerful, then spawning will happen faster. The action is continuous, since the next wave is spawned while the current wave is still active.

Hitpoint Progression Pseudocode

```
// Waves is sets of data pairs that represent the
// hitpoint percentage of the previous wave that
// should remain before spawning the next wave paired
// with the data required to spawn that wave.
Waves = {
        {percent=1.00, spawndata=SpawnData1},
        {percent=0.60, spawndata=SpawnData2},
        {percent=0.30, spawndata=SpawnData3},
        {percent=0.50, spawndata=SpawnData4}
}

// A function that is assumed to run every
// game tick (for example, every 60th of a second)
```

```
Global currentWave = 0;
Function UpdateTick()
{
    CurrentHealth = SumOfHealthOnCurrentWave();
    MaxHealth = SumOfMaximumHealthOnCurrentWave();
    HealthPercentage = CurrentHealth / MaxHealth;

    // If we are ready to spawn the next wave
    If (Waves[currentWave].percent >
      HealthPercentage)
    {
        // Spawn the next wave
        SpawnWave(Waves[currentWave].spawndata);
        currentWave = currentWave + 1;
    }
}
```

Commentary

Hitpoint Progression is a good system to use when you want the player to experience a continuous stream of enemies that is always presenting a challenge but has some ability to adapt to how well the player is doing. Similar to Spawn on Completion, Hitpoint Progression gives the designer the ability to create some waves that are particularly challenging or thematic, or stress different vectors of player power while ensuring the player doesn't get overwhelmed if they are below the designer's expected power level.

If the player is doing well, enemies spawn faster; if the player isn't doing well, enemies spawn slower. For this reason, Hitpoint Progression is a good system to use when a high variance in player power is expected due to skill or character progression and the designer wishes to create a dramatic encounter that is likely to be fun and engaging for the widest possible audience. By the same token, Hitpoint Progression is a bad spawn technique to use when you wish to test player performance.

Key Characteristics

- The most adaptive of the four spawning techniques
- Not good for measuring player power or skill
- Good for creating a dramatic combat experience

CONCLUSION

Changing even what seems like the smallest element of your procedural algorithm can result in highly varied player experiences. Timers, completion, continuous escalation, and hitpoint progression are only four of the many possibilities of spawning enemies. The correct spawning technique or combination of techniques can be selected on grounds of intensity, challenge, pacing, exploitation, balance, or other factors, depending on your gameplay's unique needs.

CHAPTER 15

Generative Artwork

Loren Schmidt
Independent

I N THE EARLY 1950S, Desmond Paul Henry found a World War II bomb guidance computer at a military surplus store. Fascinated by the movement of the analogue computer's mechanical components, he altered it in such a way that instead of expressing its processes as bomb-targeting information, it drew pictures. Its inner workings were superficially simple, on an algorithmic level not dissimilar from pendulum-based drawing machines. But Desmond Paul Henry's drawing machines have made some of the most deeply beautiful human computer art. And they achieve all this with great lightness and elegance.

Henry's machines draw with energetic, organic lines: there is a slight flutter to the weight, the edges undulate gently like bone ridges or rippling skin. They feel deeply appealing on a human level.

Much of today's digital art (especially if you work in games) has a fixation on fidelity and technical showiness. It is hard not to think this way: beyond the immediate appeal, visual fidelity is often seen as an indicator of artistic merit. This is a complicated topic, and one that I don't have space here to dissect properly. Let it suffice to say that

1. Today's particular brand of "technical excellence" is tremendously dependent on funding, available time, education, and other resources.

2. Cultural emphasis on this type of work is unnecessarily discouraging to people who don't have those resources.

3. This is not an interesting or useful metric for evaluating art.

Your art is valuable and valid no matter where you are coming from. This section aims to arm you not with new technical tools, but with general techniques and modes of thinking that are useful in addressing the human side of generative visual art. It is designed to help you quickly apply these concepts to any generative work (including games), so please apply them wherever they are useful in your own life.

TECHNIQUES

Scope is not quality; it is a separate axis: When finishing up or fine-tuning a project, one might be tempted to try and "improve" it by adding features (Figure 15.1). The generated tree gets tiny animated flowers; the sky gets heat haze and atmospheric scattering. This may seem natural, but it is not: making your project flashier and adding technical tricks is increasing scope, not quality. Instead, try taking a step back. What does your piece feel like, and how does that differ from how you want it to feel? Are your proportions good? Could you tune it better? What is the weakest part of the piece? Could it be improved by removing anything?

Thinking in terms of processes: We are usually taught to evaluate algorithms in terms of whether they work. But I'd argue that there is another more important metric here that largely goes neglected. Are your algorithms emotionally relevant to your project? Code is a rich and complex language, and there are many different ways to write the same process. Your individual decisions are a powerful expressive conduit. Also be aware that sometimes dissonance or distance can subtly insert itself when the algorithms do not feel the way you thought they would, when the tools you are using are not in harmony with your goals. If you find this happening, can you alter your algorithms or your goals so they are better in tune?

Symmetry and structure: Working digitally, one of your great strengths is the way iterative processes naturally tap into human perception. Humans have a strong natural response to symmetry, and engage automatically in pattern-detecting behavior. A few shapes with some symmetry applied can quickly start to look compelling (Figure 15.2).

Mark making: Consider the ways you are making marks. This might mean drawing pixels to a screen, rasterizing vectors, or drawing polygons in three-dimensional (3D) space (Figure 15.3). This might mean adding letters to a string. Certain tools have a very distinct fingerprint: for instance (as of 2016), much visual work done in JavaScript or Unity is highly recognizable as such. Perhaps this esthetic cast works in your favor. But if you find yourself fighting against it or wanting to try out other

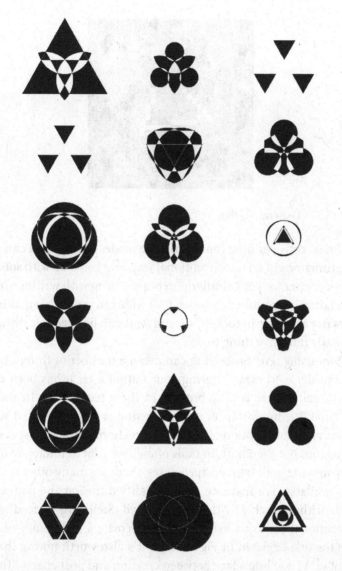

FIGURE 15.1   Generated sigils.

FIGURE 15.2   Generated flowers.

FIGURE 15.3   Generated triangle.

possibilities, consider how your marks are made. Perhaps you can use the built-in functions in an unconventional way, and come up with something that works better for you? Similarly, experimenting with writing your own low-level drawing routines can open up a wide range of mark-making possibilities not available in tools by default (this can be a technically or computationally intensive thing to do).

Postprocessing: Postprocessing can mean a number of things, but here let us consider it to mean altering your output after it has been created. Conventionally, there is little breadth in these techniques. In the realm of real-time 3D, for instance, postprocessing is largely limited to a few standbys: vignettes, motion blur, color correction, and screen space ambient occlusion. But even built-in tools often have a lot of untapped breadth. And if you write your own postprocesses, there are many other expressive options available. For instance, if you modify diffusion and pattern-dithering algorithms such as Atkinson or Floyd–Steinberg by feeding them unconventional diffusion kernels, you can create a wide range of effects, such as the one depicted in Figure 15.4. It's also worth noting that there need not be a rigid boundary between creation and post effects. There is a lot of interesting potential for feedback between the two.

PERCEPTION OF INTENT

Searching for the intent of the creator is a natural human way to interact with any artifact. One may ask: Who made this? What was their process like? What were they feeling? Sometimes people deliberately turn this capacity off or deemphasize it when looking at digital art. As mentioned above, humans are avid pattern detectors. Repetition and pattern can be beautiful. Sometimes one might make an elegant, crystalline algorithm and wish to

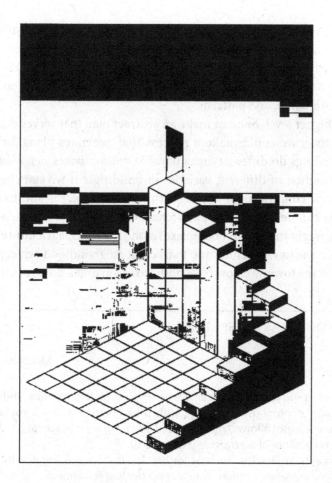

FIGURE 15.4   Generated staircase.

expose its workings and bounds. Sometimes transparency can be desirable here. In other situations, however, one might find oneself struggling against this tendency to create a process that feels more varied and intentional.

If the volume of the solid is insufficient, one can linearly increase one of its dimensions. This happens frequently when working with grammars. Suppose one is populating a town with buildings. The obvious way to reduce repetition is by linearly increasing the number of buildings in one's set. But this is a linear increase, and does nothing to address structural blindnesses or faults of pattern. When looking at the town, we see only randomly placed diverse buildings. It's still noise.

Instead of simply pursuing linear growth, one can pursue greater self-awareness. In the case of our town, we might benefit from algorithms that create different types of multibuilding complexes. Like increasing building variety, this can decrease the repetition of outputs. But more significantly, this begins to address the problem of perceived blindness or lack of intent. Suddenly, when looking at the town one starts to pick out walled courtyards, parks, and patterns.

On a higher level, one can make an abstract plan that serves as a guide. For instance, we could make a process that generates plans for towns. Which feelings do different areas have? What motivates neighborhoods, the distribution of different varieties of buildings? If we start here with a high-level concept, then our algorithms for complexes and individual buildings can be created with awareness of the plan. When viewing the town, we might find factory complexes along the water, agriculture centers away from the town's center, and markets at neighborhood centers. When we look at the town, we now have both variation and a sense of intent.

PROCEDURAL ART CASE STUDY

MARK MAYERS

Desolus is a surrealist puzzle game where you explore dreamlike landscapes and power mysterious technology with solar energy. My background as a computer scientist allowed me to create *Desolus* using procedural art, despite having no traditional art training (Figure 15.5).

Art assets in *Desolus*, such as terrain, are first roughly created by hand, with algorithms like erosion simulation providing refinement and detail. By manually creating a tree species and then manipulating its generation, unique trees are able to be grown for the game's environments as needed using SpeedTree. These elements allow for more diversity in assets than could be developed traditionally, especially by a small team (or, in this case, a solo developer).

Despite its resplendent appearance, *Desolus* contains no rigged characters or animated models. Instead, the game uses a detailed graphics processing unit (GPU) particle effect system to convey gameplay elements abstractly. Traditional animations are replaced with particles and shaders, allowing for more effort to be spent designing compelling worlds. For example, the black hole in *Desolus*, which comprises the game's core puzzle mechanic, is generated with a gravitational lens shader and GPU particle system. Tweaking various parameters of this particle system, such as colors, physics forces, emission, and shaders, produces a variety of impactful results in various scenarios. A similar methodology is used for creating the sky of *Desolus*. Shaders controlling color and atmospheric properties are manipulated to

FIGURE 15.5   Generated landscape from *Desolus*.

create a dynamic sky system, which is critical for setting the mood of scenes. Nonorganic meshes in the scene are generated through fractals and procedural meshes. For instance, the black obelisks present in every scene of the game are created by recursively cloning a simple cube in a pattern.

These individual systems combine to compose the "universe" of *Desolus*, a complex world created from simple algorithmic rules. This process of creation emulates the natural world, as the universe operates by a set of laws that humans can ostensibly describe through science. However, it is the artist who interprets what he or she finds most beautiful about these universal laws.

CHAPTER 16

Generative Art Toys

Kate Compton
Independent

EVERYONE LIKES BEING CREATIVE. And everyone likes discovering that they're more creative than they thought they were. For many years, people have enjoyed crafts like pottery wheels, Spirographs, Mad Libs, spin art, paper marbling, and tie-dye. These artistic toys helped everyday people make interesting artworks (even if those people lacked creative talent or inspiration) by producing surprising and emergent results from simple choices.

Now that we have digital systems, we can make art toys with even more surprising and emergent behavior. No longer bound by the limits of reality, we can build Spirographs in virtual reality (VR), Mad Libs that generate worlds, tie-dye that evolves over time, and pottery wheels that spin out curling tendrils of emergent geometry.

I've enjoyed building generative digital art toys, and they've helped me better understand and use generative methods. I've written this chapter as a guide to help you to design and build your own. May you find as much pleasure and fun and strange generative artwork as I have!

BUILDING ART TOYS, FOR EXPERTS AND NOVICES

So why is this chapter on art toys in a book on procedural content for games? Because generative art toys can use many of the same techniques as procedural generation (PCG), but don't have the same gameplay-based restrictions as content that has to go into a game. As someone who makes both generative art toys and PCG for games, I find I have a lot more freedom making the art toys, and I spend more time enjoying the wildness of the generativity and less time worried about gameplay issues.

Art toys are also a good way to explore new kinds of generative methods (algorithms suitable for generativity), or to try out old favorites in a new context. I've repurposed the particle-based techniques we used to create *Spore* planets to also make interactive drawing tools that come to life. Lindenmayer systems (L-systems) can create nice trees for game backgrounds, but they can also be used to make surreal flowers for a flower-arranging app (Figure 16.1). Context-free grammars can construct dungeon levels and *Mario* platforms, or can build music and poetry. Flocking algorithms can move nonplayer characters (NPCs) for combat, or can power a choreography generator. I've written a popular blog post on different generative methods you might want to try, "So You Want to Build a Generator," but I can't think of a single algorithm that couldn't be turned to making art, so keep your eyes open for new potential procedural paintbrushes.

One of the reasons I love making art toys with procedural content is that, in games, the generated content is often invisible (like artificial intelligence [AI] movement) or in the background (like sky textures and trees), but it's always serving the purposes of the gameplay. The gameplay is always the star, and the PCG plays a supporting role. What if the user were interacting directly with the content generator? What if the user were controlling the generator, giving it feedback, or exploring and curating the

FIGURE 16.1 Art toy by Kate Compton, where the user iteratively breeds new procedural flowers, generated with an L-system and an evolutionary algorithm.

things it made? Suddenly, the focus is on the generator itself; now it's the star of the show and the center of attention! As someone who loves building generators, this is a pretty delightful situation.

EXPERIENCE OF ART TOYS

Digital art toys (and the physical art toys of the past) are beloved because they help us discover the artists in ourselves, even when we aren't particularly good. We might not all secretly be great artists on the inside, but we can surprise ourselves by creating a neat mandala, abstract artwork, chiptune melody, generated poem, procedural flower, decorated pot, animated creature, or any of the many odd and interesting artifacts that you can now make with easy-to-use digital tools. The tool needs to be smarter than a pencil, but also let the user feel like they're in charge. How can you strike that balance?

Art toys should provide a good experience for users. We're familiar with the kinds of pleasures that games provide (see 8 *Kinds of Fun* or Koster's *Theory of Fun* for nonexhaustive lists), but creativity apps and art toys have their own different kinds of pleasures. I've come up with several modes that an art toy might operate in, depending on how much independence it has outside the user's interactions: it can feel like a tool, like a collaborator, or like an artist itself.

If it is a tool, it can magnify or constrain the user's input so that the output becomes bigger, more complex, and better made than the actual skill and effort they put in. As a collaborator, the art toy can provide inspiration, suggest new directions and modifications, and encourage a user who might otherwise feel uninspired and undirected. Sometimes the generator is independent enough to create content on its own, and the user can become the one providing guidance, steering the generator to explore different parts of the possibility space, as the user collects and curates and shares the subset of generated artifacts that they find particularly interesting. Sometimes we even give up understanding how to control the system at all, in exchange for the fun of chaotically surfing on a generative wave of art. Try *Become a Great Artist in Just 10 Seconds* by Michael Brough and Andi McClure for a grand example of this.

In any of these cases, the user should feel like they are exploring a rich and varied space of possible artifacts, quickly and pleasurably. They should also feel like they, personally, have ownership of the artifacts that the generator creates, whether they had the skill to build them (with the generator's assistance) or the good taste to pick them out (from the generator's output).

A user who uses a well-made art tool will often forget about the tool's role in creation altogether, which is not a bad outcome! Saying "I'm really good at this" is a much more powerful feeling than "this generator is good at this." Conveniently, a user who takes to social media to share their skill at a creativity is also symbiotically promoting the app, too! Call it the *Minecraft* effect: when the users feel creative and powerful, both the users and the apps win.

TRADING CONTROL FOR POWER

The central idea behind an art toy is that the user is trading away control and gaining power. What that means (and why it's important) becomes clear if we contrast *art toys* with *art tools*.

There are countless professional digital art tools available today. Very soon after computers developed, people created drawing software for them (Ivan Sutherland's 1963 *Sketchpad*), and this practice has continued ever since. Many of these tools were created with expert users in mind—professional creatives or skilled artists—and give users total control over the output. This brilliant user must have an idea of the final image already in their head; the tool's purpose is to help them render that idea to the screen. Not a simple demand!

But there are more users who want to be creative than just these few creative geniuses (and professional creatives). Creativity is linked to numerous positive outcomes in health and psychological wellness. Being creative is a pleasurable activity: we feel good when being creative. Interestingly, these benefits aren't correlated to how good we are at the creative activity, just whether or not we feel engaged. This means that this kind of creativity is an autotelic activity; that is, it's practiced as an end in itself, rather than to get some external result.

Professional creativity isn't necessarily an autotelic activity. Photoshop, for example, assumes that its users are professionals trying to get something specific done. So it is highly flexible and highly complex, and has to give the user total control. Likewise, three-dimensional (3D) software like Maya doesn't know whether the user is making a 3D printed teapot, an architectural rendering, or a 3D cut scene, so it has to support all three, but can't provide automated support for any given task. Automated generators aren't customizable enough; professional users require total control. However, autotelic users are willing to cede control to a generator, as long as it gives them more power; that is, the generator can magnify or superpower streamline their creative activity in some way.

There are many digital examples of this trade-off (e.g., *Spore* vs. *Maya* and *Instagram* vs. *Photoshop*). But even older childhood toys like the Spirograph show this trade-off between power and control.

An unconstrained drawing tool like a pen gives an artist complete control, able to draw in any direction. "Line drawing" encompasses a huge possibility space, containing some Rembrandts, sure, but mostly ugly and incoherent scribbles. A novice user will more likely end up with a scribble than the Rembrandt; they can draw anything, but aren't likely to find their way to the good stuff.

With Spirograph, a gear-based drawing toy from the 1950s, the pen is stuck in a socket in one of the gears, and the gear forces its motion into spiraling loops as the gear spins around its track. The user has only a few discrete decisions to make (color of pen and size of gears), and one dimension of motion (forward or backward). This creates much smaller possibility space, but that space is full of universally interesting stuff! No Rembrandts, but a lot more satisfyingly symmetrical geometry mandalas.

Pottery wheels make a similar trade-off in one more dimension. From the huge three dimensions of freedom (and accompanying possibility space) of a hand-sculpted shape, one dimension is automated by the wheel, leaving the two dimensions of freedom (in–out and up–down) to work the pot. The automation has taken away a bit of freedom, but has given us a faster, more reliable way to get to satisfying outcomes. We've given up control and gotten superpowers in exchange.

KASPAROV'S CENTAUR

Isaac Karth

Today, new AI and generative tools are creating art. A neural network can transfer the style of one image onto another or change the composition. A photograph can be made to look like it was painted by Van Gogh or Renoir.

This isn't the first time artists have dealt with new technology. Generative tools have strong parallels with early photography. As photography struggled to establish itself as a medium in its own right, some painters reacted by embracing Impressionism. Impressionism took inspiration from the more candid subject matter that photography allowed, but it also embraced the subjective visual aspects that photos had trouble reproducing.

Likewise, in the wake of his historic loss to IBM's Deep Blue, chess grandmaster Garry Kasparov became interested in a new way to play chess. In 1998, he played the first game of "advanced chess" against Veselin Topalov: each player used a computer as a partner.

This cyborg play style, sometimes called "centaur chess," created better players than individual humans or machines. Like the centaur, the human–machine collaboration lets each half of the combination overcome the weaknesses of the other. The human is still playing the game, but the rote work has been automated, freeing the player to express themselves.

An artistic metaphor for this is the generative artist Strangethink's *Joy Exhibition*. *Joy Exhibition* is a little VR art gallery, where the only painting tool is a collection of billions of procedurally generated paint guns. Each gun has a distinct and weird pattern. These paint guns are a microcosm of PCG and centaur art.

Interestingly, impressionist paintings seem to work particularly well for style transfer. Something about the loose brushstrokes appears to make it easier for the machine to generate a cohesive result. The future of game and art generation likely has similar discoveries lurking, waiting for the right artist to put the pieces together.

DESIGN AND CONSTRUCTION OF ART TOYS

Hopefully I've convinced you to build an art toy, if you weren't already planning to do so.

If you were designing a game, you'd probably start with a type of game-play (e.g., tower defense or match 3). But there aren't established genres yet in art toys, so each one seems to be a unique design solution. So how do you begin designing one from scratch? Figure 16.2 shows the common design pattern that I've seen from many of the casual creators and art toys I've studied. Each art toy has three kinds of elements (inputs, transformations, and rendering), with an optional fourth element of social or sharing mechanics. You can think of these as modular Lego bricks that can be snapped together, creating a different art toy in each configuration. I've made this into a set of physical cards that you can print out and experiment with at home.*

Inputs

Inputs can be anything from simple keyboard input or scroll wheels, to touchscreen and mouse-dragging or tablet pens, to full body tracking with a Kinect or 3D tracked VR hand controllers.

One of the important considerations here is to consider the "width" of the data pipeline. A keyboard produces very sparse data: binary keypress events, spaced out over several seconds. A mouse provides a continuous feed of X, Y coordinates, two dimensions of data recorded continuously over time. A hand tracker like the Leap Motion records the joint positions and rotations of wrists, hands, and fingers. If wrists move freely in 3D

---

* http://www.galaxykate.com/arttoys/arttoy-cards.pdf

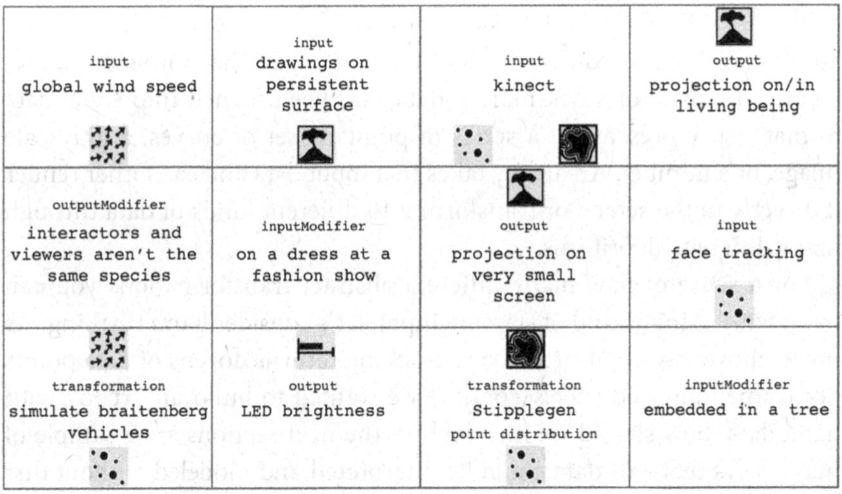

input global wind speed	input drawings on persistent surface	input kinect	output projection on/in living being
outputModifier interactors and viewers aren't the same species	inputModifier on a dress at a fashion show	output projection on very small screen	input face tracking
transformation simulate braitenberg vehicles	output LED brightness	transformation Stipplegen point distribution	inputModifier embedded in a tree

FIGURE 16.2   Example card from the printable set.

space, and each finger joint has about one-and-a-half degrees of freedom (rotation plus a bit of side-to-side motion), a hand produces 50–100 data points per sample, a huge pipeline of information to process!

Very high degrees of freedom (like skeleton tracking) require continuous feedback to the user to help them understand the system. *The Treachery of Sanctuary*, a triptych art installation by Chris Milk that uses the user's shadow as input, does a spectacular job at this. As the user raises their arms, they see their fingers' shadows extend into large feathered wings, and lowering the arms retracts the wings. As they flex their fingers in and out, they see the feathers fan in and out at the same rate. This continuity (temporal and physical) of the generated shadow gives a great stream of feedback to the user, and the gallery patrons, even children, instantly understand and begin playing with their shadow.

Contrast this to many other body-tracking apps: while *Treachery of Sanctuary* uses the entire continuous pipeline of input to generate the shadows, other apps try to detect "pose" occurrences, compressing the rich pipeline of data into a series of discrete binary events spaced out over time: the same spacing and discreteness as keyboard input. Good user interface (UI) feedback is often an issue with these apps, perhaps because they've discarded 99.99% of the user's input before they start. But generativity like that shown in *Treachery of Sanctuary* suggests that this need not be the case.

Data and Transformations

So you have some input. What now? That *real input* (the motion of a hand, a body, a crowd, or stock market data) has been turned into some data format that represents it: a series of points, a set of curves, a grayscale image, or a number. An art toy takes that input data and can either render it directly to the screen or transform it to different kinds of data through many different algorithms.

For a sense of how many different abstract transformations you can build with a single kind of starting input, let's consider hand tracking. As noted above, raw input from hand tracking returns dozens of data points per frame, hundreds per second. If we wanted to build an art toy with hand data, how should we interpret it? The next sections are a sample of many ways that this data could be interpreted and modeled without discarding information (like traditional gesture recognition does).

Points and Rotations

Leap Motion returns the hands as several arrays of positions (for each finger, the wrist, etc.). Freeze the hand for a moment in time and look at the positions of the joints. Each one has a location in space, and each location might be in front or behind some other geometry (an imaginary plane of canvas). There may be moments (and positions) where the points cross a boundary (when the fingers "pass through" the canvas). Each finger joint also has a 3D vector for the direction that it is pointing. With these two arrays, we could build geometry aligned along the bones, but extending further outward, as *Treachery of Sanctuary* does.

Connectivity and Meshes

From a set of points, we can build a connectivity graph. Between each edge of the finger is an edge representing a finger bone. But there may also be edges between fingertips showing their proximity (with edges appearing and disappearing as fingertips near and touch). If both hands are visible, we can build a Voronoi map of connectivity, a procedurally generated cat's cradle of edges.

Gestural Curves

Hands are rarely still. They wave and flex, clench and open. Each joint moves along an invisible animation curve through space, and we can record those curves as well. Google's *Tilt Brush* takes this approach, recording the curves of motion and then reskinning them with different strokes or using them as paths for additional actions (see the "Rendering" section later).

Forces and Acceleration

Each joint is moving. From that, we can calculate the velocity (as a 3D vector) and thus determine its acceleration and implicit force. If my hand were constantly shedding paint, which direction would the paint fall? Should I make a mark where my hand is now, or in the direction it is moving? If I know where each finger is on a relaxed hand, can I tell how flexed or stretched a finger is? Is that stress also a force to be recorded? If I'm swinging my hand, I often have less sense of where it is than of the direction of its movement and the forces acting on it. Figure 16.3 shows the velocity and the forces applied to many points along the tracked hand. Even just drawing these vectors as arrows creates emergent art from the hands' motion. These forces could also be applied to particles "held" in the hands, or to simulated agents, or used to manipulate a pixel buffer of colors.

Rendering

We have inputs and a way to transform those inputs into progressive layers of different kinds of data structures.

Wait, wasn't there supposed to be some art in this art toy? Certainly the most memorable part of any art toy is the visual results of the interaction.

Drawing is often defined as "making a mark on a surface," but what does it mean to make a mark, and what is the surface? For an exhaustive ontology of digital drawing tools, I recommend Alvy Ray Smith's

FIGURE 16.3   Hand-tracking image. On the left, hands are tracked as arrays and acceleration. Even drawing these forces creates interestingly emergent patterns. On the right, velocity and acceleration are drawn additively, with subsequent hand forces overdrawing each other to leave a trail of movement over time.

"Varieties of Digital Painting," but for the purposes of this chapter, here are the basic concepts that you can use to build a rendering method:

Canvas: This may be a buffer or a series of composited buffers. If we are playing in 3D, or with vector graphics, it may also be a scene graph or list of renderable shapes. Regardless, it's a way of recording what we will render to the screen.

Mark: A semipermanent element or action. It might read from the canvas, as a "blur" brush has to sample the pixels underneath before redrawing them, or a "fill" command paints outward until it encounters an edge. It is constructed, it is added to the canvas, and (because we aren't working in reality), it may morph or flow or change or be deleted. For a traditional digital paint program like MS Paint, the canvas is a simple pixel buffer, and most marks just write a color into an area of the buffer, or start a function that recursively writes color into expanding areas until a stop condition is reached. The buffer is never erased, only added to. An Illustrator graphic has no persistent buffer as its canvas, but instead has a scene graph. If the scene graph is changed (a mark is added or a color is changed), then the scene graph renders itself onto a temporary buffer and onto the screen.

Additive versus parametric rendering: In additive rendering, there's a buffer that gets added to and evolved each time, based on the previous state of the buffer. Nothing is ever discarded; it's just built over, which mathematically looks like this for some buffer with five marks or actions being made on it: final buffer = $fe\,(fd\,(fc\,(fb\,(fa\,(\text{buffer})))))$. Parametric rendering is rendering without a buffer memory. Each time, it renders the whole finished product from scratch, doing whatever subrendering or compositing it needs to do along the way: final buffer = $f(a, b, c, d, e. \ldots,$ initial buffer). But the boundary between these two is surprisingly flexible. In a buffer-based drawing engine like Processing or HTML canvas, I may have a scene graph that I want to redraw each frame. I can "erase" the buffer before drawing each time (setting each buffer pixel to a background color), and thus achieve parametric rendering. Or I can choose not to clear the buffer, and each parametric rendering will be made on top of the previous rendering. This technique leaves the past trails of a moving object visible, which can be good for inexpensive trail rendering, notably used in the Windows Solitaire win animation and the Microsoft 3D Pipes screensaver. There's also an interesting middle path, where the previous rendering is partially obscured. I often draw a partially transparent rectangle on top of the previous rendering, leaving the trails visible, but fading out over time in an attractively veiled way.

The two competing VR drawing apps, *Oculus Medium* and Google *Tilt Brush*, seem similar at first, with identical inputs, and both using a gestural curve model to record their marks. But under the surface, one is an additive and the other is a parametric rendering, and this changes their interaction. *Medium* uses voxels, a 3D version of the pixel buffer. The user can "mark" more voxels into space, or write over previous voxels (or write over them with blank space to erase). But one can't go back and edit an earlier mark, other than by undoing to the point it was made. *Tilt Brush* is fully parametric, where each stroke is stored as a vector and then "rendered" into the scene graph (which is later rendered onto the screen in 3D). This allows modification of previous strokes, and more interesting ways of rendering strokes as animated curves or particle effects or patterned ribbons.

Advanced and indirect rendering: *Tilt Brush* and *Medium* are both intended (if unintentionally) as tools for good artists (note how their promotional materials show famous Disney animators and illustrators using them). They want to be flexible enough for anyone to build anything, so they kept their rendering very directly related to the input. If you're building a smaller art tool, for more flexible users, the mapping from input to output can be much less direct. Flexibility and control can be sacrificed for generativity and power, and that can be a good thing!

Remember that the rendering being described here doesn't mean the final rendering to the screen, but the way that the abstract model turns into a mark.

One very common parametric approach to rendering is to have an array of numbers, a "string of DNA," which is rendered into some physical form. For an animated flower prototype, I turned an array of 30 floating-point numbers to a set of rules for a flower-generating L-system. This rendering process had several advantages. The space of the flowers was interesting and varied, but also continuous. This allowed me to perform an evolutionary algorithm on the flowers responding to the user input of selecting their favorite. I could also "lerp" between new values over time, mutating the flowers according to time. I also was able to hook the values up to a music analyzer, which morphed them in time to music, and then hooked it to a Leap Motion Controller, so that each hand position would generate a different flower.

This is the powerful part of this "input–model–rendering" model of art toys. Once you have it built, you can begin switching out new inputs or rendering methods, generating new, playfully strange art toys with each variation.

You can also use time as an input parameter for any parametric rendering. Rendering at frame 2 will be slightly different than at frame 1 or 0. If your parametric functions are continuous, rerendering frames (or rebuilding scenes) will create the effect of a smooth animation. The art game *Panoramical* is a lovely example of this. The user sets nine different two-dimensional (2D) sliders, creating 18 different parameters. Time is added as a 19th. Each of the many levels is a different parametric function to interpret those 19 parameters into music and a 3D scene of geometric objects. Changed over time, it creates an animated soundscape that is controllable by the user.

Another engaging way to interpret models is to have simulations or other algorithms using them as inputs. Any graph or set of points can be turned into a Voronoi diagram or Delaunay triangulation. From there, it could be rendered as a 3D mesh or as paths of connectivity for simulated agents to move along. Models and inputs can create forces that act on the elements in the world, rather than being elements themselves. The classic art installation *Text Rain* (Camille Utterback and Romy Achituv, 1999) drops text from the sky on a projection, and the users create barriers with their shadows that it can flow down or puddle upon. Art toy users could also create wind, gravitational wells, water currents, or any other force to move renderable elements. Imagination (and simulation power) are the only limits.

OUTSIDE THE GENERATOR: JUDGMENT, SHARING, AND CURATION

What happens between the user and the generator is important. Just building it will create an art toy that is intriguing and generative. But often some of the most powerful interactions happen outside the generator, in gameplay built around it or in communities that arise outside. How does the user learn to use the tool? Are extrinsic forces at play when they are creating something? All these are other things to consider when building the tool.

With the *Spore Creature Creator*, it's possible to look at a creature and instantly judge whether you like it. This is true of most visual art tools, but for artifacts like music, stories, or games, this "judgment" step can be several seconds to minutes to hours long! Sometimes art toys can play with this idea of judgment, creating artificial feedback that may or may not reflect actual judgment. *Become a Great Artist in Just 10 Seconds* pokes at both the idea of judgment and the idea of art school by asking the user to match their drawing to the given still life or landscape and judging them accordingly. But this art toy doesn't allow the user to draw directly, only by pressing keyboard keys to activate surprising and frustrating glitch-art filters, making the automated judgment a silly and surreal metric.

Another art toy that gives the player control over curation but no creation is *Picbreeder*, an online tool to browser neural network–generated images and "breed" new ones. Although the users' only interaction is clicking on the ones they like, users still show pride in finding unusual ones in the space and showing them to other users.

CONCLUSIONS: CREATIVITY FOR ANYONE

There are very many aesthetics available for art toys. From frustrating and opaque (*Become a Great Artist*) to welcoming (*Spore Creature Creator*), intensive and controllable (*Medium* and *Tilt Brush*), uncontrolled and automated (*Picbreeder*), or meditative (*Text Rain* and *The Treachery of Sanctuary*), there can be art toys for every play experience and every artifact type. Procedural content can make them more powerful, surprising, generative, and welcoming to new users.

CHAPTER 17

Audio and Composition

Bronson Zgeb
KO_OP Mode

SKIPPING STONES IS AN experiential game in which the player throws found rocks from a beach over the water, creating generated music. There are two major components to a procedural audio system like the one found in our game *Skipping Stones*: producing sound and composing.

PROCEDURAL AUDIO IN SKIPPING STONES

Sampling

In order to produce sound, I used a sample-based synthesis approach. The basic premise is that you create and record samples from your instruments first to use as a basis for all the audio. Another approach would be to synthesize all your audio in the engine, which, although possible, requires a greater knowledge of audio synthesis and audio programming. Furthermore, synthesizing complex audio can put a big strain on your CPU. A sample-based approach gives you all the power of your existing instruments, synthesizers, and sound effects (SFX) libraries, and is simpler to understand and implement.

If you're familiar with audio hardware or software, you may be familiar with the concept of a sampler. A sampler plays back short audio files while simultaneously modulating them to produce modified versions of the base sample. For example, the most basic sampler can play a sample at different speeds, which also modifies its pitch. Even this basic functionality was enough to start building my procedural audio system. But first, a little bit of music theory.

Pitch

Western music contains only 12 notes, which are then repeated over about 11 octaves, beyond which the notes become imperceptible to the human ear. These 12 notes are C, C#, D, D#, E, F, F#, G, G#, A, A#, and B. In some cases, we might call C# (pronounced "C sharp") a D flat, F# a G flat, G# an A flat, and A# a B flat, but for our purposes this doesn't matter. In fact, the names of the notes are completely irrelevant and can sometimes be more confusing than helpful. For example, octaves start on C rather than A, and there is absolutely no correlation between any of the sharps (or flats) with their corresponding nonsharps (or nonflats), that is, A# and A. The names of the notes are just names, nothing more. Octaves are used to represent how high or low a given note is. That is, an A4 (that's A on the fourth octave) is just a higher-pitched version of an A3, which is consequently higher than an A2, and so forth.

Now that you understand the selection of notes you have at your disposal when making music, it's important to understand what a note actually is. A note is a wave of sound created by an object that's vibrating at a given frequency. So when a speaker plays an A4, for example, it's because the speaker is vibrating at 440 Hz, which travels through the air until it reaches your ears. The important thing to note here is that every note in Western music corresponds to a specific frequency. Table 17.1 is a lookup table of note frequencies by name and octave.

So what does this mean? First, every note in every octave has a specific pitch. Second, the ratio between a note and its neighbors is always the same (as is the ratio between its neighbor's neighbors, its neighbor's neighbor's neighbors, etc.).

From any note, you can multiply its pitch by the same known value and land squarely on a neighboring note. This is the key to sample-based synthesis. For example, if you loaded a recording of a C3 note from a piano into a sampler, you could play it back as any other note from that same piano within limits.

What limits? A basic sampler modifies the pitch by playing back samples at a different speed. As a result, there's only so far you can stretch a given sample before it sounds terrible. How far you can stretch a sample depends on the sample itself, but you don't expect to go beyond a couple octaves up and down. If you need a wider range, you could use multiple samples, one for every other octave range, for example. Using this information, you can emulate an instrument playing any note in any octave using only a handful of samples.

TABLE 17.1   Pitch Values by Note and Octave

Note	1	2	3	4	5	6
A	55.00	110.00	220.00	440.00	880.00	1760.00
A#/Bb	58.27	116.54	233.08	466.16	932.33	1864.66
B	61.74	123.47	246.94	493.88	987.77	1975.53
C	65.41	130.81	261.63	523.25	1046.50	2093.00
C#/Db	69.30	138.59	277.18	554.37	1108.73	2217.46
D	73.42	146.83	293.66	587.33	1174.66	2349.32
D#/Eb	77.78	155.56	311.13	622.25	1244.51	2489.02
E	82.41	164.81	329.63	659.26	1318.51	2637.02
F	87.31	174.61	349.23	698.46	1396.91	2793.83
F#/Gb	92.50	185.00	369.99	739.99	1479.98	2959.96
G	98.00	196.00	392.00	783.99	1567.99	3135.96
G#/Ab	103.83	207.65	415.30	830.61	1661.22	3322.44

Implementation

Most of the instruments in *Skipping Stones* are actually just basic samplers. Each one is loaded with a sample of a C note in some octave (usually C3), and when it plays, I modify the pitch in order to play the desired note. *Skipping Stones* was built in the Unity engine, which allows you to set the pitch of an audio source as a floating-point number. So in this case, a pitch of 1 means play at normal speed, 0.5 is half speed, 2 is double speed, and so forth. I created a lookup table of pitches by calculating the ratio between a note and its neighboring note and multiplying forward until I had enough range.

Therefore, playing an instrument with a pitch of 1 will give me a C (because that's the pitch of my original sample), whereas playing an instrument with a pitch of 1.059463 will give me a C#, a pitch of 1.122462 will give me a D, and so forth. Additionally, since all my instruments are loaded with a sample in C, I know that the same pitch across all my instruments will produce the same note.

At this point, you're able to start building basic instruments, so it's a good time to start working on your procedural composition engine.

PROCEDURAL COMPOSITION IN SKIPPING STONES

In order to build the *Skipping Stones*' procedural composer, I used the principles of music theory and turned them into software. From that point, it was possible to guide the stylistic choices of the procedural composer to mimic those of our actual composer, which in your case could just be the style of a composer whose style you admire. I did this by adding extra rules that could be triggered randomly, or using a statistical model.

Beat

The first thing you'll need is a way to keep all your notes on beat. In *Skipping Stones*, the player skips stones across a lake to create music. Every bounce generates a part of the composition. Our bounces were physically driven, based on the force and angle of the throw, so we couldn't be sure that a stone would bounce on beat to the music. As a result, the music sounded more like a cat walking across a piano than actual music. So in order to fix this, I wrote a metronome system to keep time. When a stone hits the water, it submits an event to the internal metronome, which in turn submits an event to the audio system to play a given instrument when the next appropriate beat occurs. If you're familiar with metronomes, you'll know that after you set the beats per minute (BPM), it'll tick once on each beat. But in order to make interesting music, you need to play notes in between beats as well. So in order to stay rhythmically correct in between beats, you'll want your metronome to keep track of half beats, quarter beats, eighth beats, sixteenth beats, and so forth until you're satisfied with the result. Depending on how you've built your metronome, an easy solution is to double your BPM for every beat division you'd like to add. For example, for our purposes 180 BPM is the same as 90 BPM if you consider every tick of the metronome as a half beat instead of a whole beat.

My metronome implementation was based around the InvokeRepeating function, as shown below:

```
InvokeRepeating("ProcessAudioSources", (60/
bpm), (60/bpm));
```

This was a quick and accurate way to implement a consistent beat. You may be tempted to try using multithreading (or in the Unity engine, using "Coroutines"), returning a call to WaitForSeconds(), but in practice, this is prone to drifting off beat over time. InvokeRepeating is a function that schedules a call to another function, in this case ProcessAudioSources, after a given time and then repeatedly calls that function again after another given time. So in this case, I'm calling a function called ProcessAudioSources on every tick, as determined by my BPM. Put simply, ProcessAudioSources fetches a list of any queued audio and plays it back. In my particular case, it also fetches the next available audio source (because we operated with a limited number of audio sources that can play at once) and applies any volume, pitch, or filter values before playing.

In *Skipping Stones*, the length of a note was controlled by the length of the sample in almost all cases. However, it would be fairly straightforward to add a simple envelope to audio sources. The purpose is to have procedural control over your note lengths; that is, are they whole notes, half notes, quarter notes, and so forth? This is done by dynamically lowering the volume of an audio source after a given amount of beats, and turning it off once it reaches zero.

Scale

Here I cover some basic principles of music theory so that we can encode them into our composer. My goal is to provide as little information as possible in order to get started, so I take some shortcuts. It's also important to understand that the "rules" of music theory were developed over centuries of observation and experimentation, which is to say that it is not a science. Music theory should be thought of more as guiding principles to lead you toward something that's generally accepted as "sounding good."

The purpose of a scale is to provide structure by telling you which notes you're "allowed" to use, that is, out of the 12 notes in Western music, which ones are OK and which are off-limits. For our purposes, you probably only need to understand the purpose of a scale and how it works, and then let the computer do the rest.

Most of the scales used in Western music are just a variation on the major scale, so I'll focus on that one. The major scale is seven notes long, but we can't say exactly which seven notes until we've chosen a root note. For our purposes, the root note is simply the first note of our scale, and choosing it is entirely up to us, or the algorithm.

Steps

It's important to understand the difference between whole steps and half steps in music. A half step means moving one note forward, whereas a whole step is two notes. First, I'll remind you of the order of the notes used in Western music:

C C# D D# E F F# G G# A A# B C

So, for example, if we're on E and we take a half step, we'll be on F. If we're on E and we take a whole step, we'll be on F#. So let's say we choose

E as our root note, how do we know the rest of the notes that comprise our scale? We're going to start on E, make seven steps forward, and every note we land on is part of our scale. In the case of the major scale, the seven steps are whole, whole, half, whole, whole, whole, half. So, referencing the note order above, that would give us

E F# G# A B C# D# E

And that's our E major scale, which composers refer to as the key of E major. But this isn't a book on music theory. For us as procedural designers, it's more important to understand how we got here, so that we can encode it into our composer. We'll want to encode other scales as well, as they can have a big effect on the perceived mood of the music. It's important to experiment with different scales and root notes while you're trying to find the right mood, and make sure to take note of anything you find particularly beautiful.

In *Skipping Stones*, I usually pick the root note at the start of the game, and change when the time of day changes. In general, the root isn't something you want to change very often unless you know what you're doing. The major scale is generally considered happy sounding, and our game aims for a moody atmosphere, so we mostly use the minor scale. When the game starts, or when we start a new composition, I make an array of notes by cross-referencing my scale tables (pictured below) with my pitch table (Table 17.1) and my chosen root note.

```
int[] Major = {2, 2, 1, 2, 2, 2, 1 };
int[] Minor = {2, 1, 2, 2, 1, 2, 2};
int[] PentatonicMajor = {2, 2, 3, 2, 3};
```

Once I have this information, I have to decide exactly how to traverse the scale. Just traveling up or down the scale in order isn't very interesting, as it sounds more like somebody practicing piano than playing a piece. I use a state machine–like technique that starts on the root note and travels no more than a few scale steps up or down. The state machine has a bit of momentum, so if the piece is going up, it'll keep going up for a bit before coming back down again, and vice versa. Be aware that some notes in the major and minor scales create tension, while others relieve that tension. In other words, it's not necessarily a good idea to jump around the scale entirely randomly.

The pentatonic major scale is a great example of a scale that doesn't have this property. The pentatonic major scale is just the major scale, but with the fourth and seventh notes removed. As a result, any sequence of notes sounds good, but it's impossible to build a sense of tension and release.

A quick example rule you could deduce from this is that whenever you play the fourth or seventh note in the major scale (which produce the most tension), you'll want to follow it up with the root note (which releases the most tension), but ultimately this is a stylistic choice and you should experiment for yourself to determine what sounds good to you.

At this point, you can start to experience your procedural composer in action, which means you can start to experiment with it and build stylistic rules that appeal to you and your game.

Chords

Chords are simply notes that sound good when played together. Chords usually consist of three notes, but they don't have to. Here's my quick and dirty guide to constructing chords. Once you know your scale, start on any note in the scale. This is your chord root. From here, take the note two up (in the scale), and finally the note two up from there. So, for example, the first, third, and fifth notes of a scale make a chord, as do the second, fourth, and sixth, or the third, fifth, and seventh. Now you know how to construct chords.

Depending on the scale you're using, the interval between those notes can differ, and this will change the mood of the chord. For example, the chord made of the first, third, and fifth notes of the major scale is a major chord, and as a result sounds more uplifting. By contrast, the chord made of the second, fourth, and sixth notes of the major scale is a minor chord; therefore, it has a moodier sound.

This is the most basic way to construct chords, but there are ways to modify a chord to give it different voicings. For example, normally the root note is the lowest note of a chord, but this doesn't have to be the case. Let's say we have a C major chord, played C3-E3-G3, where 3 represents the octave in which the notes are played. We could play this same chord as E2-G2-C3 or G2-C3-E3, which are known as the first and second inversions, respectively. Notice we're playing the same notes, but the resulting sound has a subtle difference.

Motif and Repetition

In music, we use the term *bar* to describe a section of music that consists of a certain number of beats. Since the music in *Skipping Stones* is controlled by the player throwing stones on the water, there's no guarantee that a piece of music will be constantly playing, as opposed to a normal song where once you hit play, it'll play until the end. As a result, *Skipping Stones* doesn't use the traditional concept of a bar of music. Instead, I considered every stone thrown as a single bar of music and I grouped together every four bars as a section.

In order to make this come through in the music, I used a repeated motif throughout the section. A motif is a short melody often repeated throughout a piece of music. When the player throws the first stone, I record the note sequence and consider this to be my motif for the upcoming section of music. Then, on the second throw I'll recall this motif by randomly inserting notes from the first note sequence among the newly generated notes for this second bar of music. On the third throw, I completely disregard this motif, generating a completely new sequence. And finally, the fourth throw repeats the motif, but with some notes replaced by chords using that note as a root.

In addition to this, when a stone sinks I play either the second, fifth, or seventh scale note, except in the case of the final stone, where I end on the root note. As a result, each bar feels as though it's building tension until the final throw, which resolves the tension and brings the section of music to a logical conclusion, and every four stone throws generates and completes a new musical idea.

So the idea of motif and repetition gives procedural composition structure, but after some time it can start to sound predictable and dull. For variety, I added in little flourishes here and there to give the music a more improvisational feel. The first of these was to randomly play a short arpeggio, often on the first skip of a given stone. An arpeggio is simply a chord where the notes are played in succession, instead of simultaneously. The arpeggios in *Skipping Stones* are played quickly in order to give a little contrast to the otherwise slow pace of the music. Aside from the arpeggios, I also play a few well-placed chords instead of single notes. This is really just the tip of the iceberg when it comes to adding a bit of life into the music, but for us, it was enough to fill what was missing, while working within our time and budget.

Finally, I added accompanying instruments. For every time of day in *Skipping Stones*, we built a primary instrument and an accompanying instrument. Often, the primary instrument would be some kind of "lead," that is, some kind of piano or "powerful" (in sound) synth. The accompanying instruments were more dreamy, with lots of reverb and slow release.

Earlier I said that every four stones made up a single musical section, but actually that's not true. The player had the ability to throw two stones simultaneously, and would then have to wait for one to sink before he was able to throw again. The first stone controlled the primary instrument. This is the stone that generated the musical structure. The second stone controlled our accompanying instrument.

The accompanying instrument didn't have as many rules associated with it as the primary instrument. Because of its generally softer and dreamier quality, nearly anything it played sounded good, as long as it supported the primary instrument. In order to do this, it operated in the same key as the primary instrument, and would sometimes make vague mentions of the motif or play short arpeggios, but otherwise, it was free to explore the music however the random number generator felt it should.

CONCLUSION

I could have continued to improve the composer of *Skipping Stones*, but we had to end the project. While working on it, I found that every addition to the engine made an enormous impact on the quality of the music it produced. If you're willing to learn some music theory and experiment, I'm certain you could build a more impressive procedural audio composer.

To this end, I recommend that you seek books that give concrete and practical ways of applying music theory. I've found *Improvise for Real* by David Reed to be one of these books, but you'll need access to some kind of instrument to get the most out of it. Another excellent read is *Making Music* by Dennis DeSantis, which focuses on giving solutions to actual problems when making music. Not every problem will apply to procedural composition; however, many of the ideas are directly applicable.

It's important to understand that the beauty and expressiveness in the *Skipping Stones* audio engine didn't come from just the procedural composer, but also the instruments designed by our human composer to work within the engine. As in other aspects of procedural game design, we must find a balance between authored and algorithmic elements, and the two must collaborate in order to achieve the best results.

III

Procedural Narrative

GENERATING GAME CONTENT OR assets is often the first instinct for designers, but even the story experienced by the player can itself be generated using similar methods. For more than 30 years, interactive fiction and roguelike games have relied on a variety of techniques to build narratives, sometimes using nothing but the most elementary components. Other games have attempted to control pacing and tension with artificial intelligence (AI) directors that can detect properties of the user's ongoing playthrough and react accordingly. The text that the player reads and the words that the player hears can all be generated. Nonplayer characters can be created with personalities and histories that interlock with the other elements of the setting. Everything in the author's toolbox is at our disposal.

Perhaps even more so than other methods in this book, techniques of narrative generation must be applied with care, because the results can easily fall well short of what can be produced by a human author, while draining a team's resources across disciplines. Be cautious with the scope of your project, and remember that scripted and generated elements can be favorably mixed. If you choose your goals well and understand the interactions of your game's systems, you can create entirely novel situations that will surprise and delight players that come into contact with your story engine. We can dream of a generated world in which the player has a joint creative role, taking an active part in writing the story that is being woven before them.

CHAPTER 18

Story and Plot Generation

Ben Kybartas

Independent

T HE ROLE OF STORIES in modern video games can be viewed as a growing field of experimentation and refinement. Stories in games may simply be a way to provide causality and motivation to the actions taken by a given player or players in a game, or even go so far as to use the mechanics and interactions to reframe the player as a storyteller, eschewing traditional gameplay in favor of narrative experimentation. Stories may be narrated, discovered in the environment, unfolded through cut scenes, presented in dialogues, given as quests, embedded in mechanics, read in wikis, and embedded within artificial intelligence, as well as emerge through simulation, and much more. The point, in essence, is that what it means to *generate* stories for video games is a heavy and complex question. Any approach to procedural story generation will need to make assumptions about both what a story actually means to the game and how it will be represented. *Façade* (Procedural Arts, 2005) and *Left 4 Dead* (Valve, 2008) both had systems to measure the supposed level of drama and player tension in the game, using marital turmoil and zombies, respectively, to create the feelings of rising and falling tension associated with stories. Contrarily, games like *Dwarf Fortress* (Bay 12 Games, 2006) and *Crusader Kings* (Paradox Interactive, 2012) rely more on complex simulation to structure the player's experience into emerging sequences of causal events that create the feeling of a grand narrative. Thus, *Façade* and *Left 4 Dead* focused on representing stories through emotion and dramatic tension, while *Dwarf Fortress* and *Crusader Kings 2* utilized complex world building and simulation to create a player-guided form of storytelling.

This chapter, alternatively, focuses specifically on the generation of sequential stories that occur successively within a game world, similar to quests in role-playing games or episodes of a television series. Relationships and character attributes are used to drive a custom story grammar that generates the actual story content, which in turn can impact the relationships and characters of the game world. Grammars were chosen as the representation for story in that they are relatively simple to author, understand, and implement. Some disadvantages to grammars is that the results tend to be highly structured and, at worst, could be perceived as repetitive. This chapter is divided into several sections, starting first with an introduction to grammars and story grammars. Second, we provide the representation used for both the game world and story. Finally, we present the design of the actual grammar rules, and discuss ways to improve the generation process.

GRAMMARS AND STORY GRAMMARS

The approach to story generation taken in this chapter makes use of grammars, particularly graph grammars. Probably the most well-known and common use of grammars is the grammar used in language and sentence construction. While obviously different, the grammars used in this chapter follow the same philosophy. Essentially, a language grammar is a vocabulary and a set of rules that can be used to construct "valid" sentences. For our purposes, we will be designing a vocabulary and set of rules to construct valid stories. In this section, we introduce the basic concept of grammar using a simple string grammar as our example. Grammars are built up of *symbols* that form the content of the grammar, and *rules* that dictate how these symbols may be constructed. In this example, we will use the symbols A, B, and C and the following three rules:

1. $A \rightarrow C$

2. $A \rightarrow B$

3. $B \rightarrow CC$

These are more formally called *rewrite rules*, where the symbol to the left of the arrow is the *pattern* that, if it exists in our string of symbols, can be *rewritten* to the symbol on the right-hand side of the arrow. For example, if we start with the string *A*, we can rewrite that same string as either *C*, using rule 1, or *B*, using rule 2. Furthermore, we can rewrite the string *B* as *CC* using the third rule. Therefore, strings *C*, *B*, and *CC* are all valid strings that can be made with the *starting symbol A*. While this may seem limited, if we add a fourth rule, say, *C→A*, then *CC* can be rewritten as *AC*, *CA*, or even *AA*, which in turn could become *AB*, and then *ACC*, and then *ACA*, and so on. Using only rules 1–3, we are always guaranteed to reach a point where the string can no longer be rewritten for any starting symbol; with the fourth rule, we can now expand the starting string *A* infinitely.

While the string grammar above may seem interesting, it doesn't have any explicit story "content" yet. However, while the symbols above are only strings, there is nothing that prevents symbols from being actual story content, such as story *events* or structures. Early story structure research actually proposed that grammars could be developed to represent every story structure in existence. Such a magical (likely fictional) grammar has yet to be found; however, grammars have still found use for modeling structured types of stories, such as children's fairy tales (see Vladimir Propp's "Morphology of the Folktale" for such an example). Imagine instead that we were to create a simple grammar for creating sidequests in role-playing games, which are also typically highly structured. We might break down the potential events of a given sidequest into its own set of symbols, say [*Journey*], [*Encounter*], and [*Discovery*]. Next, we create a set of rules:

1. [*Journey*]→ [*Journey*][*Encounter*]

2. [*Encounter*]→ [*Encounter*][*Encounter*]

3. [*Encounter*]→ [*Discovery*][*Journey*]

Now, with these three rules, and starting with a [*Journey*], we can get quests like [*Journey*][*Encounter*][*Discovery*][*Journey*][*Encounter*] or [*Journey*][*Encounter*][*Encounter*][*Encounter*]. The next step could then be to write to expand our set of rules and symbols, which take the abstract quest structure we just developed and turn it into a more concrete set of actions and events. Consider the following new rules and symbols:

1. [*Journey*]→ [*Go to town*]

2. [*Journey*]→ [*Go to the forest*]

3. [*Encounter*]→ [*Fight a goblin*]

4. [*Encounter*]→ [*Fight a dragon*]

5. [*Discovery*]→ [*Find gold*]

6. [*Discovery*]→ [*Find weapon*]

Applying this set of rules to our previous examples gives us much more specific quests, such as [*Go to town*][*Fight a goblin*][*Find gold*][*Go to the forest*][*Fight a dragon*]. We still don't need to stop there, and could create a new set of rules and symbols to state what possible dragons could be fought, what weapons could be found, and so forth.

In implementation, grammars are often used as procedural content generators by taking one or more symbols as a starting set and then randomly applying a number of valid random rules until either a point is reached where no more rules can be applied or a certain number of rules have been applied.

One advantage to the two grammars discussed in this section is that they are visually easy to understand and reasonably straightforward to implement. One disadvantage to the grammar-based approach is that by keeping the grammar entirely dependent on itself, we avoid any meaningful connection with the game world. Most stories are structured around characters, and in particular conflicts between these characters. Essentially, without tying the grammar more directly to the characters of the world, we can't hope to have stories that meaningfully involve the game world in the generated story. As such, we will want to create a new form of grammar that operates simultaneously on both a story grammar and a representation of the social game world. In this way, each rule contains both a social pattern and a story pattern, followed by a change to both the story and the social world.

GAME WORLD

One of the driving assumptions of this investigation was the idea that stories are based around character relations, and specifically about conflicts between characters. The role of the story then surrounds the resolution of conflicts one by one, usually with one major conflict driving the entire plot. Therefore, interesting stories can only meaningfully occur as the result of an interesting set of characters and relations. This means we should first aim to model the game world in such a way that all this information is made explicit. Within this particular investigation, we chose to model the characters and their relations as a social network—essentially, as a directed graph where each character is a node, and the edges represent the relation of one character toward another. We define each character as minimally having a unique ID and a set of attributes, which are essentially a set of key–value pairs for each character, where the keys are the same for each character, with only the value being different. "Name" and "age" might be two examples of keys, where each character is expected to have a name and age, but their actual names and ages will likely be different. Likewise, we will define the relationships between characters in a similar way, with each relationship containing a set of keys and values. "Trust" and "friendship" may be two such keys. It is also useful to keep each edge one directional, meaning that the relationship one character feels toward another may not be the same as the relationship that character feels for them. As a disclaimer, this is by no means the only way to have a model of characters and relationships, but such a structure is intuitive and relatively straightforward to author and implement. Likewise, similar representations of characters and relations are relatively common, and seen frequently in role-playing games and interactive fiction.

We assume a dynamic game world, in the sense that we expect that the relations and even the attributes will change over time. In fact, given that the core of the stories we are creating is related to characters and conflict, it is arguable that a dynamic game world is necessary to represent the changes needed to construct interesting stories. It is also a lack of dynamism that many players note (and lament) in a lot of branching choice-based narratives or story-rich video games.

The very simple social model shown in Figure 18.1 will be used as the basis for our subsequent examples in this chapter. Here, we have a Western-inspired social world comprised of three nonplayer characters (NPC) and the player. Each character has four attributes: a name, number of bullets, money, and a certain level of gambling skills. There are three types of relations: the money owed, the level of trust, and the affection level between characters. For clarity's sake, we do not show all relations between all characters in the world.

STORY MODEL

For our model of story, we will break away from the linear model used in traditional story grammars and instead adopt the directed graph model more commonly seen in interactive fiction and hypertext. Essentially, in this model discrete sections of the story content form the nodes, with edges indicating different branches of the story that a player can select. In

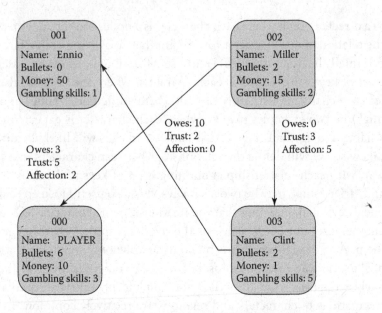

FIGURE 18.1   Diagram of relationships between four characters.

this model, the actual story experienced by the player relates to the path they take from one of the starting nodes of the narrative to one of its terminal nodes. It should be noted that by doing this, we are now technically working with a *graph grammar* rather than a string grammar. This means that rather than just rewriting one symbol into one or more different symbols, we are instead rewriting nodes in a graph with new graph pieces.

RULE DESIGN

Now, given both our models of game worlds and story grammars, we can begin to create a new rule structure that makes use of both. We'll start by dividing the types of rules we want to make into two categories, which we'll call *initial rewrite rules* (IRRs) and *secondary rewrite rules* (SRRs). We'll define the IRRs as the set of rules that give us a basic story skeleton with which to work, and the SRRs as rules that rewrite and expand the story skeleton. Essentially, our process to build a story will be to apply one IRR to get our initial story, and then apply a number of SRRs to progressively make the story more complex. One advantage to this approach is that we always ensure that at every step of the generation we have a complete story; that is, even if we only apply one rule, we still have a story.

For the IRRs, we only care about searching for patterns in the game world; that is, when designing the IRRs, the main question to ask is "What interesting stories can arise out of the possible patterns in our social graph?" Returning to our Western example from before, we can see that it is quite possible for someone to owe more money than they currently have. Thus, we can use this need for money as the main conflict for a possible story. Following the example of many typical Westerns, we can envision a potential story where a character in debt tries to win back their earnings in a poker game. Given that in many cases we want to involve the player in the story, a possible IRR may look like that shown in Figure 18.2.

Put simply, the pattern on the left of the arrow is the game world pattern we're searching for; in this case, we are looking for a situation where there is a character X who has less than 5 money and owes more than that to another character, Y. If this pattern exists in the game world, then we can initialize the story on the right, in which character X plays poker against the player and takes whatever winnings they have to character Y. We use the circle with the dotted line to indicate possible starting points of the story, whereas the plain circle marks the possible ending points of the story. In this case, there is only one start and one end to the story in question. Looking Figure 18.2, we can see such a pattern existing between Clint and Ennio, so it is valid for us to generate the above story with Clint taking the role of character X and Ennio taking the role of character Y.

When designing an IRR, it is usually advised to use relatively simple game patterns, such as using only two characters and their relations. The reason for this is twofold. First, it can be quite costly performance-wise to search a large graph for very complicated patterns, and it is a non-trivial search to implement. Those familiar with performance issues in

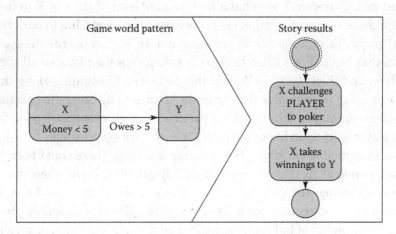

FIGURE 18.2   Effect of a rewrite rule.

computing will recognize that it is actually NP hard to search a graph for any arbitrary patterns, whereas it is much simpler and faster to search with only two characters. Second, simpler patterns are far more likely to exist in the game world than complex ones. While it is easy for a pattern like the one above to exist, if we had a large pattern with many characters and rules, the likelihood that that pattern would exist in a given game world is increasingly unlikely. This is a problem, though, as complicated relationship patterns and large complex stories are far more interesting than the simple story we generated above, and it's for this reason that we design the SSRs.

SECONDARY REWRITE RULES

SSRs are similar to IRRs, except that we are not creating a new story. Instead, we are looking to rewrite specific events from our story, again using patterns in the game world, to expand and complicate the existing story. This means that while IRRs are used to create general stories, the SRRs should be much more malleable, and should be able to apply to many events in many different stories. Returning to our example, we can assume that there will probably be more than one story where playing poker occurs as an event. We also know that cheating in poker is yet another staple of Westerns, so we might want to define an SRR in which two characters can mutually agree to cheat someone out of all their money in poker.

Such a rule might look like Figure 18.3. This means that in order to apply this rewrite rule, there must be a poker event in the story *and* there must be a character Y who has a high enough level of trust of X to help them cheat. One such relation exists between Miller and Clint in our original graph. This means that in our sample story, we can rewrite the event such that Miller helps Clint to cheat at poker, robs the player of all their money, and then has Clint deliver that to Ennio. Continuing along this line, we may want to give the player the chance to discover the cheating in question. Maybe Y in the above pattern has high enough affection for the player to let them in on the truth. Or maybe the player simply has high enough gambling skills to tell something is wrong. These could both be two separate SRRs that can be used for any gambling event where cheating is occurring. Then, we can author rules where the player is allowed to confront characters they catch doing something illegal at gunpoint, given a certain number of bullets. This could then devolve into duels, or surrenders based on how many bullets the criminal has, and so forth. In this way,

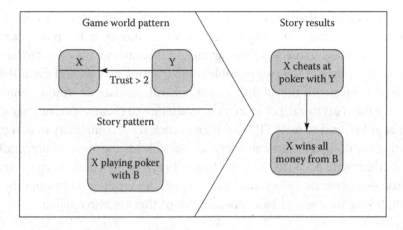

FIGURE 18.3   Another rewrite rule in effect.

we end up with a list of SRRs that could end up with our card game ending in a violent duel, but those same rules could be used to duel wagon robbers in the desert, or to catch people cheating at sharpshooting contests. Ideally, there should always be more SRRs than IRRs, with many different possibilities for all potential story events.

In terms of the actual application of SRRs, in practice it was reasonably effective to first search for all valid SRRs, and then choose one at random and apply it. This process could be repeated a fixed number of times for each story. As an alternate approach, one could continuously apply SRRs until there are no more valid SRRs to apply. However, it is easy to design SRRs that may be applied infinitely and can break the generation. As such, even if the designer is very cautious, it is still good practice to cap the generation process after a certain number of rule applications.

GAME WORLD SIMULATION

At this point, it's important to discuss the dynamism of the game world. Currently, our stories do not have any concrete effect on the game world, but in reality, we want our game world to be dynamic. In our Western world, for example, we should have ways to gain trust and affection, as well as ways for new characters to get into debt, and so forth. In this way, while we may be generating similar stories, they will be occurring as the result of an ever-changing, dynamic game world. To achieve this, we extend our definition of the story model to include preconditions and postconditions. Essentially, things in the game world must be true for certain events to occur, whereas each event can in turn make changes to the game world.

If we go back to the IRR defined above, we may want to have X take the winnings of poker to Y, only if X actually won money in the poker game (e.g., if the poker game was a minigame). In this case, we may want to have the story branch at the two possible results, with a new second event that X leaves defeated if they didn't win at poker. Likewise, we would want to reduce the trust toward characters who attempt to cheat a specific character at poker, and so forth. This adds an extra level of complexity to design, in that the designer must consider each possible arrangement of preconditions that could occur in the story. In practice, it is often good to run a pass through a generated story and assert that each event has its precondition met, taking into account any postconditions that are also applied.

METRIC-GUIDED GENERATION

In this section, we discuss a brief and slightly more technical alternative to the application of SRRs. Previously, we stated that simply selecting valid SRRs at random and applying them was a valid way to generate stories, and this is still true. Interestingly, though, since we are calculating all valid SRRs, it is quite possible to be more selective about which SRRs we choose. Essentially, if we define certain features we would like to see in the resulting story, we can prioritize which valid SRRs we choose based on how we want the final story to be structured. We may, for example, want to prioritize player choice, and so we prioritize valid rules that add one or more branches to the resulting story. Likewise, we may want our Western to be filled with shoot-outs, and thus we prioritize any SRRs that add gunfighting events. Conversely, if we want to keep characters alive longer, then we may want to avoid actions that involve their death. (It is morbidly easy to end in Shakespeare-like scenarios where all characters have murdered each other.)

As a more complex example, imagine we kept track of all the postconditions resulting from each individual story. This means we know all changes to the game world that occurred as the result of a story that the player directly experienced or influenced. Now imagine we prioritized any valid SRR whose game world pattern is met due to the changes the player has made in previous stories. In essence, this means that when we generate stories, we prioritize stories that occur as a result of something the player did in the previous story. This adds a great deal of causality between stories and helps the player to feel that their interactions are valid. For example, if the player chooses to duel with someone and loses all their bullets, and then we prioritize the generation of a story where the player is held up and can't defend themselves, then the consequences of the previous stories can affect all the subsequent stories. This, on top of a simulated game world, is another way to keep the stories interesting, because even though the types of stories generated may be similar, the context out of which those stories are being generated is dynamic, ever changing, and sensitive to all the actions taken by the player.

CONCLUSIONS

Story generation is by no means an easy task, and to date there are relatively few games that have focused on story generation as one of their main features. By consequence, story generation presents an interesting alternative to the traditional means of authoring stories, by allowing the author to focus more on the structures and rules that guide the player story, rather than try to tie them to a particular story created by the author. And this seems relevant, especially with an increased level of criticism toward the minimal effects players typically have on the stories and worlds in game. As the horizons of what a game is expand further and more experimental works gain serious interest, it seems that games can be used not just as a way to tell stories, but also to challenge traditional storytelling methods. By focusing on experimental and generative elements, designing stories becomes an exploration into how stories may be formed, opening that up to the player, as opposed to simply telling them a good story through audio logs and journals.

CHAPTER 19

Emergent Narratives and Story Volumes

Jason Grinblat

Freehold Games

MOTIVATION

In April 2015, I was fortunate enough to join a live stream that featured Nick Scratch, Austin Walker, and Cameron Kunzelman—members of a group of streamers called Stream Friends—playing my roguelike game, *Caves of Qud*.* *Caves of Qud* is set in a far-future, postapocalyptic Earth populated by mutated animals, robots, and sentient plants. The Stream Friends were cooperatively playing as a single character, and they had just descended into the depths of the game's first dungeon, a shale cavern called Red Rock. As they paraded into the darkness, they stumbled on a pack of aggressive, humanoid hyena creatures called snapjaws. Carefully, they assessed the danger of the situation. They scanned their surroundings for corridors to use as choke points, boulders to hurl at the snapjaws, and anything else that might help them survive.

At this point, Nick noticed that one of the snapjaws looked different than the others. He moved his cursor over it and examined its description, discovering that it was a named snapjaw faction leader (Figure 19.1). Its name was Ugo, and it was known as the "calloused tot-eater." Its description also included details about procedurally generated relationships it had with some of the game's other factions. It turned out that Ugo was loved

---

* https://www.youtube.com/watch?v=4ewMeqsjtTI

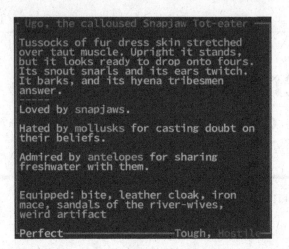

FIGURE 19.1   Description of Ugo, the calloused snapjaw tot-eater.

by snapjaws (predictably), hated by mollusks for "casting doubt on their beliefs," and admired by antelopes for "sharing freshwater with them."

Reading this description shot sparks into the streamers' conversation. Immediately, they began to ponder, what *do* mollusks believe? And why was Ugo so kind to the antelopes? After all, freshwater functions as currency in *Caves of Qud*. Sharing some with another clan would serve as an act of great friendship. They conjectured that the mollusks were feuding with the antelopes, and Ugo was caught in the middle. At this point, they accessed their character's reputation screen. They were dismayed to discover their dismal reputation with antelopes. The creatures actively disliked them. All of a sudden, it made sense that Ugo and his pack would be hunting their character.

The battle commenced. The streamers hacked at Ugo with their bronze battle axe, while Ugo and his compatriots retaliated with crude clubs, claws, and bites. The battle turned sour for the streamers, and they were forced to flee. They put distance between themselves and Ugo's horde and rounded a nearby corridor, only to find another pack of snapjaws. They sighed collectively, knowing it was over. Resigned to their fate, they accessed their character's inventory and took a swig from a canteen of precious freshwater. Then, at Austin's suggestion, they defiantly emptied the canteen over their character's head. Ugo would be sharing no freshwater with antelopes on that day. Charging toward Ugo, they were felled by the snapjaw horde.

When we designed *Caves of Qud*, we had no idea who Ugo was or that he would exist at all. We didn't craft a narrative about a water feud between mollusks and antelopes, nor did we tell the story of a bold adventurer who in his last moments defies his enemy by spilling his precious cargo. We didn't tell these stories, but we set the stage for them with procedural systems.

Emergent narratives like the one that unfolded before Nick, Austin, and Cameron have a special home in procedural games. As designers who seek to evoke certain experiences, they offer us a tool beyond the reach of traditional narratives. They're personal—no one will repeat Stream Friends' experience, as no narrative track has been laid out with it in mind. The stories that emerge from games that dive deep into the realm of procedural systems are some of the most shareable precisely because the conditions that produce them are ephemeral. Think of *Dwarf Fortress*, whose myriad systems and starting conditions engender all sorts of emergent stories with only the barest narrative framework.

Emergent narratives are also authentic. In resulting from the collision of systems rather than the script of an author, they mirror the experiences we have in our everyday lives, the stories we hear from our family and friends, and the tales we read about in history books. In his book *Persuasive Games: The Expressive Power of Videogames*, Ian Bogost argues that "videogames open a new domain for persuasion, thanks to their core representational mode, procedurality."* He calls this domain procedural rhetoric, "the art of persuasion through rule-based representations and interactions rather than the spoken word, writing, images, or moving pictures." Stories that emerge from game systems are manifestations of an argument those systems make. Part of their power is the authenticity they possess on account of their scriptlessness.

Games have a unique power to enable player narratives. This chapter sets out to explore that power and guide designers toward using procedurality to cultivate the kinds of stories they want their players to tell.

THE VOICE IN THE MACHINE

The leading lament of designers considering a foray into the world of emergent narrative is the loss of authorial voice. The power of a scripted narrative lies in the author's use of literary elements like theme, tone,

---

* Bogost, Ian, *Persuasive Games: The Expressive Power of Videogames* (Cambridge, MA: MIT Press), ix.

voice, and mood. The expressiveness of the narrative form, then, lies in the author's faculty to leverage those elements in their stories. On account of their uncontrollable nature, do emergent narratives occupy a space inaccessible to the author or designer who seeks to express not just something, but something *in particular*?

I argue that there is room for authorial voice in procedural systems that enable emergent narratives, although the designer's role diverges from that of the traditional author. In procedural design, it's possible to insert elements like themes and mood into both the rules of generative systems and the handcrafted atoms that get procedurally combined. The result is less precise than the traditional story but richer in other ways. Whereas the author crafts a storyline that traverses narrative space, the procedural designer crafts a *story volume** that contains numerous adjacent stories exploring similar themes or invoking a similar mood. It's important to note that a story volume doesn't enclose an arbitrary lump of narrative space. Instead, it encloses a family of emergent stories, all of which are begotten by a set of carefully curated system parameters (Figure 19.2).

For example, with *Caves of Qud*, while we didn't anticipate the precise story of Ugo, we did want our players to explore certain themes present in his story. For one, we were interested in how we (as humans) relate to our morphology. The exploration of what drives a sentient mollusk's beliefs taps into that theme. We were also interested in a world where the social structures are built on the scarcity of resources we take for granted. The streamers' defiant act of water wasting only resonates in such a world. By observing the inhabitants of that world's relationship with water, we get some insight into our own relationship with it.

Consider the story volume constructed by another game that leans heavily on procedurality yet manages to maintain a clear voice. Red Hook Studios's 2016 dungeon crawler *Darkest Dungeon* explores the psychological stresses of dungeoneering. When you lead an adventuring party of procedurally generated characters from your gothic manor into the rotted Weald, the outcome is undetermined. The narrative that emerges is your own. However, the game's systems—such as the afflictions your characters accrue from traumatic events—constrain the space of possible narratives

---

* Project Horseshoe Group Report, "Generative Systems, Meaningful Cores," "Story Volumes Rather than Storylines" section, http://www.projecthorseshoe.com/reports/featured/ph15r3.htm

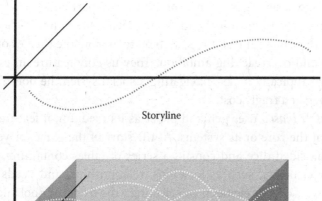

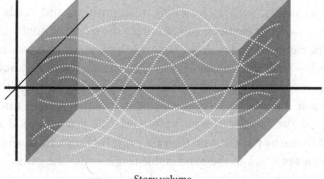

FIGURE 19.2   Single storyline contrasted with several storylines that share themes and comprise a story volume.

to those that explore the effects of trauma and evoke the mood of hopelessness. Even success stories are premised on overcoming your afflictions rather than avoiding them altogether.

FIASCO: A CASE STUDY

Let's examine the particulars of a procedural game whose rules create a well-defined story volume of emergent narratives. *Fiasco* is a collaborative, tabletop role-playing game published by Bully Pulpit Games in 2009. It follows in the tradition of other pen-and-paper role-playing games like *Dungeons & Dragons*, but it distinguishes itself in a few key dimensions. It's designed for short play sessions, it privileges role-playing over rules complexity, and it eliminates the role of the game master in favor of a collaborative approach to story creation.

Fiasco also distinguishes itself with its explicitly articulated themes. As argued by media researcher Felan Parker, "*Fiasco* is designed to simulate the caper-gone-wrong subgenre of film."* In particular, *Fiasco* draws heavily from the films of Joel and Ethan Coen. These films, although disparate in their plots and settings, all tend to explore the themes of human stupidity and overreaching ambition. They usually feature an everyman character—typically male—navigating a social system he doesn't understand, often at a tragic cost.

Although *Fiasco* uses pen and paper as its medium, it features procedurality at the core of its systems. At the start of the game, players roll a pool of six-sided dice and consult a series of tables containing plot and character elements, such as locations, relationships, and needs. Taking turns, players choose elements by selecting a die from the pool and matching it to the element's index in the table. Each player must have a need and a relationship with the players next to them. Then, the players role-play a series of scenes based on these plot elements. Halfway through the game, players reroll the dice and choose elements for the Tilt, an unexpected event that shakes up the story. The players role-play a second series of scenes informed by the Tilt, and then they resolve the game in an epilogue.

The stories play out to their inevitable tragic ends. The game supplies a variety of settings—a Western-style saloon, sleepy suburbs, and a remote research station in Antarctica—for the capers to go wrong. How does *Fiasco* constrain narrative space to include only those emergent stories that touch on its themes? It embeds the restrictions in its game rules. By requiring each player to select a need and a relationship with their neighbors, and by constraining player choice through the use of dice assignment, the rules coerce players into choosing conflicting needs and relationships primed for souring. Furthermore, the rules ripen the conditions for conflict and tragedy by introducing an unexpected event during the Tilt—one that's usually at odds with the goals of the characters. Players can't avoid the Tilt; they must simply adjust to its ramifications.

Fiasco also encodes its themes in the handcrafted units that get procedurally combined during the game's Setup and Tilt phases. These are the individual entries in the plot and character tables. Let's examine one of the

---

* Parker, Felan, "The Set-Up, the Tilt and the Aftermath: Role-Playing the Caper-Gone-Wrong Film in *Fiasco*," http://www.academia.edu/4530327/The_Set-Up_the_Tilt_and_the_Aftermath_Roleplaying_the_Caper-Gone-Wrong_Film_in_Fiasco

tables from the *Tales from Suburbia* setting. These are relationships from the Work and Crime categories.

Work	Crime
1. Business rivals in a dying industry	1. Drug manufacturer and dealer
2. Service worker and client (restaurant, bank, janitorial)	2. Gambler and bookie
3. Professional supervisor and employee	3. Thieves (shoplifters, burglars, car thieves)
4. Tradesman/homeowner (lawn care, plumbing, HVAC)	4. Small-time vandals, ne'er-do-wells
5. Salesman/homeowner (siding, drive resurfacing)	5. Embezzler and company accountant
6. Professional/client (pastor, doctor, lawyer, banker)	6. Organized crime figure and wannabe

Most of these relationships entail a degree of tension. A gambler and bookie, business rivals in a dying industry, service worker and client—we can see how they're primed to erupt when combined with contentious needs or unexpected obstacles. Introducing a Tilt element like "someone develops a conscience" into the relationship of an embezzler and company accountant is likely to bring the powder keg to its inevitable conclusion.

Fiasco's designers could have chosen to include any number of relationships from among the myriad ways we relate to each other as human beings. They chose these relationships because they work to constrain narrative space in a thematically resonant way. While each story plays out differently, they're all bound by the themes *Fiasco* explores. In its own words, *Fiasco* is "a game of powerful ambition and poor impulse control."*

UNPACKING YOUR THEMES

The first step in approaching a procedural design that yields a particular story volume is to identify your themes. This process can be trickier than expected, especially if you don't have experience engaging critically with media. Many creators, myself included, are driven by intuitions around what makes for compelling ideas. I get a vision in my head, such as a strong-willed and principled mollusk, and I think, "This needs to be in my game!" The goal is to examine these intuitions and try to unpack them. Once you've teased out the kernel that makes your idea tick, you

---

* *Fiasco* back cover.

can formulate it as a broader theme. Then you can envision narratives that explore other aspects of that theme. Finally, you can develop systems that enable player stories within your desired story volume.

With *Caves of Qud*, we started with fond memories of our *Gamma World* campaigns. *Gamma World* is a tabletop role-playing game originally published by TSR in 1978. It's set in a pulpy, postapocalyptic North America that's been transformed by nuclear fallout into a bizarro ecosystem of mutant flora and fauna. As teens, we at Freehold Games played *Gamma World* extensively. Over the course of our gaming sessions, I role-played as, and interacted with, teleporting tortoises, psionic pelicans, and parasitic fungi. These experiences were absurd, hilarious, and wonderful. They served as our primary inspiration for *Caves of Qud*.

Guided by our intuitions, we transposed the simplest of these experiences to *Caves of Qud* by designing mechanics that enacted them. For example, we wanted to let the player play a character with a carapace, wings, telepathy, or all three. So we designed a character creation system that includes mutations, which combine to produce morphologically diverse characters. As we started to explore more complex social interactions, and systems that could mimic them, we examined our intuitions around what made these interactions compelling. For instance, why did I enjoy the thought of a mollusk bristling at a challenge to its beliefs?

After much meditation, we concluded that the kernel of these interactions is *our relationship with our morphology*. When I'm imagining how a mollusk might respond to a social exchange, I first imagine how I might respond as a human. Then I extrapolate by imagining how the morphological differences between mollusks and humans might inform their interactions. I go through a process of anthropomorphizing the mollusk, and then deanthropomorphizing it. All the while I'm implicitly examining how my own morphology informs my interactions.

This formulation helped us envision how other creatures' morphologies might inform their social exchanges. As we went further, it helped us start to parameterize these exchanges and design a system to reproduce them. We followed a similar process for the theme of scarcity. Originally, the idea to use water as currency came to us as a play on familiar roguelike mechanics, hunger and thirst. Then, we started to tease out the ramifications of our idea. In particular, we observed how roguelikes are some of the few games to accurately model our utter dependency on water. We realized our extension to the mechanics could be used to explore the social dynamics that emerge from that dependency.

Ultimately, these examinations led to the design that produced the network of relationships between Ugo, mollusks, antelopes, freshwater, and the player. The narrative that unfolded from these relationships, along with all the other narratives that unfold from its variations, comprise the story volume articulated by our design.

GRIST FOR THE NARRATIVE MILL

As a final point, let's look at how simple touches can help players narrativize the events they experience in your game. I argued for how systems themselves can work toward shaping your story volumes. For example, the presence of the Tilt in *Fiasco* works toward creating narratives where characters can't anticipate their outcomes and are often devastated by them. But small details in your content can facilitate narration and shape your story volumes as well. Character and place names, item descriptions, level layouts, and sound effects can all serve as grist for the mill when it comes to enabling thematic player stories.

Take our decision to give Ugo a name. By virtue of his position as a snapjaw faction leader, we gave Ugo unique art and a descriptive title. For the purpose of communicating his mechanical distinctiveness, his name is superfluous. But a name is thematically resonant. It implies certain characteristics about Ugo's culture, and so it acts as a narrative springboard for players' interaction with him. If we were handwriting a story about a snapjaw faction leader, we'd almost certainly give him a name to personalize him. By the same principle, emergent narratives emerge more discernibly when their subjects are positioned as components of a narrative. Stories need characters, and Ugo's name positions him as a character.

Beyond facilitating narration, you can also shape your story volume with your choice of details. Ugo's descriptive title of "calloused tot-eater" evokes a certain mood. In conjunction with other details, like the aggressive attitudes of snapjaws and the scarcity of water, we know that the narratives likely to emerge around Ugo involve hostility and conflict. Ugo's affable relationship with antelopes adds even more texture, and a portrait starts to emerge of a complex figure mired in unusual social relationships premised around scarce resources. With this amount of context, the player's interactions with Ugo take on new meaning. As the Stream Friends discovered, Ugo was more than a monster in a dungeon.

CHAPTER 20

Poetry Generation

Harry Tuffs
Independent

1. "Tales of the Lunatic Horn of Pride"

   Dramatic verse. 88 lines, 22 stanzas. Extract:

   As prophets foretold, the ladies will distil
   Never march pleasant into rusty mystique
   Disdain be not mean, though some call thee still;
   So remember this ballad of vanity and technique.

2. "Hunting with the Magnificent Horse"

   Heroic epic. 642 lines, 107 stanzas. Extract:

   The stallion of chaos is burning perfumed
   Mythic, tough, lusty, and consumed
   Always move gentle into lusty rocks
   Such was the pony whose madness was locked.

3. "The Dancing of the Politician"

   Satire. 56 lines, 2 stanzas. Extract:

   Politician! At last I behold thee, dirty and fair!
   Bloody, dumb, dirty and fair
   With monkeys as cheap as your bloody light,
   The sister of wrath and wounded flight.

These are three examples of the procedurally generated poetry in my RPG, *A House of Many Doors*. The poems I generate share a few common qualities: they are all presented in game as four-line "extracts" from a larger piece. They all (attempt to) deal with a single overarching theme—a horn, a horse, a politician. And most importantly of all, they're all pretty bad. Just not very good at all.

Why are they bad? Well, because procedural generation of text is difficult, and our brains are such finely tuned word tools that "language" is basically a synonym of "thought." When we generate rocks and trees and continents, they are imperfect, but unless they're really misshapen, we don't notice. When we generate poems, their lack of quality is immediately obvious because we are deeply familiar with how language works. It's an effect of uncanny lexis, similar to the uncanny valley—we can make beautiful trees in computer-generated images (CGIs), but we haven't mastered the human face. Familiarity breeds difficulty.

Now some insanely clever people at Google—people who are far better at this than I am—have also been teaching computers to write poetry. But instead of procedural generation, they've been using staggeringly complex neural networks. I include an example below:

i don't like it, he said.
    i waited for what had happened.
    it was almost thirty years ago.
    it was over thirty years ago.
    that was six years ago.
    he had died two years ago.
    ten, thirty years ago.
    "it's all right here.
    "everything is all right here.
    "it's all right here.
    it's all right here.
    we are all right here.
come here in five minutes.

Now, this is hugely impressive for many different reasons. This represents the struggle toward true artificial intelligence (AI). AI that can learn and adapt, AI that actually understands grammar rather than being told by a programmer to generate text in a way that obeys grammatical rules.

In almost all respects, this is much more impressive than anything I've done. One area that it doesn't impress, though, is the quality of the poetry.

See, my proc gen poems are bad. But not that bad.

By qualification, I am not a computer scientist. I am an English literature graduate, giving me an appreciation for—and understanding of—poetry, and I think this helped when it came to coding a proc gen engine that created the stuff. I went into the process with a different perspective, I suspect, than most computer scientists might have had. One of my biggest priorities was to categorize my word database not only by rhyme, lexical category, and meaning, but also by number of syllables.

See, meter is important in poetry. Especially in the kind of premodernist poetry I wanted my engine to write. And while I wasn't quite up to the task of categorizing each word by which syllable was stressed, I could at the very least ensure that the number of syllables was taken into account.

And just like that, I had a way of ensuring my proc gen poems had appropriate cadence. It made an immediate difference, and I suspect I'd never have thought about it if I approached this as a computer science problem rather than a poetry problem.

So what's the takeaway from this? Real-world knowledge of what you're trying to generate can be helpful at worst. At best, it can cause you to totally reevaluate your approach. If you don't have three years of college study on hand, a week or two of intense research will probably do the trick.

Let me take you through my process of poetry generation, top to bottom, beginning with a terrible admission: I originally didn't intend to generate poetry at all.

Part of the premise of *A House of Many Doors* was that the player character would collect memories and experiences in the course of the story—A Moment of Melancholy, say, or a Horrifying Ordeal, or a Droll Recollection—and spend them to write poems. It was essentially just a way to collect experience points and level up. I created a system to generate the poems' titles, and then told the player, 'You wrote a poem!" The poetry itself was left to the imagination.

Then, in the run-up to the ultimately successful Kickstarter, I carelessly mentioned that the game allowed the player to write generated poetry. This caught people's imaginations like wildfire. With trepidation and excitement, I realized I'd have to actually generate proper poems.

I'd already been interested in doing this, but I was under the impression that it would be a waste of time—I didn't realize that so many people were actually interested in the idea.

Why am I telling you this? To explain one of the central pillars of my poetry system—it selects a genre first, titles second, and then everything else after, based only on these first two. This is the opposite of how real poems are written. It wasn't a part of any plan, but it ended up working rather well! Let's take "Hunting with the Magnificent Horse" as an example.

If the player spends Breathtaking Spectacles to write a poem, then the poem will be a heroic epic. A title will be collated from a database of appropriate words—since this is an epic, it might be a grandiose adjective like *magnificent* and a martial-associated noun like *horse*. Then a title will be created from these words. At this stage, it's essentially poem title Mad Libs.

Along with the genre, the title becomes the basis for everything after. Synonyms are collected for *hunting* and *horse*—and then when the poem needs to find a noun or verb, it has a high chance to choose one of these (e.g., *stallion* or *pony*). Loosely related words, but not exact synonyms, are also collected—there is a slightly lower chance of these being picked (e.g., *lance* is associated with *horse*, but is not an exact synonym). Then there is a chance to choose something completely unrelated, but otherwise relevant to the genre (for a heroic epic, this could be something like *sword* or *hero*). Finally, there is also a very small chance of totally random deviation (just for fun).

This has the effect of creating a (mostly) coherent subject matter and theme that runs throughout the poem, but which isn't totally rigid. And remember that all these words are categorized by syllable, too, and by rhyme for the words that end each line.

Now that the important nouns and verbs and adjectives have been chosen, the system runs through a similar process for lines. Let's take a line from "The Dancing of the Politician," "With monkeys as cheap as your bloody light"—before the important words are added, this would be "With _____ as _____ as your _____ _____." Which lines are chosen is weighted by genre and by the grammatical construction of the preceding lines. Again, there's a very small chance of utterly random deviation here, because sometimes it's fun to throw a spanner into all my hard work.

The word database in *A House of Many Doors*, with all its synonyms and rhymes and syllable counts and genre weighting, consists of almost 10,000 words. It can spit out more poems than there are atoms in the universe.

I tried to give the player as much control over their poems as possible. In retrospect, though, I wish I'd gone further.

The player in *A House of Many Doors* isn't passively clicking a button labeled "Generate poem." With hard work and in-universe justification, they acquire a resource, and then choose where to spend it—choosing what kind of poem they wish to write. An epic saga? A melancholic lament? A satire, a romance, a dream vision? The player feels involved in shaping the poem that ultimately results, even if the code does the heavy lifting.

This is part of the appeal of the very best world builders, too. Clicking a button labeled "Generate world" is fun. But choosing world size, population demographics, continent layout, or—as will be the case in *Dwarf Fortress*—the magic system? That makes it a process that the player can endlessly delight in. Rather than a novelty act—a "look what the computer can pull out of its hat" one-time trick that gets dull quickly—the process of procedural generation becomes an experiment.

I encourage other proc gen pioneers to hand over the reins to their players as much as possible. By allowing your players to experiment like this, you're not just ensuring they have fun—you're exposing the complexities of the system in an intuitive way that would never be apparent otherwise. Your world builder can model rainfall distribution and no one will notice. But give the player a slider to alter rainfall distribution, and let them watch as deserts form—suddenly they will admire the depth of the simulation that much more.

Like I said, though, I wish I'd gone further with this in *A House of Many Doors*—it wouldn't be unfeasible to allow the player to choose to write about a politician!— but I'm too far along in development to change this now. Perhaps in my next project.

Another regret is the relatively short time span I had. This is an inevitable side effect of commercial game development. If I had a few more months to spare, and the will to remake the system from the bottom up, there's a lot I'd do differently. I would categorize words by metric feet as well as syllables. The syllable count system helped created poems with an approximation of meter, but with (a lot) more time I could add a system that checked for stressed and unstressed syllables too. Then I could generate poems with proper, ruthlessly administered iambic pentameter in the Shakespearean vein—and almost anything in iambic pentameter sounds nice and literary.

Even with all this theoretical extra work, though, the poems would still be bad. As discussed already, all computer-generated poems will be bad and stilted and suffer from uncanny lexis (when this rule stops being true, we will all have been enslaved by our robot overlords anyway).

So I suppose if I had any one piece of advice it would be, embrace badness, as long as it's funny or interesting or both. Your proc gen system might be very complicated and probably took a lot of work, but it will occasionally produce bad results. If you can make sure those are funny–bad, rather than frustrating–bad, you've already won.

CHAPTER 21

Characters and Personalities

Emily Short
Independent

INTRODUCTION

When we talk about procedurally generated character and personality, there are several things we might mean by that:

Description: A system that procedurally creates *descriptions* of characters or personalities, but which is not primarily concerned with making those characters interactively meaningful.

This type of system might be used to fill in background detail, for instance, by offering small profiles of the antagonists one encountered in a sandbox video game environment, or as part of a generative art project.

Realization: A system that procedurally creates nonplayer character (NPC) *dialogue and actions* in response to the player's actions, interactions with other NPCs, and/or events within the world model.

This type of system finds the best way to perform predefined character traits, allowing a character to demonstrate a depth of responsiveness that we could not accomplish purely through writing. However, the characters' essential traits have been chosen by the game writer or by the player during a character creation process.

Creation. A system that procedurally assembles NPC character profiles, compositing personality traits, appearances, loyalties, and other features that are both fictively meaningful and functional within the game world, so that the player encounters a perennially changing cast of characters.

This type of system can verge on story generation, since in some cases narrative events might arise from the dynamic interaction of characters. Highly simulation-focused systems such as *The Sims* can produce emergent (if not always consistent or well-formed) stories when characters with conflicting personalities are put in the same household, for instance.

In this chapter, we focus primarily on realization and creation techniques. Character description has a number of applications in game development and procedural art—in fact, it is the kind of procedural character work I have had the most call for over the course of many different text-based game projects. However, autogenerating a character description often uses many of the techniques already outlined in this book. We might, for instance, use a context-free grammar to build up a paragraph about a character, drawing on a preexisting corpus of character traits.

Character realization and character creation, on the other hand, require some additional techniques.

SOURCE MATERIAL

In discussing these issues, I'll be referring to examples from several of my past projects.

In *When in Rome 2*, the player has to encounter, identify, and subdue an alien life-form. The game selects the alien type randomly at the beginning of each play session. Different behavior rules correlate with different alien traits, so the player can learn about the alien by watching how it interacts with its environment. *When in Rome 2* is available at http://ifdb.tads.org/.

Versu is a game platform that Richard Evans (*Black & White* and *Sims 3*) and I developed together. *Versu* modeled characters as agents with independent desires; each agent would choose the action they most wanted to perform out of a list based on the current social situation. Although this system is no longer under production and the games written with it are not available, it has been fairly extensively documented. More information about *Versu* is available at versu.com, including papers for both lay and academic audiences about the underlying system and the toolset that we used to create new content.

Blood & Laurels was the final game I wrote for the *Versu* platform, and it was released as a stand-alone app for the iPad. (It is no longer available due to incompatibilities with recent versions of iOS.) *Blood & Laurels* was set in a fictional version of ancient Rome, and was a story of intrigue and conspiracy to overthrow the emperor. The story had a preauthored branching narrative structure, but within each scene the interactions were highly procedural, allowing characters to share information and flirt with and fight, betray, and poison one another before moving on to a fresh scenario—a sandbox embedded in a preauthored structure.

The Mary Jane of Tomorrow is a game about training a robot to exhibit some personality traits (enthusiasm, courtesy, and knowledge of particular subject matter) and suppress others (ennui and knowledge of other subject matter). Because the player can assemble traits in almost any combination, this project relied heavily on text generation techniques to realize the robot's evolving speech patterns. The game can be found at http://ifdb.tads.org/.

REALIZATION

For most of my projects, procedural realization has meant choosing what to say, and then how to say it.

Choosing what to say might be dictated by the needs of the plot in a story-based game—for instance, we might know that a particular NPC needs to set a quest during the course of the next scene. We might also choose dialogue in response to a question from a player, or as part of a social interaction that we're modeling.*

If our character doesn't speak English or isn't primarily engaged in social interactions, this might translate instead into choosing what to do and how to do it: for instance, in *When in Rome 2*, a meat-eating alien from a low-gravity planet might choose to steal and eat a salami, but have difficulty eating the salami because of its low strength.

Selecting Dialogue

Versu modeled characters who had their own unique dialogue around certain topics and ideas. *Versu*'s conversation rules then controlled transitions

---

* There's a great deal more to say about dialogue modeling than fits into this chapter, especially as it isn't our primary focus here. My blog at emshort.wordpress.com contains a number of posts in the "conversation modeling" category that deal with particular approaches.

from one piece of dialogue to another, encouraging characters to stay more or less on topic.

In one of our unreleased demo projects, we wrote a scene in which any *Versu* characters could be brought together to play a game of cards and chat freely from their corpora of dialogue. One of the characters, Patrick, was a modern frat bro; another was an early nineteenth-century admiral. When Patrick told a story about his numerous dates, the admiral followed up with a story about sexually transmitted disease running rife on his ships during a Pacific voyage.

Both pieces of dialogue were tagged as pertaining to the topic of sexual behavior, so the social affordance allowed a transition from one to another although the characters had never been explicitly written to talk to each other. This topic structure provided a useful generality that let components from different genres interact.

Players who encountered this transition read more into it than was actually there. The admiral was not intentionally *scolding* Patrick for sleeping around or expressing an equivalence between Patrick and his own sailors. But because the stories were written to be specific to the characters' experiences and offer some subtextual depth, they seemed to mean more when juxtaposed.

Layering Dialogue Features

In *The Mary Jane of Tomorrow*, the procedural system spends little time working out what to say in a macrosense. There are only a few questions (on the order of a dozen or so) that the player may ask. Most of the system's content focuses on rendering the nuances of the dialogue to demonstrate the robot's current settings.

For instance, we can ask the robot to do us a favor, and we get this response from a robot who is trained in flirtation, enthusiasm, and faux medieval diction:

> The robot crosses her legs. "If thou wishest it, yea!"

The gesture of leg crossing is available because the robot is flirtatious. She agrees in medieval language because of her diction training, and she uses an exclamation point because she's enthusiastic. If we asked when she was bored instead, we might get

> The robot shrugs. "Verily."

This is implemented as a grammar. The response to a request consists of two tokens: [gesture] [consent]. Each of these tokens is then expanded using a corpus that takes into account mood and diction features. The consent token breaks down to [consent phrase] [final punctuation], where the final punctuation will be . if the robot is bored, but ! if the robot is enthusiastic.

Handling all in-game dialogue this way could become overwhelming fast in a large project; in *The Mary Jane of Tomorrow*, it works because there are few initial utterances, and because this level of variability is the main point of the game experience.

But even in a situation where we need to produce a much higher volume of content, we can identify dialogue elements that we can usefully treat as tokens to be expanded in the moment, such as

- Gestures or tone-of-voice indicators that might accompany a speech act.

- Social moves, such as greetings, farewells, compliments, and insults, that might be included in a longer piece of speech.

- Exclamations.

- Names of other characters or in-game entities, which might be substituted differently depending on the speaker's relationship to that character ("Eunice," "Dr. Yeung," "Mom," or "that genius").

- Hesitations and framings—If the character has a piece of information to convey, do they say it outright or do they frame it with some hesitation or uncertainty? "I think...," "I hate to contradict you, but...," and so forth, all convey a more cautious personality.

You can also transform generated text after it has been constructed. In *Versu*, we had a "drunk character" filter that would create slurred speech for a character after they'd drunk too much, by converting *s-* to *sh-* and doing other similar conversions. Simple as it was, this effect was a dramatic favorite with players.

Stutters, word repetitions, sentence fragmentation, and self-interruption can also add to the performance, communicating that a character is nervous, confused, lying, or in some other state of distress.*

---

* The SpyFeet project of the University of California, Santa Cruz (https://games.soe.ucsc.edu/project/spyfeet) digs deeper into some of these forms of speech filtering, and connects these elements with studies of personality traits in general.

In *Versu*, our drunk filter meant we autogenerated profanity when a character slurred the word *sit*. It would have been possible to add some special case checking to make sure that this didn't occur, but in practice, we didn't consider that problem a game killer in the specific case of *Versu*. However, as always, it's a good idea to be ethical about the construction of output: if you're altering words before they're printed, check to make sure that the generated text is not more offensive than is otherwise appropriate for your work.

Character and World Interaction

Versu treated its world model more like a stage than like a fully detailed simulation. The objects in a room were interesting more for their expressive capacity than for any functional purpose—which meant that we often defined objects with expressive hooks. The main purpose of a vase was to be smashed in anger. A fireplace might afford the possibility of staring thoughtfully into the flames or destroying a dangerous letter or stabbing the coals viciously with a poker. Food at a dinner party could be eaten, criticized, or (in extreme cases) thrown at other diners.

Providing expressive hooks in the world model augments the sorts of dialogue-layering techniques described above. Characters seem connected with the space they're in—and if they're interacting with props that the player is also able to move, alter, and destroy, these interactions drive home that the player is not interacting with something purely scripted.

CREATION

Realization and creation are not independent of one another. A system that allows dynamic character creation often needs realization techniques in order to present that character in an interesting way.

But dynamic character creation introduces further constraints, especially if we intend the player to interact with a character in different ways depending on the character's strengths. In this case, designing our vocabulary of character traits becomes a subset of game design, since we are now in essence constructing a gameplay system with character features as elements of that system.

Such a system relies on a robust selection of combinable character traits, skill sets, or behaviors that are

- Orthogonal to one another, or else tagged with information about mutually exclusive features

- Mechanically significant

- Easy to communicate to the player individually

- Likely to combine in interesting and evocative ways

Orthogonal

When we say that traits are orthogonal, we're saying that they apply to different aspects of the character's life and therefore can be combined freely. A person's height is orthogonal to their strength: a person could be tall and strong, tall and weak, short and strong, or short and weak, without any inherent contradiction.

On the other hand, if we chose traits such as flirtatious–standoffish and outgoing–shy, we might find ourselves generating characters who are both flirtatious and shy. It might be difficult to realize that character convincingly, since the qualities describe overlapping aspects of a person's behavior.

If we really wanted, we could still use those traits, but include a rule during generation that any generated character who was both flirtatious and shy should be discarded and rerolled (or restrictively generated in the first place). However, it's often easier and more productive to avoid these problems initially by rethinking the trait axes until we come up with some that are genuinely orthogonal. For instance, instead of flirtatiousness, we might measure a character's *interest* in romance, giving us a romantic-aromantic axis to pair with our outgoing–shy axis.

Then we might generate romantic and outgoing characters who would behave flirtatiously, romantic and shy characters who were hesitant daydreamers, aromantic outgoing characters who wanted to be friends with everyone but date no one, and aromantic shy characters who standoffishly kept to themselves.

Each of those combinations is interesting and plausible, so we've maximized the descriptiveness of our procedural system.

Mechanically Significant

If a game is heavy in story or meant to be played only once, the fiction probably carries quite a bit of weight with the player, coloring her experience of the entire game.

The more the player encounters different scenarios built with the same ruleset, the more the fictional layer abstracts away *unless* it is supported by mechanical content as well. An NPC with an aggressive facial expression becomes no different from an NPC with a passive expression unless the two characters also respond differently to the player.

This is something we discovered in writing characters for the Austenesque stories in *Versu*. One of the characters, Mr. Brown, was a bad-tempered poet loosely based on Lord Byron. We wanted him to be arrogant, romantic, flirtatious, swift to anger, and a constant source of irritation.

Initially, we gave him a number of special lines of dialogue to use when speaking to other characters, allowing him to give flowery speeches that none of the other characters could use. With repetition, though, the flowery speeches felt like what they were a fictional decoration of the character, rather than a deep mechanical feature. Brown emerged more powerfully as an individual character when we translated his dramatic qualities into a mechanical function instead, and made Brown prefer to escalate situations. If you insulted him, he'd take maximum offense; if you flirted with him, he'd come back twice as warmly; if you rejected him, he'd gripe and sulk.

Easy to Communicate

The more complicated the trait, the less likely it's going to come across to the player. Some traits also don't read well in particular stories because there are few opportunities to exercise them.

In our *Versu* stories, a character who was habitually unpleasant to high-ranking men didn't read clearly to players: he appeared in a story where most of the other male characters were rich, and therefore he just seemed generally surly. There weren't enough cases where the player could see him interact with lower-ranking men and perceive a pattern.

Meaningful in Combination

If you present a player with a character description made up of three emotional styles (say, aggressive, friendly, and passive) and three hair colors (blond, brunette, and black-haired, perhaps), you've created a system in which there are 3 * 3, or 9, possible total combinations.

However, the player will *experience* this system more as if there were only 3 + 3, or 6, possible combinations. Because hair color and emotional style are largely irrelevant to one another, you don't get a dramatically new play experience by making a blond aggressive character as opposed to a black-haired aggressive character. Once players have seen each emotional style and each hair color, they'll feel, correctly, that they've exhausted the system.

Making your elements mechanically significant will help with this, of course, because then a black-haired aggressive character will (somehow) play differently than a blond aggressive character. But it's also productive to think of elements that resonate with one another as *symbols*, so that a pair together takes on a meaning that wasn't inherently there in the individual elements.

RECURRING STRATEGIES

Combining Output from Several Layers of Simulation or Gameplay

In *Blood & Laurels*, the player could acquire poison from one of the characters and then subsequently poison any NPC in any banquet scene. The procedural effects of poisoning took hold slowly: at first, the victim would seem not to react at all, and would go on with what they were already talking about. But soon afterward, they'd start to choke and sputter, and then their conversation would be cut off in a dramatic death scene and flurry of servant reactions.

That delay was part of what made the poison so satisfying to play. Because you could poison someone at any time in these scenes, and because the poisoning was interlaced with the rest of the scene's drama, it could turn out variously funny, dark, or sad, just as a result of whatever else happened to be layered with the poisoning death. Cutting instantly to the poisoning death would have felt much less rich.

Bringing Character into Every Interaction

We want to juxtapose features that come from gameplay *context* (what are we currently talking about, and how does this character currently feel about the protagonist) with long-term character *traits* (what kind of person is this, and how do they tend to behave in general?)

Writers of screenplays try to write dialogue rich in subtext. Each line exists to convey information not only about what is happening, but also about the characters' relationships and inner life. Dialogue without this characteristic is called "on the nose": it's boring, predictable, and impersonal. In a procedural context, we can layer different aspects of the story in order to get that feeling of subtext.

For instance, we might imagine a system where

- The content of the next beat of dialogue is chosen based on the needs of a prewritten narrative; it's specific to this one moment and will never be repeated.

- The emotional content of that beat is chosen based on character relationships built up via gameplay.

- The text, voice, or graphical rendering of this dialogue and emotional content is determined by the character's traits and behavior; it reflects some ongoing realities.

Juxtaposing Events and Interpretation

Players fill in gaps in the narrative with their own explanations of character motive. This is a tremendously useful opportunity for a designer. In the simplest case, this means that the player will interpret text output like

> The robot sighs. "I'd love to," she says.

as sarcastic or exasperated, but read

> The robot grins. "I'd love to," she says.

as sincere. If we imagine the tone of voice used in those two performances, they come out quite different, even though nothing in the text specifically says that the first tone of voice is sarcastic and the second tone of voice is genuine. Text is particularly versatile in this respect, but even if we're using graphics, we can do some of the same things—for instance, by combining different gestures with lines of dialogue. The gesture provides a context for interpreting the dialogue.

The player can build larger bridges as well. Here's one of the poems the robot character will compose in *The Mary Jane of Tomorrow*:

> Peasants at the joust
> every jaw agape:
> defeat is ready to spring.

This robot is trained in medieval diction, so it draws a medieval image from its corpus of possible images. The final line, meanwhile, is pulled at random from a separate corpus of proverbs and general situations. By putting together a specific, detailed circumstance (peasants gaping) with a broad interpretive remark (defeat is ready to spring), we invite the player to come to her own conclusion about what is going on here. Perhaps the joust is about to go horribly awry; maybe one of the contestants is fighting badly and in peril of death. But, as the author of these passages, I never imagined or intended that specific juxtaposition.

Callbacks to Earlier Events

In *Versu*, if the player did something that caused a character to change their opinion of the protagonist, the system would not only register a numerical change in the character's reaction, but also record a string of text describing why the NPC had changed their opinion. We could then reuse the string when the character wanted to report on how they felt about someone.

For instance, if Fred has decided to insult Miss Bates by saying he doesn't have a good opinion of her intelligence, his dialogue might be rendered like this:

> *Fred:* Miss Bates is a fool. She would not stop talking about turtles at supper.

Callbacks create perceivable consequence: the player can see how earlier events have affected the current state of the system.

PITFALLS

Overgeneralization

A piece of character generation or character behavior code is rarely as completely universal as one might hope, especially across different genres or lengths of story.

Versu was designed as a platform for many different stories, and indeed for many different types of story. The initial suite of stories released were a murder mystery and a ghost story set in Regency England and reflected a Jane Austen–derived environment, with characters in some cases lifted from her books directly and in some cases adapted from similar behavior. The second set of stories were shorter office comedies set in the modern day.

We anticipated (correctly) that we would need to create different behavior sets to account for these different genres of story, since a character flirting in a modern office setting would likely say things that would be considered wildly scandalous in the Regency setting.

The less obvious challenge was that we also needed our social actions to have different impact depending on context. The office comedies were meant to be farcical, with social situations that rapidly escalated into more and more ridiculous problems, and gameplay took place over perhaps half an hour. The Regency stories were meant to be more serious and dramatic, with character relationships evolving over closer to an hour of playtime and through many different scenes. The models we developed for how a character might react to an insult in one were wrongly tuned for the other.

Multiplying NPC reaction numbers by a scaling factor did not always resolve this problem, because the Regency social practices were designed with the idea that characters would spend some time sending social signals and then confirming that those signals were actually intended. In the office comedy, by contrast, we needed characters to over- rather than underinterpret what had been said to them—to start throwing pies right away, rather than politely trying to clear up any misunderstanding.

In practice, any system of procedural character realization designed for narrative is likely to be tightly bound to the underlying story genre and gameplay system. A system created for one context may not easily transfer to another.

Overrealism

For *Versu*, we developed a model of the social practice of conversation. It procedurally expressed ideas about conversation flow taken from studies of real-life conversational pragmatics: rules such as "it is a violation of social norms to fail to answer a question you've been asked" or "it is socially normal to keep talking about the same topic that is already under discussion" or "if there are several conversational partners available, people are more likely to respond to those with whom they have the strongest relationship."

The latter rule turned out to be realistic but ill-suited to a game. In early testing of the system, we found that players complained because when they entered a room, the NPCs in that room might respond to the player briefly but then go back to talking to one another. When we investigated, we found that the system was behaving as specified: the player just happened to be playing a relative stranger walking in on two close friends. The scenario of the friends acknowledging the newcomer just long enough to be polite is true to life, but it violated the players' expectations of agency and centrality in the game universe.

When we added a weighting factor to the simulation so that NPCs would always prefer to interact with a player character, testers said the results were much more realistic.

Untamed Simulation

In one of the *Versu* office comedy scenarios we worked on (but never published), the story included a meeting where all the characters came together to work on an advertising strategy. In testing, I was taken aback when two of the characters, who had been flirting all game long, had sex in the middle of the meeting, in front of their coworkers.

To some extent, this outcome was the fault of not having enough rules in the simulation: we hadn't added strong enough controls to indicate that it was a severe social violation to participate in such intimate behavior in front of other people, or in a work setting. But it was also a manifestation of a problem we frequently faced in general, in which the simulation generated outcomes that damaged the intended behavior of the story.

For *Blood & Laurels*, we solved this problem by adding scene-by-scene constraints. In each scene, we would specify which characters were allowed to die, leave the room, or have sex—those being the extreme points that we felt could derail the narrative.

In some games, this doesn't matter. For sandbox games and roguelikes, there is no pregenerated narrative to destroy; it's to be expected if all the dwarfs die in *Dwarf Fortress*, or if the Sims in *Sims 3* are trapped in a doorless bathroom and starve to death. But in a more narrative context, we often need to make sure our simulation does not stretch our narrative framework beyond what we're prepared to handle.

IV

The Procedural Future

GAMES AND SOFTWARE HAVE been procedurally generating interactive experience for decades, yet at the time of writing, most can agree that we remain in the infancy of our field's potential. While procedurally generated levels and chatbots are becoming commonplace, the future remains unknowable. Designers debate whether satisfying stories can be truly generated, or whether a player's perception of content as machine authored changes its value. Perhaps these questions will be answered definitively, and perhaps not.

As we've seen throughout this book, procedural generation is a diverse field even within the confines of game design, as if it resists generalities by nature. In this final section, we see the nigh-infinite directions we can continue to explore, whether we create as scientists or as artists. How we talk about generators, test them, categorize and quantify their properties, select specific algorithms, or even generate games and generators themselves is all touched on here.

Ultimately, the steps forward will be as surprising as they are exciting, and it is difficult to speculate about the next disruptor to the mainstream conversation about procedural generation. However, the tools used to achieve that paradigm shift will undoubtedly include those provided within this section.

CHAPTER 22

Understanding the Generated

Gillian Smith
Independent

P RESSING THE "GENERATE" BUTTON and seeing the surprising results that come from a system you made is one of the joys (and frustrations) of creating procedural generators. It's easy to determine the success or failure of a generator based only on what we witness come from the system as developers. But unless the generative system is intended to create only one artifact, at some point we need to understand the generator as a whole: what types of things it tends to make, whether it makes things that have sufficiently high quality, or if it has any biases in it that aren't obvious from just eyeballing the output manually. As makers of generative systems, we are making entire spaces of potential content that a player or viewer or other designer may need to interact with. Instead of needing to do quality assurance on handcrafted content, we need to do it for every potential piece of content that could come out of the software we create.

This chapter offers a method for automatically critiquing what is being generated and, in doing so, better understanding the generator's capabilities. I'll be talking about the notion of understanding how *expressive* a generator is and some strategies for visually understanding that expressiveness. And finally, I'll close with some general thoughts about how and why and when it makes sense to grapple with the overall generative space of a system, rather than individual pieces of content.

EXPRESSIVE RANGE AND GENERATIVE SPACES

Generators are like little minidesigners who operate in a very specific domain. They have their own style and quirks and strengths and weaknesses. A generator's style is highly sensitive to the data and algorithms we employ in their creation. Being able to understand this style and how it changes based on player and/or designer input is a crucial aspect of generator design.

I like to think about the *expressive range* of a generative system as the *potential* range of content the system might be able to create. A single instantiation of the system—with a fixed set of parameters and fixed codebase—has what I'll be calling a *generative space*. A system's expressive range is made up of many potential generative spaces. When you change an input parameter or a line of code, you are creating a new generative space filled with a lot of different pieces of content.

For any given generative space, we might be able to say that a system can create thousands, even millions, of unique pieces of content that fill that space. But, how different are those pieces of content from each other? Is the system biased toward creating certain kinds of content? Are the few examples you see when you hit the "generate" button representative of the overall generative space, or accidentally only in one small corner of it?

It's impossible to answer these questions by examining small samples of content that come from a generative system, and looking at every piece of content is prohibitively expensive. This chapter presents a method for understanding expressive range automatically, using the *Launchpad* level generator as a running example. *Launchpad* is a parameterized generator for Mario-like two-dimensional (2D) platforming levels. It supports static platforms, moving platforms, gaps, springs, enemies that pace on a platform, and stompers.[1]

QUALITIES OF THE GENERATED

Types of Qualities

If a generative space is a collection of generated content, then let's begin by understanding individual pieces of that content. When we look at generated content ourselves, we are usually judging its value along several measures that are custom to the domain we're working with. The first step in understanding a particular generative space is to capture the qualities we care about in pieces of generated content, so that we can see how well those qualities are distributed across the space. Maybe you care about seeing a particular number of challenges in a level, or a distribution of resources across a map, or a pleasing color scheme. There isn't one universal set of qualities to look for, although there are some types of qualities you can think about for your own system. These types of qualities are adapted from previous research.[2]

- *Topological*: Topological properties are based on the underlying structure of the content created, independent from how it is skinned. For a level generator, this might be properties such as the presence of loops and cycles, or how much the player's path branches. For a story generator, it might be the story's length or the shape of the narrative arc.

- *Experiential*: Experiential properties describe how the player will interact with and experience the generated content. Is there a particular rhythmic quality to player movement through the space that you are hoping for, or a method for estimating level difficulty? In a puzzle game, is there a certainly desirable number of solutions, or set of characteristics for what a good solution should look like? Are there particular strategies you want a player to use, and what might be indicators of those strategies being adopted?

- *Aesthetic*: Aesthetic properties describe the visual and auditory qualities of the generated content. Qualities like the kind of color palette used, the extent to which it uses warm or cool colors, and the use of contrast and salience to highlight particular features are all examples of artistic properties.

- *Semantic*: It is important to consider not just the gameplay properties of content made by generators, but also the real-world, semantic meaning behind what is created. For example, a character creator may generate characters from a library of clothing types—how many of those clothing types read as masculine or feminine?

Example

For some concrete examples, Figure 22.1 shows three example levels from *Launchpad*, zoomed all the way out so we can see the entire map at once. Two qualities that we are interested in based on seeing these levels are

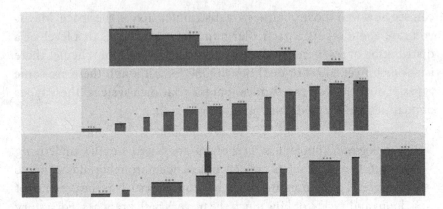

FIGURE 22.1   Three levels created by *Launchpad*.

- *Linearity:* This is a *topological* property, describing the vertical change in heights of platforms across an entire level. A level that is highly linear is one that follows a straight path (be it flat, sloped upward, or sloped down). A level that is nonlinear is one that follows a curve, with many changes in vertical orientation. The first two levels in Figure 22.1 have high linearity, as they follow a straight line; the second has medium linearity.

- *Leniency*: This is an *experiential* property, describing how lenient the level is to players when they fail. A highly lenient level is one with challenges that do not tend to kill the player if they fail, such as jumps to new platforms with no gaps underneath them. A nonlenient level is one that has mostly challenges where the player is likely to come to significant harm if they fail. The first level in Figure 22.1 has high leniency, as there is only one challenge that could bring the player to harm. The next two levels have low leniency, with many gaps that will kill the player if they fail to jump over them successfully.

Linearity and leniency are the two qualities that will be examples for the remainder of the chapter, but there are some other example qualities we could imagine caring about as well:

- *Density*: An *aesthetic* quality describing how much of the screen space is taken up with level elements versus left as open space

- *Risk–reward ratio*: An *experiential* quality that describes the average reward given for each risky maneuver in the level

Formalizing Qualities into Metrics

In order to automatically assess these qualities and compare many pieces of generated content using them, we need to develop metrics that correspond to them. These metrics should be determined using some algorithm that can give us a score that can be compared with other pieces of content from the same generator. Often, metrics will be defined on (or normalized to) a [0, 1] scale, to make it easier to perform comparisons between individual pieces. Ideally, these metrics will be efficient to compute for each piece of content, because—as we'll discuss in the next section—they will need to be run for many pieces of content each time you want to assess the current state of the generative space.

In any formalization of some aesthetic quality into a numerical score, there will be some aspect of that quality that is not fully captured—and that's okay! Our goal here isn't to come up with the perfect mathematical definition of *fun* or *beauty* or *difficulty*. Instead, we want to come up with some formal expression that gives us insight into a very specific quality we care about. Keeping in mind how well your mathematical definition maps to the fuzzier concept you are trying to capture will be useful when interpreting the generator's expressive range, as described later in the chapter.

Example

Let's look at the qualities we pulled out for *Launchpad*—linearity and leniency—and see how they can be formalized into a metric.

- *Linearity*: With this metric, we want to capture how much change in vertical movement there is across a level—whether the player will feel like they are moving along a series of hills and valleys, or moving in a straight line. To describe this as a single number, we treat the midpoint of each platform as a data point, and perform linear regression to find a line of best fit through the platform midpoints. We can then calculate how far off from that line each individual platform is by taking the absolute value of the distance between the actual height of the platform (y) and the expected height of the platform if it were to fit on the line (y_{exp}). Summing up all those values and dividing by the number of platforms (n) gives us a score that tells us, on average, how far away from the line the platforms are. To boil it down into an equation, a linearity score for any given level is

$$\text{linearity} = \frac{\sum_{p=1}^{n} |y - y_{exp}|}{n}$$

Because we divide by the number of platforms in the level, this score can be used to make comparisons between pairs of generated levels. A larger number means there's more distance overall from the line of best fit to the platforms. But to get a number that tells us how linear a level is in comparison with other potential levels produced by the same generator, we will need to normalize the score to a [0, 1] range. More on that when we talk about analyzing a generative space, rather than an individual level.

Note that this number can tell us how linear a level is, but doesn't tell us anything about the actual line it follows. A level that is completely flat will have the same linearity score as a level that follows a continuous upward or downward slope. For our design purposes, that was okay. But if we also wanted to know some information about the kind of line that we're following, rather than just how well we're following it, we could define another metric that uses the slope of the line of best fit.

- *Leniency*: Here, we want to create a metric that gives us a sense for how likely the player is to come to harm in any given level. There are a lot of factors that could be considered for this, but in the spirit of keeping with our design goal of creating lightweight metrics that can be calculated quickly, let's just consider the hazards that players encounter and how much harm can come to the player by interacting with them. *Launchpad* supports seven major kinds of obstacle that players interact with: gaps, enemies, long falls, springs, stompers, moving platforms, and jumps to new platforms with no gap underneath. To calculate the leniency of a level, we assign a leniency score to each of these elements:

Leniency	Element
0.0	Gaps, enemies, long falls
0.25	Springs, stompers
0.75	Moving platforms
1.0	Jumps without a gap

These points are chosen based on design intuition for how harmful the element can be to a player. Gaps, enemies, and long falls have low leniency because the failure state for interacting with these elements is death, and we've observed them to be the hardest elements for players to interact with. Jumps with no gap underneath them, even if technically difficult to overcome, will never be responsible for player death—thus they are given a high leniency score.

Summing the score for each level component and dividing by the total number of components gets us a leniency score between 0 and 1 that can be used to compare levels:

$$\text{leniency} = \frac{\sum_{e=1}^{n} \text{leniency}(e)}{n}$$

Again, some information relevant to level leniency is lost in creating this metric. It does not consider the challenges that come from ordering or frequency of level elements; for example, a player may be more likely to come to harm if they face three difficult jumps over gaps in quick succession, rather than three jumps over gaps that are spread far apart from each other. The goal with this metric is to provide a rough estimate based in our design intuition and that will later be interpreted with this caveat in mind.

Metrics versus Requirements

If you've used some generation method that already aims to create desirable content (perhaps a generate-and-test or optimization-based approach), then you have already gone through the step of creating some formal, mathematical definition of desirable features in the content. These may be interesting metrics to look at on their own: How often does your generator hit the requirements you specify for it? But bear in mind that understanding the emergent qualities of what is created involves examining features that aren't necessarily already encoded in the generator. Perhaps some of these metrics will move to the generator's fitness function at a later point, if it's decided that you actually want all of your generated content to have a particular value for a given metric.

For example, *Launchpad* uses a generate-and-test approach to creating levels where it aims to meet specific criteria set by a human designer in terms of the underlying rhythmic structure. A designer can specify that they want levels to be made up of fast-paced segments where the player takes regular actions, or slow-paced segments where the player has more time to rest between each challenge. While the way these parameters are set has an indirect impact on the expressive range of the overall system and provides different generative spaces for each parameter combination, the parameters themselves are not directly tied to the metrics of linearity and leniency.

QUALITIES OF THE GENERATOR

Now that we've got a way to automatically assess the quality of individual pieces of content, we can talk about what qualities we might care about for the generator itself with respect to the content that it creates.

We can use these metrics to get some insight into the generative space for an instance of the generator, by considering a generative space to be the n-dimensional space defined by those metrics. Every piece of content created by the system can be measured by each metric and plotted somewhere in that generative space. For *Launchpad*, with its two metrics of linearity and leniency, this means we have a 2D view on the generative space.

With this way of thinking about a generative space, we can now ask ourselves what kind of qualities we might want to understand with respect to a particular generative space, as well as the overall expressive range of the system.

- *Variety*: We often talk about creating content generators that can produce a wide variety of content. Now we know what it would mean to produce high variety within a given generative space: there should be large coverage across the entire space, with at least one piece of content at each point in the space. But more importantly, we can characterize variety. It's rare for a generator to uniformly produce a wide variety of content, but we can look at a generative space and see what kind of variety is produced—perhaps a level generator produces a high variety of levels with respect to their use of color palettes, but low variety with respect to a risk–reward ratio.

- *Unintentional bias*: Related to the sense of uniformity in variety of content is the notion of consistency. Examining a generative space lets us see areas where the generator is biased toward creating more or less content. This may or may not be desirable, but is a helpful insight to gain before deploying a content generator in a game or tool. We can gain a sense for how likely a player is to see a generated character wearing feminine clothing by looking at the generative space.

- *Responsiveness*: Generators can have unpredictable emergent behavior, where a single parameter change propagates and gives unexpected results. If our generator permits changing its inputs in some way (e.g., by altering the data it builds from or twiddling with input parameters), it is useful to see how the generative space changes as well, and to build up an understanding of the expressive range of the generator.

- *Content families*: Any generator will have a particular style of content that it typically creates, whether that style is deliberately and carefully crafted, or merely an artifact of the generative system. We can use analysis of a generator's generative space and expressive range to understand that style and see if there are particular common "families" of content being created: clusters of content that are similar to each other but far away from other kinds of content.

VISUALIZING EXPRESSIVE RANGE

So we now have a way to think about the generative spaces for our system and its overall expressive range. What are some useful ways to visualize that expressive range so we can understand what is being generated? In this section, I talk about two ways to visualize a generator's expressive range: comparing histograms that are cross sections of a particular generative space, and seeing clusters of similar content.

Histograms

A generative space has dense regions, inhabited by pieces of content that have similar metrics scores, and sparse regions, where there are few or even zero pieces of content that will ever be produced with those scores. A useful way of viewing these regions of differing density is to use a heat-map-based histogram, where the brightness of a region corresponds to its density. Visualizing a generative space in this way lets us see at a glance how varied content is, as well as if there are particular regions that a generator is biased toward or against. We can easily look at different histograms side by side to visually scan for changes in the generative space based on different input data or parameters.

However, visualizing a generative space with a 2D histogram comes with the trade-off of only letting us view a 2D "slice" of the generative space at a time. For visualizing many metrics simultaneously, it may be worth using a plot, such as a box-and-whiskers diagram, which gives a high-level overview of the mean, median, and standard deviation of each metric score at the expense of getting a sense for the overall shape of the generative space. This kind of visualization can also be useful for rapidly comparing different versions of the generator side by side.[3]

Example

Figure 22.2 shows a generative space heatmap for a particular parameterization of *Launchpad*, produced by generating 10,000 levels and scoring them with the leniency and linearity metrics described earlier. The linearity metric has been normalized across all generated levels to be on a range [0, 1], by first calculating all the linearity scores for all the levels, and rescaling so that the maximum score is 1 and the minimum score is 0.

This particular parameterization generates levels that are chains of 5-second-long, medium-density level segments separated by a resting platform. The player's actions follow a regular, rhythmic beat. The histogram shows that for this configuration, the generator is biased toward creating two types of levels, marked by bright green and red areas of the heatmap. The two types of levels it most commonly creates are levels that are highly nonlinear with medium leniency and levels that are highly linear with medium leniency. This heatmap also lets us see that with this

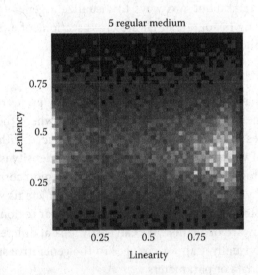

FIGURE 22.2 Example generative space histogram for a particular configuration of parameters to the *Launchpad* level generator.

configuration of parameters, the generator never makes levels that have a very high leniency score, and is most likely to create levels with a leniency score between 0.2 and 0.6.

It's useful being able to quickly see at a glance what kinds of levels the system can create. However, the real power of the heatmap visualization comes where we can compare different visualizations for different configurations of parameters, thus uncovering hidden biases. Figure 22.3 shows a set of generative space histograms for all possible combinations of the rhythm input parameters for *Launchpad*—the length of the rhythm, its type, and its density. These parameters control the "rhythm" that an ideal player will feel with their hands during gameplay as they hit different movement buttons on a controller: from short, regular, fast-paced segments to long, irregular, slow-paced segments.

Seeing these graphs side by side lets us see some unexpected biasing in the generator for particular rhythm parameters. In particular, setting the generator to produce regular rhythms biases the system toward creating highly linear levels, while setting it to create short swing-beat rhythms allows it to suddenly create segments with greater variety in leniency. This

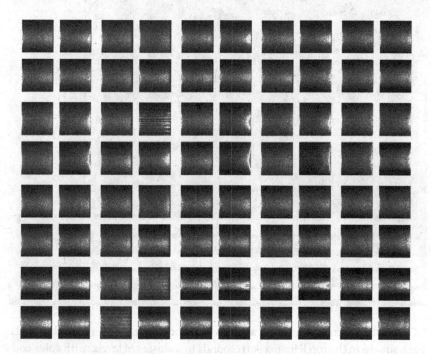

FIGURE 22.3 Set of expressive range histograms for *Launchpad*, each representing a different configuration of input parameters.

kind of biasing wouldn't be possible to see just from a quick visual inspection of single pieces of content produced by the system, because roughly the same areas of the expressive range are still covered—just with a very different frequency in certain regions than before. So hitting the "generate" button and playing a few levels would show that the same kinds of levels are being created with these parameters, and we would actually need to play and take note of thousands of levels before we could start to get the sense that the system is biased.

Distance-Based Clustering

An alternative for visualizing high-dimensional spaces is to determine clusters, or families, of content. While this method takes more implementation effort up front, it can be a helpful way to visualize over time how different clusters are changing in size and character. Clusters can show emergent patterns or families of generated content. For example, Figure 22.4 shows a cluster map for the *Launchpad* level generator. Each colored rectangle

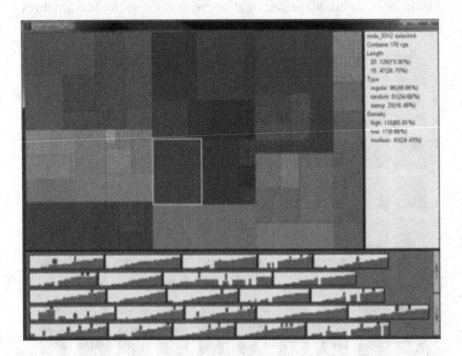

FIGURE 22.4 Screenshot of an analysis tool showing clusters of similar levels. Each square in the top left area corresponds to a cluster of levels, with color coding for levels that are similar to each other. The bottom panel lets the user scroll through to see all the levels in that cluster.

corresponds to a cluster (the size of the rectangle is proportional to how many levels are in that cluster), and selecting a rectangle shows the levels that are part of that cluster—the selected cluster in Figure 22.4 shows a family of upward-sloping levels that have many stompers in them.

In order to perform this kind of cluster analysis, it is necessary to be able to define the "distance" between two individual levels. In the case of our example, we defined an "edit distance" between two segments— the distance between two levels, A and B, is equal to the number of edit operations that would need to be made to convert level A into level B (see Ref. 1 for more details on how this was calculated). However, we could also use the metrics that we defined earlier and define the distance between levels as the Euclidean distance between them in the generative space. Any function that can compare two pieces of generated content and return a number that is small if they are similar and large if they are dissimilar will do!

CONCLUSION

In this chapter, we've seen a systematic method for understanding a generator's capabilities in terms of its generative space. Instead of looking at individual pieces of content by hand, we now have a method for looking holistically at all pieces of content generated by the system to understand the full range of what can be created, as well as for diagnosing any unintentional biases in a generative space. While implementing and maintaining metrics and expressive range visualization is additional development overhead, this method for "understanding the generated" can help with both the design and development of generative systems. For designers, having a sense of the range of content a user might see—or not see—can guide the creation of both the generative system and the larger game context that uses it. For developers, visualizing a generative space and how it changes during the course of development can help them track down bugs (e.g., if a small code change suddenly radically alters the generative space) and understand the emergent ramifications of seemingly small development decisions.

REFERENCES

1. Smith, Gillian, Jim Whitehead, Michael Mateas, Mike Treanor, Jameka March, and Mee Cha. 2011. Launchpad: A rhythm-based level generator for 2D platformers. *IEEE Transactions on Computational Intelligence in AI and Games* 3 (1).

2. Canossa, Alessandro, and Gillian Smith. 2015. Towards a procedural evaluation technique: Metrics for level design. In *Proceedings of the Foundations of Digital Games Conference*.

3. Horn, Britton, Steve Dahlskog, Noor Shaker, Gillian Smith, and Julian Togelius. 2014. A comparative evaluation of procedural level generators in the Mario AI framework. In *Proceedings of the Foundations of Digital Games*. Fort Lauderdale, FL.

CHAPTER 23

Content Tools Case Study

Kepa Auwae

Rocketcat Games

A S DISCUSSED IN MANY chapters of this book, handcrafted elements can create memorable moments in procedural levels and break player-perceived patterns. But how do you support the creation of those moments, so that they are influenced nicely by the generator, and prevent them from becoming repetitive themselves?

In building the level editing tools for *Wayward Souls*, we were inspired by *Dungeon Crawl: Stone Soup* and *Spelunky*. The example is for a two-dimensional (2D) game, but many of these concepts could be applied to a three-dimensional (3D) game. Through trial and error, we created a highly functional handcrafted room editor. Our goals for these tools were

- *Easy visualization*: This is great for coordination, as this way the editor could be used by anyone on the team. Someone handling the design could build a basic room based on what would encourage interesting combat or exploration, and then an artist could load it up in the editor and do a visual pass. It's also great just to make the development process easier, as it is less cumbersome than typing out each tile by hand in ASCII into a text file.

- *Conditional elements*: Some modifications depended on other modifications to happen or not happen first. For example, we wanted to give the algorithm a chance to place a pillar in the middle of a room, with a further chance to place decorations around the pillar with a torch on the front of it. Nested random chances were ideal to make a modular system where there were many possibilities that could combine with each other.

- Allow for shaping the room geometry by both addition and subtraction, based on chance or a conditional being fulfilled. Allow for adding doors or passageways, taking out chunks in the wall. Based on the previous nested chances, the same room could look very different if you saw it multiple times in a single play.

- Allow for easy further scripting, for things like dialogue triggers, doors being closed or opened by crossing an area, ambush encounters, cut scenes, and more.

- Be easy to learn for new people. Using layered image files and a parser for them as a level editing tool means that it's easier to visualize and make the modular content. This is again mostly for team coordination. If we wanted to get a new designer to help make modular rooms, it would be preferable if they didn't have to spend large chunks of time deciphering complex text files.

We ended up using the usual rooms in *Wayward Souls*, with the procedural bits mostly being short hallways. For the current game we're working on, these modular rooms are being attached to and placed in more purely code-generated areas. This approach is the best of both worlds. You get freeform generated spaces to explore and maneuver in, punctuated by a large amount of varied handcrafted modular geometry (Figure 23.1).

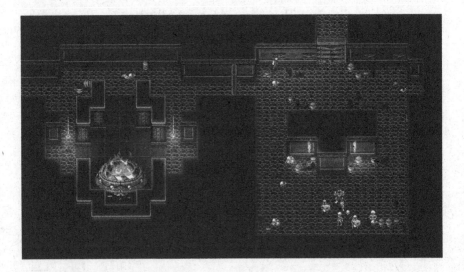

FIGURE 23.1   Generated level.

In our previous games, we used a web-based tile level editor, but over time, we found it was too cumbersome for more complex cases. We had way too many things in *Wayward Souls*. Tile types, decorations, monsters, and other entities would be too much to track. The main tool we ended up using was Photoshop/GIMP.

SYSTEM OVERVIEW

Every pixel in a map image represented a tile. Every color represented a different kind of tile. A separate palette file served to associate the colors to specific tiles.

Data from a layered PSD file would be run through a web-based parser (Figure 23.2). This processed all the graphic layers and converted them to tile data, which was stored in an SQLite database on our server. This would then be assessable in the test build of the game, instantly, for all developers and testers.

The level image files were layered so that different layers could be flipped on and off at will. The layer names served as scripting to determine the conditionals as to when and how often that layer's pixels could be drawn onto the map by the game. The layer name scripting had many different uses, many of which were compatible to be applied to the same layer:

- Set pixels in that layer to be an entity rather than a tile. Set the pixel as a specific monster, a breakable piece of furniture, a torch, a door, or a large art asset.

- Set what percentage chance the layer has to spawn.

FIGURE 23.2 PSD file, ready for processing.

- Set a name for a group of layers from which only one layer is chosen. Give the same name to two other layers; the game picks one out of the three. Have different group names so one layer from each set gets chosen.

- Set layers as associated with another layer, so it only has a chance to spawn if the previous layer does, for example, 50% chance to spawn a torch on a wall that only has a 50% chance to spawn.

- Set pixels drawn on the layer as invisible triggers for the player to step on, calling a function also set by the layer scripting. Go past this line, and it will close all doors in the room, and then spawn in waves of enemies that need to be defeated to open the doors.

EXAMPLE ROOM

1. *Geometry*: This is the base room. Every other layer would be drawn over this layer, should it appear. The geometry is very simple: it's a big square (Figure 23.3). The two light center pixels are possible spawns of items the player can use. In the corners are spawn points for possible larger, breakable decorative objects. The darker pixels are possible spawn points for things that the player can walk over, and can also be broken in the heat of combat.

2. *Entry*: This layer was designed to only appear if a hallway connected to the room from the east. Not only did it draw a door on the base of the room, but it also drew spawn points for decorations (Figure 23.4).

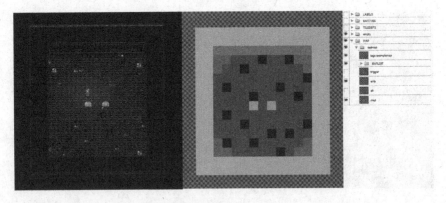

FIGURE 23.3   Simple room, in game and in editor.

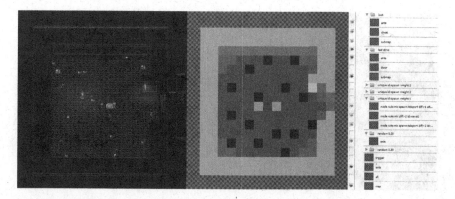

FIGURE 23.4   A new door added to the room, which only appears if the room is connected from the east.

Part of the wall was indented further out, and another part of the wall came in to create a shallow alcove in the top right of the room.

3a. *Random elements*: Now the game chose from a pick-from-one group. There were three groups to pick from, and the behavior of this one was to potentially add pillars of various sizes to the room. It picked that group, and then picked three possible large pillars to spawn (Figure 23.5).

3b. *Random elements*: Here's the same room, but with a different pick-from-one group selected (Figure 23.6). Also, new decorations were randomly picked to be spawned in the room. Also, a new possible door spawn point was added to the west, above the previous one.

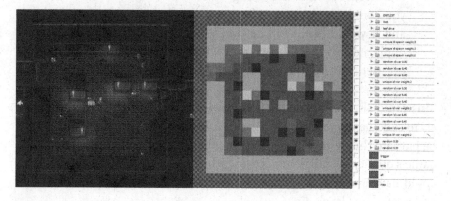

FIGURE 23.5   Large pillars added to the room.

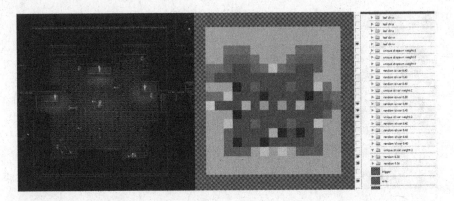

FIGURE 23.6 Different variant of the same room.

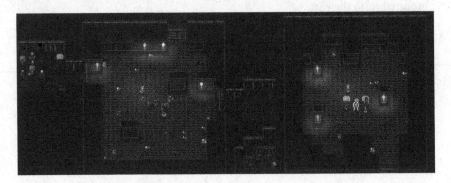

FIGURE 23.7 The room with monsters added, in two different conditions.

4. *Artificial intelligence*: Finally, monsters get added to the room by the game, set by parameters based on the dungeon area and floor (Figure 23.7). On the right is the same room, but with another set of different conditionals being chosen at random. With this system, you could use the same inserted room multiple times on the level, and it would likely still be different. If you really wanted to avoid duplicates, you could also track which by chance conditional layers get used, and put them on a stack that isn't used twice.

This could also be applied to other ways to add details and points of interest to code-generated areas in a game. Anything your game supports could be put into this system. It also makes collaboration easier, improving your game's quality overall. With designers being able to easily add things, you could have a very large variety of interesting set pieces in an otherwise code-generated level.

CHAPTER 24

Automated Game Tuning

Aaron Isaksen
NYU Game Innovation Lab

As game designers, we use adjustable game parameters to tune a game to achieve a great player experience. For example, for a two-dimensional (2D) platformer, we have to tune the size of the character and enemies, how strong gravity pulls down, how high the player can jump, and so forth. For a turn-based puzzle game, you might need to tune the probabilities of different pieces arriving on each turn.

Each unique combination of parameter settings creates what we call a new game variant. These settings directly affect both the designer and the player, so getting them just right has a major effect on what is possible in the game, how the game feels, and how enjoyable and difficult a player might find the game. After all, getting Mario's jump to feel right is more about adjusting parameters than coding accurate physics.

Exploring all these possible game variants to find specific settings for the best player experience was a really time-consuming part of my job as a game designer. So when I decided to go back to grad school and work on automated game design techniques and computer-aided game design, my first project was to come up with a system that could use artificial intelligence (AI) to explore many game variants and report back the difficulty of each one in a way that matched how human players would feel about the game. This technique could also find some new interesting game variants we hadn't thought of. One of the goals of the project was to make sure the technique could be used by game programmers that were good coders, but that they didn't need to have an advanced degree in computer science or experience with a lot of mathematics.

Part of what makes this problem so challenging is that there are so many parameters that can be changed at once, so it's often impossible to search exhaustively—imagine adjusting hundreds of independent control knobs to search for the perfect game. While tuning games, designers rely on intuition, experience, and user feedback to iteratively search for better parameters. The designer must estimate player skill; set game parameters; playtest; evaluate the player experiences using interviews, observations, or analytics; revise design parameters; and then repeat the process until the game reaches an appropriate level of difficulty.

Additionally, when a designer and playtesters become experts at the game, they can lose perspective on how it is experienced by new players. As the designer repeatedly plays the game, they get better and better, and the adjustments they make to the game can target those expert players. This can make the game too difficult or obtuse for new players. So one of the constraints for our system was to make sure that there was an adjustable skill level to control for both low-skilled and high-skilled players.

By changing parameters alone, we can also find surprising and interesting game variants that can inspire new ideas. When working on a game for a long time, it can be difficult for designers to break out of the current design and try some creative new ideas. This is especially a problem if all changes break the game; the designer might need some large changes to multiple parameters to find something else that works. Algorithms, on the other hand, don't get frustrated with temporarily bad results and are willing to keep searching until they find something else worth investigating.

Automated playtesting and visualization help with this process, guiding designers in their exploration to create games best suited to individual skill levels and play styles.

In this chapter, I describe the method we used to tune game parameters that can be used by everyday game designers without requiring human playtesters. Our general approach is shown in Figure 24.1. To explore a new game variant, we select parameters from a valid range of reasonable values. Using these parameters, we generate a level and simulate playing it using an AI.

The trick here is to use an AI that doesn't try to play the game perfectly, but that makes the kinds of errors that humans make. Because the AI doesn't need to be a champion, you can write a less complex AI than you might need if competing against human players. I suggest starting with a simple AI and then add complexity only if needed. We repeat the process of running simulated players through the game, collecting lots of data.

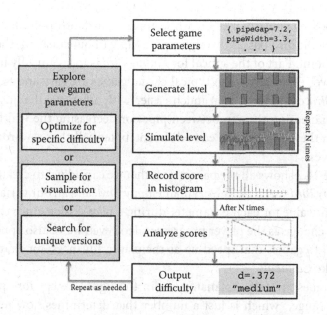

FIGURE 24.1   Diagram of how to explore game variants. We explore game space by simulating game variants and estimating their difficulty using survival analysis.

Then, we look at the data we collected and decide if the game is too easy or too hard. If it's too easy, we can make some adjustments to make it harder and try again. If we feel it's too hard, we can make it easier. We don't have to guess which knobs we should adjust to make it easier or harder, as we can just try different settings and let the computer quickly figure out the effect of the changes.

If this overview leaves you with some questions, there are also deeper details in our publicly available research papers hosted at game. engineering.nyu.edu/exploring-game-space.

STEP 1: SET PARAMETERS

To begin, we need to decide which game parameters we can adjust, and set them to some values. For our example in this chapter and for our research, we decided to work with a game that is popular and has relatively few adjustable game parameters. We chose *Flappy Bird* because it is a commercially successful phenomenon, spawning hundreds of similar games, and the rules are simple to implement and understand.

In *Flappy Bird*, a player must fly a constantly moving bird without crashing into a series of pipes placed along the top and bottom of the screen (Figure 24.2). Each time the player taps the screen, the bird flaps its wings, moving upward in an arc while gravity constantly pulls downward. Each time the bird passes through a pipe gap without crashing, the player scores a point. Part of the appeal for *Flappy Bird* is the comically high difficulty level, especially when typical casual games are easy and forgiving. *Flappy Bird* could have been much easier with a few small adjustments, such as increasing the gap between pipes or decreasing the width of the pipes, but these would have led to different, potentially less rewarding play experiences.

Figure 24.2 shows all the parameters that we can adjust to create different *Flappy Bird* variants. The original *Flappy Bird*, and all our variants, has a constant value for each parameter during a play session since the game does not change as the player progresses. However, we've also applied our approach to games that speed up as the player advances, for example, in games like *Canabalt*.

The values are self-explanatory from the figure except for "pipe gap location range," which is just a number that determines how much the pipe heights vary from pipe to pipe. Larger numbers mean more changes from pipe to pipe and are harder because there is more distance to travel between a high gap and a low gap. By varying the parameter in the figure within sensible ranges, we can generate all variants of *Flappy Bird* that use the same set of rules.

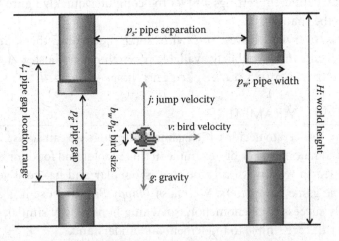

FIGURE 24.2 Gameplay of *Flappy Bird*. In *Flappy Bird*, the player must navigate the bird through a series of pipes without crashing. We modify the labeled parameters to generate unique game variants.

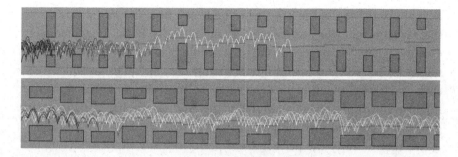

FIGURE 24.3   Two different generated levels given different parameter sets. More simulations complete the second version, so we can see that it's easier for the AI to play. The horizontal lines indicate the target location for the AI to flap.

STEP 2: GENERATE THE GAME LEVEL

Once we've set some game parameters, we can generate our new game variant. This involves placing the bird and pipes in their starting positions and randomly distributing the pipe gaps. In Figure 24.3, we show two different generated game variants.

Because the levels are generated using a random process, it is important to generate a new level each time the AI runs, even though the parameters do not change. Otherwise, if the same random layout of pipe gaps is used repeatedly, artifacts can arise in our data caused by a particular placement of the gaps. For example, the gap locations can randomly come out approximately equal for a section of the level, making that section easier. These problems are averaged out by generating a new level each time.

STEP 3: SIMULATE THE GAME

We now have an AI play the game for us. Accurately simulating human game play with an AI requires an understanding of how players react to game events: this is the process of player modeling. The idea is not to make your AI so good that it can always beat the game, as happens a lot when people think about AI for games. Instead, we want to model how humans actually perform—we ultimately care about how humans perform, not the AIs. As long as the model properly predicts human perception of difficulty for novice, intermediate, and advanced players, it fits our purposes.

To make the human-like AI, we first begin by creating a simple AI with perfect motor skills—a perfect player with instantaneous reaction who would never lose at the original *Flappy Bird*. Our AI is very simple and is very fast to run. The AI looks forward to the next pipe and tries to stay a bit above the top of the lower pipe, and each time the bird drops below that target height (the horizontal lines in Figure 24.3) the AI immediately executes a flap. Whatever AI is used, it should play with very good performance on solvable levels, and should mainly only fail on impossible levels, such as a level with a tiny pipe gap where the bird cannot fit through. You might want to use an A* or Monte Carlo tree search–based AI for your game, or write your own simple one, like we did.

We then modify the perfect AI to perform less well by modeling the main components of human motor skill that impact difficulty in these types of action games: precision and actions per second.* Adjusting these values lets us model different player types, since novices react slower and are less precise than experts. Our model relies on a predetermined value, which we determined using a user study to figure out how precisely players can tap an onscreen button, and we can reuse those numbers for other games too.

When a player plans to press a button at an exact time, they execute this action with some imprecision. We model this error as a normal distribution (aka a bell curve), as shown in Figure 24.4. The width of the normal distribution is proportional to a player's imprecision. Imprecision is a trait that all humans have, but it is also related to the time a subject has to react to an event, called the speed–accuracy trade-off: the less time they have to react, the less accurately they will respond.

For simplification, our player model assumes precision is an independent variable and not dependent on bird speed. We measured precision as an error, with standard deviation ranging between $\sigma p = 35.9$ ms and $\sigma p = 61.1$ ms, and use this range for game space exploration. Unity, C#, and JavaScript don't have built-in functions for generating normally distributed random numbers (also called Gaussian distributed random numbers), but you can search the web for some libraries or functions that will do this.

Humans can only perform a limited number of accurate button presses per second. In our user study, we measured an average 7.7 actions per second, or about once every 130 ms. We also limit our AI to this same number of actions per second so that it can't play unrealistically well. We simplify our model by keeping this constant, although a more complex

---

* We also modeled reaction time to an unexpected event, but that didn't matter as much, so I left it out of this chapter. You can refer to our research papers if you want to implement it for your game.

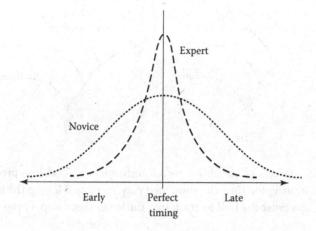

FIGURE 24.4 Timing curve graph. Expert players are more precise than novice players.

model would account for fatigue, since players can't keep actions per second constant for long periods.

This is how we actually coded this approach for use in our system. At each frame of the simulation, we predict the next time t in the future when the bird will drop below this ideal flapping location—the ideal player would flap at exactly this time t. We predict this by just running a copy of the game as fast as possible without drawing to the screen, and figuring out how many game loop ticks until the bird will drop below that line; this takes less than a millisecond to calculate. We then make the player less precise by adjusting this time t by adding a random normal distribution with about a 30 ms standard deviation, as shown in Figure 24.5. By reducing or increasing the width of the bell curve for our precision model, the AI plays more or less well. To keep the AI from flapping faster than a human could tap, t is limited by the number of actions per second. If t happens too soon after making another flap, we force t to be at least 130 ms.

Keep in mind that it's important that the AIs we are using here don't learn or improve. If you make a change and the scores increase, you just made the game easier for the AIs. You can't necessarily do that with human testers, because they are also learning and improving each time they play the game. So if a human plays two variants and performs better on the second, it might be that they are just getting more skillful at playing the game. But AIs that don't learn are reliable in the sense that they can be

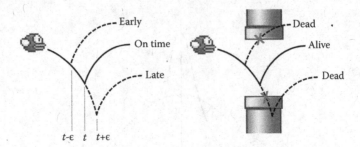

FIGURE 24.5 Effects of variable t on AI performance. Modeling precision by randomly adjusting the time the simulated player jumps. Moving the jump earlier or later can cause the bird to crash into the lower pipe or upper pipe.

reused repeatedly with the same skill settings to determine how difficulty changes as you modify game parameters.

For each simulation, we get a score s, equal to the number of pipes that the AI passes before crashing, and we record each score s for analyzing in the next step. If the AI reaches a goal score of 20, we store a score of 20 and terminate the run so we do not get stuck simulating easy games where the AI will never hit a pipe. Although *Flappy Bird* can theoretically go on forever, human players tire or get distracted and will eventually make a terminal mistake, but the AI can truly play forever unless we enforce a maximum score.

The generate and simulate steps are run repeatedly until we have enough data samples to adequately analyze. The more times you run the simulation, the more accurate an answer you'll get, but it will take longer. We found doing about 10,000 simulations was plenty, and this only took about a second for the computer because *Flappy Bird* is a simple game and we had our own version that had no graphics to draw. If your game is more complicated, it will take longer, but you can speed things up by turning off any graphics rendering and just run the game simulation without anything being drawn. You can also adjust the goal score when you will stop the simulation—lower goal scores will run faster. The important thing is to try some different values and see what works best for your game.

STEP 4: ANALYZE THE DATA

Given our game parameters and player model, we can now estimate the difficulty of the game variant. One way to analyze your game's difficulty is to keep track of all the final scores that players get, and then figure out how likely each score is. We do this using a histogram. A histogram is a type of data structure that keeps track of how many times a value (or a range of values) has appeared.

To make a histogram, first you keep track of all the final scores in an array. When you want to figure out the probability of getting each score, you just go through the array and count how many times each score appears, and then divide by the total number of scores in the array. If you've got many scores, then you can use bins to keep track of scores in a range. For example, you might count scores of 49, 10, and 22 as being in the same bin for scores between 0 and 50.

Figure 24.6 shows some examples of how you can use histograms to compare different game variants. In Figure 24.6a, we see a pretty hard game, such as a difficult variant of *Flappy Bird*. In this game, the most likely score is 0, the second most likely is 1, and so forth. This means low scores are very likely and high scores are very unlikely. In Figure 24.6b, we see the same histogram as in Figure 24.6a, but now compared with a second histogram in gray. The gray histogram represents an easier game. We know this because the probability of getting a low score has gone down, and the probability of getting a higher score has gone up.

In Figure 24.6c, we see another shape for the histogram, which is representative of games that start out easy and then get harder as you score

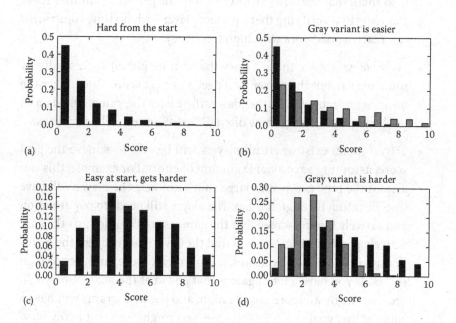

FIGURE 24.6   Examples of final score histograms.

higher. That gives a low probability of achieving a low score, since the game starts out easy; a high probability of achieving a medium-valued score; and a low probability of achieving a high-valued score. In Figure 24.6d, we can see that the game data shown in gray is a harder game than the game data shown in black. We know this because it is more likely to get a low score for the gray data than the black data.

Using this histogram, we can use some relatively simple statistics to determine how difficult the game is. In our research, we used a technique called survival analysis, which figures out how the score frequencies change as a player continues in the game. In practice, a simpler method of just taking the median or mean of the histogram would also be reasonable and is easier to code. If the median score decreases, then the game is harder; if the median score increases, then the game is easier.

A couple of situations might come up:

- *Impossible games* are those games that can't be played successfully by any player, no matter how much skill. These games will have a very low mean score with no cases of high scores in the histogram. This can happen, for example, if the jump velocity is much stronger than gravity, so the player crashes into the ceiling, or if the pipe gap is so small that the bird can't fit through the gap. We eliminate these games by first verifying that a perfect player with no time adjustment can reach a goal score with high frequency.

- *Playable games* are those games that can be played successfully by some players but the player won't get a perfect score. The higher the mean score achieved by the player, the easier the game. The data in the histogram tells you how often different scores will be achieved.

- *Trivial games* exist where all players will be able to achieve the goal score, assuming a reasonable amount of effort. For example, this can arise if the pipe gap is very large so it's unlikely the player will have trouble fitting through the gap. The player still needs to pay attention and actively tap the screen, but the game is trivial as long as they are actively participating. You will find these variants because the histogram will have few low scores, a high mean score, and lots of high scores. If you have a lot of games that ended at the goal score, you'll see that the mean score is quite high, and the histograms will have a spike at that goal score. In this case, you might find that many players are able to get very far into your game, and it might be too easy.

STEP 5: VISUALIZE THE DATA AND MAKE ADJUSTMENTS

There are a couple ways we can visualize the data we've collected, and see how the game changes depending on the skill of the player (remember that we can adjust the AI's skill by making it have more or less error in its time estimate of when to flap).

Beginning with the original *Flappy Bird*, we can keep each parameter fixed and vary just one at a time, exploring a bunch of different values of that parameter, and estimate the game difficulty of each variant. Figure 24.7 shows a plot of pipe gap versus difficulty for several AIs of different skill. Each line uses a different value for player precision. Lighter lines in the figure have a higher standard deviation, and so the AI makes more errors, and the game is more difficult for the player model. As one expects, the model predicts that players with less precision will find the same game more difficult to play, and narrower gaps are harder for everyone.

We can also examine how two parameters are dependent on each other, which can help designers find interesting relationships. We visualize these results using dot plots, displaying varying difficulty by the radius and color saturation of each point.

For example, we see in Figure 24.8 that jump velocity and gravity are dependent. When gravity is too high or low relative to jump velocity, the bird crashes into the floor or ceiling. In the middle, gravity and jump velocity are balanced, and we see that as they increase together, the game

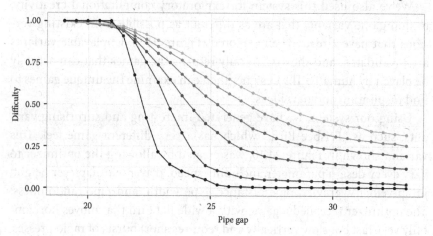

FIGURE 24.7 Line graph of difficulty. Increasing pipe gap decreases difficulty. Each line shows a different setting for player precision. Lighter lines plot lower precision, modeling poorer performance, and so are more difficult for the player model.

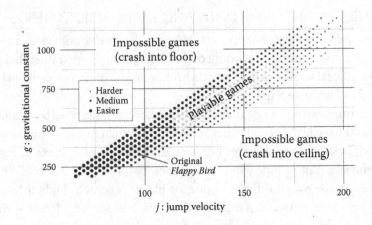

FIGURE 24.8 Graph of parameters that make playable games. Jump velocity and gravity are related and should be adjusted together.

gets more difficult—faster reaction times are required as the bird is moving rapidly up and down. Lower values of gravity and jump velocity give the player more time to react and are easier to play.

By exploring different parameters, the system can find different versions of the game for you. If you want an easier or harder version, the system can try a bunch of different parameters to find one easier or harder. Using an optimizer, you can even have the computer find an exact target difficulty.

We've also used this system for exploratory computational creativity, to find game variants that are as different as possible from existing versions that have already been explored (Figure 24.9). Unplayable variants are invalidated, and the system only returns the games that can actually be played by humans. The designer then can examine the unique games to find inspiration and new ideas.

Using our system, we have generated interesting and surprising variants, such as "Frisbee Bird," which has a very different game feel. This variant, shown in Figure 24.10, was created by allowing the optimizer to vary every design parameter, including speed, player width, player height, jump velocity, gravity, pipe distance, pipe width, and pipe randomness. The optimizer returned a game with a wide flat bird that moves horizontally very fast but slow vertically and requires short bursts of rapid presses, followed by a long pause while the bird floats in the air. This unexpected variant, discovered by our system while using the optimization algorithm, still relies on the mechanics and rules of the original, but is a significantly different play experience.

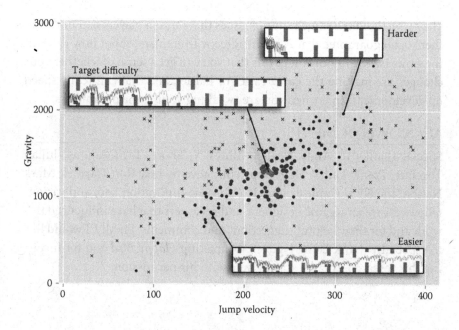

FIGURE 24.9 Scatterplot graph of game variants. We can search different game variants for a target difficulty. Each point indicates a variant tested to find the target; × indicates impossible games; dot size indicates closeness to the target.

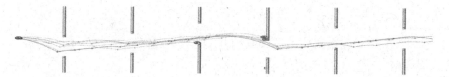

FIGURE 24.10 New *Flappy Bird* variant. "Frisbee Bird" was unexpectedly created by our system, an example of computational creativity. We show six simulated paths with jump points indicated by triangles. The player is very wide and thin, with weak jump velocity and gravity that gives the feeling of floating.

CONCLUSION

I hope this chapter has convinced you that using some simple player modeling and human-like AI players can help you understand the difficulty of your own game. These techniques can be implemented without any complex libraries or significant experience with statistics. You can analyze the data using a separate program, perhaps Excel, or doing some simple data processing in Python (which is how I do it).

The ultimate goal here is not to replace human testers, but to enhance your game testing with AIs that can reliably play at different skill levels.

They won't find the same kinds of issues that human players can find, and there is no guarantee that AIs will agree with humans about how difficult the game is. The important part is that you can get a sense of whether your changes are making the game easier or harder, and that can really speed up development time when you are tweaking your game parameters.

ACKNOWLEDGMENTS

Special thanks to Andy Nealen, Tanya X. Short, Tarn Adams, Julian Togelius, Frank Lantz, Dan Gopstein, Steve Swink, Ron Carmel, Mark Nelson, the NYU Game Center, NYU Game Innovation Lab, and various fellow researchers, game designers, and reviewers that have influenced this work and for their helpful suggestions and comments. Finally, I would like to especially thank Dong Nguyen for making *Flappy Bird* and for inspiring this research. Images appear here with his permission.

CHAPTER 25

Generating Rules

Dr. Michael Cook

Independent

A S PROCEDURAL GENERATION BECOMES more and more important to people, we look for new ways to make it a part of the things we create. Throughout this book, you've already seen a huge variety of ways to generate content for your games—the artwork, the audio, the worlds your players walk through, the people they meet, and the problems they are tasked with solving. Some kinds of content we see generated all the time in games, like dungeons in a roguelike. Then there are the rarer cases, like storylines. Then there are kinds of content that are so rare we hardly ever see them in games at all—like the actual rules your players are following and playing by.

Depending on the kind of game you're making, the rules and mechanics of a game can either define everything about your game or just form a sort of suggestive space in which the player can freely express themselves. Think about the block-pushing puzzle game *Sokoban*, for example—the player can push blocks by moving into them, but can't pull them. They win by getting all the blocks onto goal tiles. The game is entirely defined by this set of rules, and by changing the rules, we change the format of the game. Compare this to a real-world children's game like hide-and-go-seek. The rules here are a setup for creative play, and players might add their own adjustments to the game according to the situation, who is playing, or what they want to do.

We don't see rules or mechanics generated by a game very often, and it's partly because of how fundamental they are. Often, we have a very strong vision about what we want a game to be like, and altering the rules too much might completely change that. It's also very hard to know how to even represent things like a game's rules—rules don't fit into neat templates like dungeons or quests. They often are unique bits of executable code that we wrote once to express a certain idea. They're also very hard to test. If a dungeon has a dead end or is a bit boring, it's not the end of the world, and we can try and detect these issues and work around them. If a ruleset is broken, though, it might make your game unplayable. As any game designer knows, it can be really hard to see that a game is broken, even if you're a human being.

In this section, we walk through a few basic things you can try out if you want to play with rule generation in your games. The exciting thing about this area is that because it's relatively unexplored, it's a wide-open playground for new ideas and discoveries—so don't be afraid to go off on your own and try out your own designs, too.

MIX AND MATCH

The process we're going to look at breaks rules down into little components that we can snap together and rearrange, in the same way that simple generators snap together parts of mazes, sentences, or songs. The smallest thing you can start changing are parameters within your game system. A lot of game designs are only a few changes away from entirely different game variants—think about all the different match 3 games there are out there, each with a little tweak. You may have already added lots of parameters to your game in order to help you balance its design. If you group all these parameters together into one list, that list defines a variant of the game. Generating values for each parameter will result in a slightly different game. Those parameters might include how the player moves, how much they have to do to finish a level, or how hard the game is to play. There will be more subtle tweaks than full rule changes, but it's a good place to start.

To really get into rule generation, a nice simple place to start is to build a simple language you can express rules in without writing code. The simpler the rule is, the easier it is to build a language for. One of the best things to start with is something like collision—when two things touch each other, what should the game do? We can do this by having a list of game objects and a list of simple effects. The list of game objects won't have things like "enemy" or "health" in it, though. Instead, it should be more general descriptions like "turtle" or "mushroom," because we won't know what's an enemy or what heals the player until after the rules have been fixed! For the effects of colliding, we can think about the general events we want to happen in our game. Can the player gain score? Can the player die? Can the player get power-ups? All these bits of code become separate effects.

All our generator has to do then is pick two object types and one effect, and it's got a little collision rule generated. It's our job to convert it into real game code, though, but usually it's just a case of having lots of code to check each building block and point it toward some code you've already written.

This format of rule generation is really easy to expand by adding in more options for the generator. We could add extra elements to our rules, for example. Maybe instead of collisions only having one effect, they have two effects, one for each of the objects involved in the collision. Now you can do things like have one object kill another object and survive (like PAC-MAN ghosts), or have effects only target one object. We can also add more types of rules, like rules for when things leave the screen or rules for when a button is pressed on the keyboard. To get more variety out of this technique, it's important to add things that you might think are useless or not interesting. Don't just add obvious game objects to the collision object list. Add in the floor. Add in background objects. Add the user interface in—anything you can think of. If you only put predictable things into a system like this, you're likely to only get predictable things out the other end.

GAME DESIGN 101

This system of rules and building blocks we've described is sort of a miniature slice of game designing, which your generator is exploring by generating rules. The most obvious way to write your generator is to make it select rule components entirely at random, maybe generating three or four of these random rules before adding them to the game. As you can probably imagine, a lot of these rules combinations will be bad or boring or, in extreme cases, completely unplayable. A totally random rule generator isn't as good a game designer as you, which won't come as a big surprise.

You can help it get better by encoding some of your knowledge about game design into the system. You've already done a bit of it simply by writing the rules language—every object you selected and every effect you wrote down, you decided to add them in because you suspect they will be relevant to game design. You didn't let it adjust the volume of the music, or the resolution of the screen. You didn't let it edit memory values directly or delete files from the player's computer (at least, you probably didn't). You decided that some things would be better for games than others, and that's an example of you helping the system design games.

But we can do better—we can write *heuristics*, little rules of thumb or guidelines for the system to follow that will help it create better rulesets. These are things that we believe to be true about our rules regardless of anything else going on in the game. Some of these guidelines we know to be universally true, no matter what rules come up. For example, if we're making a *Candy Crush*–style game, there has to be at least one rule that destroys blocks. Our game is about destroying blocks, so if there aren't any rules that destroy blocks, we can safely say that the ruleset isn't very good, and our generator can scrap it and go back to the drawing board.

These heuristics might seem very simple, but they can be very powerful. Even a basic one like "Can the player do anything?" can cut out a huge percentage of bad ruleset designs. Sometimes we can't know enough up front, though. Much like designing a game for yourself, you can't tell what a game will be like just by looking at all the rules written down—that's why people playtest their games or give them to others to play. If we could get our generator to playtest the rulesets it makes, we could maybe take the data from those playtests and write even better heuristics.

Right now, there's a lot of research funding being put into a field called *general game playing* (GGP). The aim is to develop artificial intelligence (AI) capable of playing any game, even one it's never seen before, by rapidly learning rules and strategies. One of the uses for AI like this is to automatically evaluate games and investigate any problems the designs might have. It's a long road toward that goal, though, and you might not feel like developing cutting-edge AI systems just to play with rule generation. Instead of using the cleverest AI possible to play our games and test them, what we can do instead is use the *stupidest* approach possible, and get our games played entirely randomly by a system that has no idea what it's doing.

This might sound like a waste of time, but even a random agent tells you something about how the game works. Suppose we run a random AI player on our generated ruleset 10 times. Our agent can record things as it plays—we can get it to record if it completes the game, perhaps, or whenever it gains score or touches an object. At the end, we have 10 samples of how the game looks. Suppose we're making a game like *PAC-MAN*. If all 10 of our random players never died, or if they all completed the level in under 3 seconds, there might be something wrong with our ruleset. We can write more heuristics, more guidelines, that use this new data to think about what it says about our game. Our random player isn't clever, but it represents a kind of worst-case scenario for gameplay, which is a step up from just looking at the rules without any kind of gameplay.

THROWING OUT THE RULEBOOK

Lots of people have experimented with rule generation in the past, from inventing new chess games to making completely automated game designers, but it's still a very new field without many accepted ideas. The little system we designed, with a series of building blocks for rules, guidelines to filter out bad ideas, and a random player to test the game for us, is a really basic recipe for experimenting with rules. But the exciting thing is that no one really knows what the best ideas are for creating rules, mechanics, and systems using procedural generation. There are amazing new games, entirely new genres, out there waiting to be found. So whatever ideas you have about this topic, there's a good chance no one's ever tried it before. There's only one way to find out how good they are—go and give them a go!

CHAPTER 26

Algorithms and Approaches

Brian Bucklew

Freehold Games

T HE INTENT OF THIS chapter is to serve as your first-time hiker's map of the most well-worn and pedestrian trails in the vast (and mostly unmapped) wilds of procedural generation. If it does its job, you should come away with a couple basic tools. First, an idea of where you should be able to get started without too elaborate a preparation. Second, a set of landmarks that almost anyone you meet in the field will know.

However, like any public park pamphlet, it won't attempt to fill in the vast tracts between marked trails. Eventually, you'll find that once you gain confidence and skill, the most rewarding adventure is found among the brambles.

RANDOM NUMBERS

Pseudorandom Number Generators

Since the goal of most procedural systems is to present a varied experience from player to player, and from session to session, random numbers play an important role. Although it's possible to produce varied choices in a completely deterministic manner, the most common approach is to use a series of random numbers that are different each time the game is played in order to produce the desired variety.

Almost all development environments provide one or more random number generators to use. These are almost always *pseudorandom number generators.* The "pseudo" in this case refers to the fact that these typically do not return a truly random set of numbers, but only a series of numbers that appear to be random.

Pseudorandom number generators start from an initial *seed* value and then perform a mathematical operation on that seed value that produces the next value in the random series and increments the seed in some way so the following call will produce a different (but statistically random) value. Whenever you give a pseudorandom number generator a particular starting seed, it will always produce the same sequence of random values.

For example, a particular pseudorandom number generator that is given the initial seed 5 and gives you 3, 23, 195, and 1 when asked for the first four random numbers in its series will always return 3, 23, 195, and 1 as the first four numbers when its initial seed is 5. The same is true of all remaining numbers in the series it generates for the seed value 5.

If that particular pseudorandom number generator is given a seed value different than 5, the series of numbers it would return when asked would likewise be different. For example, if you gave that exact same pseudorandom number generator an initial seed of 6 (instead of 5), it might give you 55,129, 4, 51, and 0 (instead of 3, 23, 195, and 1) when asked for the first four numbers of its sequence.

Making Use of Repeatable Series

The fact that the series of numbers a pseudorandom number generator generates is completely predictable when it is starting with a particular initial seed has a number of powerful applications for procedural systems.

- Two players on completely independent computers can share procedurally generated worlds by sharing a single seed value. The same "random" choices can be made on two completely different computers, no matter how many choices are needed, as long as those choices are made in the same order. Many roguelikes, including *Caves of Qud*, use this property for daily or weekly challenges to be shared across otherwise disconnected players. They need only share the same seed value. We'll discuss how to generate those shared seed values in the next section.

  Many multiplayer games with procedural aspects use pseudorandom series to reduce the amount of information that needs to be shared over limited network bandwidth. Small seeds can be shared instead of large swaths of generated data.

Large worlds with information that can be regenerated from seeds do not need to save a potentially large (or even infinite) amount of data to disk but can instead regenerate complex systems from those small initial seeds. The original *Elite* used pseudorandom series to generate (and regenerate when revisited) an enormous, apparently permanent, explorable universe on the very memory-constrained computer systems of the time (http://www.filfre.net/2013/12/elite/).

Seeds and Hashing

The seed for a typical random number generator is a 32-bit integer. This value, by default, is most often a simple current timestamp for a random number generator whose output you aren't interested in repeating or sharing. This will cause each execution of the program to produce different output each time it is run. For random number generators whose output you would like to repeat or those seeds which you'd like to share, a different, more structured, strategy is required.

A raw 32-bit integer like 1235100523 is not a particularly memorable or shareable value. A much more useful method that many games take is to allow the player to enter a more memorable phrase like "a magic monkey." Since the pseudorandom number generators require a 32-bit integer, and not an arbitrary string, you need some method to convert each different phrase into a different 32-bit integer.

If you're technically minded, you might already be imagining a method to squish a string into a 32-bit integer. Since it's applicable in very many areas of computing outside of this discussion, this is actually a well-studied problem. This process, of taking an input (which may be much longer than the desired seed value) and creating a value based on it, which is different for each input value, is called a *hash function*.

A hash function's job is to take some input data and transform it into an output value (typically, but not always, shorter in length than the input data). This output value needs to be the same for any given input. That is, whenever you give a hash function the value "watermelon," if the particular hash function you're using returns 81, then it should always return 81 every time you give it "watermelon." Giving the same hash function the value "lemons" or "watermelon2" should return a value that is statistically unrelated to the value that you get for "watermelon."

That doesn't necessarily mean it won't return 81 for "lemons"—it may—but for a good hash, the chances of it being 81 for both "watermelon" and "lemons" is vanishingly small (e.g., 1 in 2^32 for a good 32-bit hash).

Another helpful use of the fact that the hash values are statistically random is that you can use as much, or as little, of the hash function's return value as you want since a smaller chunk of bits pulled from a perfectly random number are themselves perfectly random. This means if a hash function generates 128 bits of data, and you want a 32-bit integer as a pseudorandom number generator seed, you can simply grab the first 32 bits of the value the hash function returns to use as your random number generator seed.

There are many common hash functions, including MD5, the SHA family, xxHash, and Murmer. Some, like SHA, produce more statistically random output, which is useful for cryptography, and some, like xxHash, produce less statistically random output but with much higher performance. Games typically do not need the statistical strength that the slower hash families provide, so a typical choice for game projects is a fast hash function like MD5 or xxHash.

Examples of hash functions in use are

- A game allows a player to enter an easily memorable string like "watermelons," which is then hashed via MD5 into a 32-bit integer for the world generation's pseudorandom number generator.

- A game generates a string describing the current date, like "June 7, 2016," which is hashed by MD5 into a 32-bit integer to generate a daily challenge that is the same across all players for any particular day.

- A game generates a string combining the current world's seed and a specific solar system's identifying information: "Worldseed51234 Galaxy 5 Solar System 118," which is hashed via xxHash into a 32-bit integer. This provides a unique seed for that solar system, which would allow the solar system to be regenerated again in exactly the same way if the player later visits it again without storing all the procedurally generated information about the solar system.

Rolling Dice

It is common to talk about random numbers in terms of rolling a number of dice. These dice are not restricted to the familiar six-sided cube dice. "1d6" means the result of one six-sided die, which you might find in any common board game, resulting in a value between 1 and 6. "1d8" means the result of one eight-sided die. "3d6" means the result of three six-sided dice added together, resulting in a value from 3 to 18.

Some pseudorandom number generators will only generate an integer between 0 and the largest representable integer. Since you often want to generate smaller ranges of values to simulate things like die rolls, it's very often useful to generate a range of integers between two given numbers (say, 1–6 for a d6).

Although many random number generator libraries give you the ability to specify a minimum and a maximum value for the next number you generate, if they don't, you can write your own:

```
RangeInclusive(max,min)
{
    return ((rng.next() % (max-min+1)) + min);
}
```

It can also be useful to generate a floating-point value between two given numbers, instead of an integer:

```
FloatingPointRange(max,min)
{
    Return ((rng.next() / MAX_INTEGER) * (max-min)) +
    min;
}
```

Examples of dice in use are

- d100s are commonly used as a percentile success roll, checking if that roll is less than or equal to the percentage chance of something happening.

- Small dice pools can be used for any numbers that need to have highly tunable ranges, for example, weapon damage. One die produces an equal chance of any number in the range, whereas multiple dice create a bell curve, making numbers in the middle of the possible range more likely.

Normal Distributions

It's often useful to generate a normal ("bell curve" or Gaussian) distribution of numbers instead of a linear one. Adding several dice of the same type together will generate a curve that approximates a normal distribution. The more dice you add, the closer you get to a truly normal distribution.

A bell curve can be useful for generating many types of content. A bell curve in one dimension can approximate the natural variety of properties that many types of things can have, with the lowest and highest values for those properties being much rarer than the middle values (Figures 26.1 and 26.2).

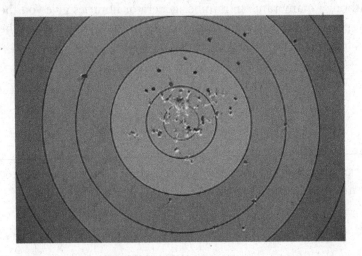

FIGURE 26.1   A normal distribution in two dimensions can approximate a cluster of plants, or a marksman shooting at a target.

FIGURE 26.2   A normal distribution in three dimensions can approximate a whole globular cluster.

A normal distribution is described with two terms, the mean and the standard deviation. The mean is the value at the "peak" of the bell curve. The standard deviation describes how "wide" the curve is. In a truly normal distribution, about 68.27% of the values fall within one multiple of the standard deviation and about 99.73% of the values fall within three multiples of the standard deviation.

Here's a basic implementation that will generate a normal distribution of random numbers with a given mean and standard deviation (std).

```
GaussianRandomNumber(mean,std)
{
    A = rng.nextfloat(); // from 0 to 1
    B = rng.nextfloat(); // from 0 to 1
    C = SquareRoot(-2 * Log(A)) * Sin(2 * PI * B);
    return mean + (std * C);
}
```

Other, faster methods are known, like the Ziggurat algorithm, if higher performance is required.

Examples of normal distribution use are

- Generating a random temperature for a particular day, with the seasonal average at the median, uncommon possible hot and cold days

- Deciding what time a nonplayer character (NPC) prefers to go to bed, with 10:00 p.m. at the median but a wide standard deviation, creating smaller populations of morning larks and night owls

- Deciding the size of a planet in a solar system, with a typical Earth-size planet at the median but rarer very large and very small planets possible

Weighted Distributions

Another very useful tool is the weighted distribution. For example, you might want a common result 9 out of 10 times, and a rare result on the 10th. You can think of this weighted distribution like a bag with nine balls marked "common" and one ball marked "rare" in a bag. The weight for each item in a weighted distribution describes the number of balls in the bag with that item's result.

Result	Weight
Common	9
Rare	1

```
WeightedResult(mean,std)
{
    Roll = rng.RangeInclusive(1,sumOfAllWeights);
    WeightAccumulator = 0;
    foreach( currentItem in Items )
    {
        WeightAccumulator →
WeightAccumulator+currentItem.Weight;
        if( WeightAccumulator >= Roll ) return
currentItem.Result;
    }
}
```

A useful variant of this algorithm simulates not returning the ball back to bag after drawing it, preventing it from being drawn again in future picks. In order to accomplish this, you simply reduce the weight of the selected item by one after it is selected.

```
WeightedResultRemovePickedItem(mean,std)
{
    Roll = rng.RangeInclusive(1,sumOfAllWeights);
    WeightAccumulator = 0;
    foreach( currentItem in Items )
    {
        WeightAccumulator →
WeightAccumulator+currentItem.Weight;
        if( WeightAccumulator >= Roll )
        {
            result = currentItem;
            currentItem.Weight--;
            return result;
        }
    }
}
```

Examples of weighted distributions in use are

- Picking the template for a random encounter from a list of possible hand-created templates, with high weight for common encounters containing a few grunts and skirmishers and low weight for a rare special encounter with a powerful leader and his retinue.

- Selecting the material for a random weapon, with common ore like iron having a very high weight and rare diamond swords having a very low weight.

- Selecting the items for a shopkeeper, with common items having a high weight and rare items having a low weight. A large table of items might be possible, and the shopkeeper would pull balls from that bag without replacing them until his shop inventory is full.

HEIGHTMAPS

The shape of a lake, the layout of continents, clumps of weeds, and a topo-graphical map are just a few of the many kinds of map features that are common in procedurally generated environments. All of them require the generation of a two-dimensional (2D) grid of values that vary with some degree of smoothness from cell to cell. These types of 2D grids of smoothly varying values are called heightmaps (Figure 26.3).

Box Linear Filters

A box linear filter (or box blur) provides a means to create a smooth heightmap with a controllable method of placing the peaks. A box blur starts with a grid with cells initialized to a set of values. Typically, a cluster of high initial values is placed around areas that should contain peaks in the final result. These initial values are then smoothed across the grid by setting the value of each cell to the average value of its neighbors. This smoothing is applied a number of times, with each pass "spreading" the initial peak values out across the grid.

A matrix of weights is often used to weight the contributions of each cell's neighbors to the average in order to control the shape of the resulting

FIGURE 26.3 Example heightmap created with Perlin noise layering. Whiter pixels have higher values.

smoothed area. This is an example set of weights that creates a "hill-like" shape when applied to each cell of a grid:

1	3	1
3	5	3
1	3	1

Midpoint Displacement

Square-diamond midpoint displacement generates a heightmap by starting with random values for the corners of a grid. The center grid square of that square (M in the grid below) is then given a value of the average of those corner values plus or minus a small random variance. Then the middle grid of each edge (E in the grid below) is given a value of the average of the two corners and midpoint plus or minus a small random variance. This creates four subsquares, and the process continues on these subsquares iteratively until the whole grid is populated. Typically, during each iterative step the amount of variance applied to each new point is reduced exponentially.

The corners are given a random value:

2	E	8
E	M	E
10	E	5

The center cell is given a value equal to the average of the corners plus or minus a small random amount:

2		8
	9	
10		5

The midpoint of each edge is given a value equal to the average of the corners and midpoint plus or minus a small random amount:

2	8	8
5	9	6
10	4	5

This continues recursively for each of the four new subsquares.

Perlin and Simplex Noise

Perlin and simplex noise are algorithms that produce gradients that have rolling waves that appear at similar rates in every direction you look, with valleys of 0 and peaks of 1. You can visualize this looking something like an egg crate foam pad, with the peaks randomly placed but statistically evenly distributed across the whole surface. These noise functions are not limited to 2D heightmaps, but can also produce one-dimensional (1D), three-dimensional (3D), and higher dimensionalities of noise (Figure 26.4).

Because most surfaces don't have an egg crate–like topography, it's typical to combine several layers of noise, each having a different frequency and amplitude. The first layer is usually a fairly high-amplitude, low-frequency layer, with big peaks and valleys that are very broad. You can imagine this as laying out the overall mountain ranges and valleys.

Additional layers that are each higher frequency but lower amplitude are added. Since they are lower amplitude, they don't affect the overall structural height as much, but the higher frequency allows them to add interesting detail to the existing peaks and valleys. You can imagine the highest-frequency, lowest-amplitude noise layers creating little potholes in the road and anthills on the ground of the larger formations that were laid down by the earlier layers.

Simplex noise has many advantages over Perlin noise. It's faster to generate. It is visually isotropic in all directions, whereas Perlin noise has some directional artifacts. However, its popularity is curtailed because it is patented under U.S. Patent 6,867,776. A similar open-source algorithm

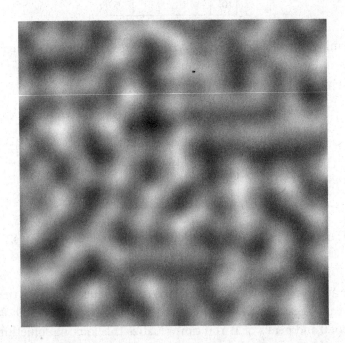

FIGURE 26.4 Example of a single 2D layer of Perlin noise; whiter pixels have higher values.

called OpenSimplex was developed in 2014 that shares many of the positive qualities of simplex noise without patent encumbrance.

SEQUENCE GENERATION

Lindenmayer Systems (L-Systems)

L-systems produce a fractal-like sequence by taking a seed string and repeatedly applying a set of transformation rules to that string (Figure 26.5).

Input string: A

Rule 1. (A→AB)

Rule 2. (B→A)

Initial value: A

(Iteration 1: A becomes AB via rule 1.)

AB

(Iteration 2: A becomes AB via rule 1; B becomes A via rule 2.)

ABA

(Iteration 3: A becomes AB via rule 1; B becomes A via rule 2; A becomes AB via rule 1.)

ABAAB

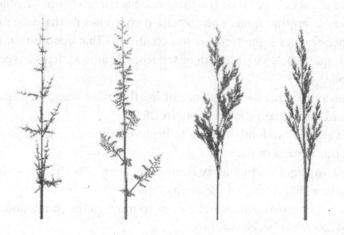

FIGURE 26.5   Weeds generated by drawing instructions generated by L-systems.

(Etc.)

ABAABABA

ABAABABAABAAB

The individual elements can be interpreted in a variety of ways. One common approach is to transform each element into a different type of input to a drawing program. For example, A = move forward 1 step, B = turn right 45°.

Examples of L-systems in use are

- Generating road divisions and building placement sequence for a city layout

- Generating the branching headwaters of a river system

- Generating the branching road systems and satellite villages around a major trade hub

Markov Chains

Markov chains produce a sequence by utilizing a directed graph of nodes. Each edge has a percentage weight assigned to it. The result of a Markov chain is generated by starting a particular node. That node's value becomes the first value of the sequence.

The next node is chosen randomly from among all the edges directed away from the current node. That next node's value is used as the second value of the sequence. Then the third node is chosen from the edges leading away from that node, and the chain continues in that way until the sequence reaches some termination condition. That condition might be, for example, a particular length of sequence or a node that's flagged as an end node.

In order to generate a sequence of weather for a week, we can use the simple Markov chain shown in Figure 26.6.

Let's say we randomly choose to begin on the rainy node. So the first day in our week is rainy.

The two edges leading away from rainy are a 25% chance of the rainy node and a 75% chance of the sunny node. Let's say we choose randomly between those two options and choose to move to the sunny node, so the second day of our week is sunny.

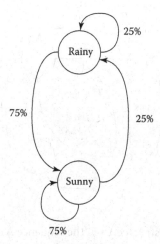

FIGURE 26.6   Simple Markov chain sequence generating a sequence of rainy and sunny days.

The two edges leading away from sunny are rainy with a 25% chance and sunny with a 75% chance. We choose one of those two edges at random to generate the weather for our third day. We continue moving between these two nodes until we've generated seven days of weather, and then our sequence is complete!

If you have an existing sequence of data, you can construct a Markov chain from it in order to create more data that shares similar stochastic properties.

Let's say we have a sequence of the letters ABCD. Each of these letters becomes one of the nodes in our chain.

ABCAABACBACDB

We then look at each letter and determine the number of times each node is followed by each of the others.

A is followed by A, B × 2, and C × 2 (A 20%, B 40%, C 40%)

B is followed by C and A × 3 (C 25%, A 75%)

C is followed by A, B, and D (A, B, and C 33.3%)

D is followed by B (B 100%)

With that information, we can construct our graph.

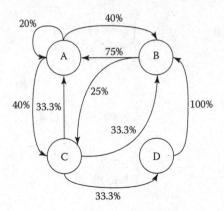

FIGURE 26.7   Chain constructed from the sequence ABCAABACBACDB.

The example chains in Figure 26.7 are "order 1," which means each single element is used as a node in the chain. The order number is the number of elements per node. An order 2 Markov chain would operate on pairs of elements instead of single elements. So in Figure 26.7, our nodes in a second-order chain would be AB, BC, CA, and so forth.

Examples of Markov chains in use are

- Generating music from note patterns

- Simulating the volatile mood swings of dwarves

- Generating random recipes

FILLING SPACE

Random Walks

Random walks are produced by starting at a given point and then taking steps in random directions. Many natural processes, like molecular motion, can be described by random walks, and they can be useful for generating all sorts of naturalistic paths and features.

One-Dimensional Random Walks

The simple 1D random walk shown in Figure 26.8 is generated by moving randomly either up or down a single unit for each step to the right. This simple technique could be used, for example, to produce a sequence of hills and valleys for a platform game.

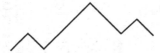

FIGURE 26.8   A 1D random walk.

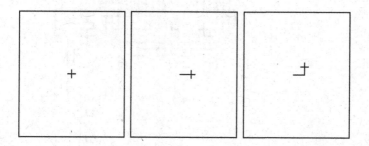

FIGURE 26.9   Two steps in a 2D random walk, first east then north.

Two-Dimensional Random Walks

Two-dimensional random walks are produced by starting at a specific location and then stepping a random direction. In Figure 26.9, each step can be either north, south, east, or west.

It's very common to make many attempts to generate a path via a random walk and simply discard those paths that don't meet your necessary criteria (Figure 26.10). For example, when using a random walk in order to generate a river system, you might discard any path that moves into a cell that is higher in altitude than it started, or that crosses a desert tile.

A powerful method of maze generation is a series of loop-erased random walks (Wilson's algorithm). During a loop-erased random walk, any time a walk crosses itself during generation, that walk is thrown out entirely and a new walk is attempted.

To generate a maze via loop-erased random walk, first a start and an end point are selected. A loop-erased random walk is then made between the start and end points. Then a random point on that random walk is selected and a new loop-erased random walk is made until that walk reaches any point that has already been walked by a previous walk. Again, if that walk crosses itself while it is being generated, it is thrown out and a new one is started. This process continues until all the grid spaces that belong to the maze are filled by random walks.

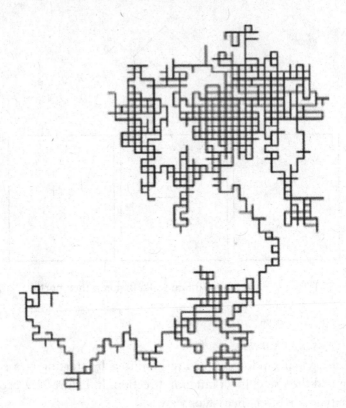

FIGURE 26.10   A 2D random walk after hundreds of steps.

Examples of random walks in use are

- Creating river systems between mountains and bodies of water
- Creating road systems between points of interest
- Creating systems of caverns
- Connecting the doors of rooms generated by a separate method
- Creating sewer layouts

Cellular Automata

Cellular automata are a broad category of systems that operate on a graph of discrete cells. They define a set of states for each cell and a set of rules that describe how the state of each cell changes based on the state of adjacent cells. These rules are typically (but not always) applied to every cell in a stepwise fashion, with each cell computing the next state based on its current neighborhood, and then all the cells changing in one step to the next state defined by the rules.

A common and familiar cellular automaton is Conway's Game of Life, which is played out on a regular 2D grid with two states for each cell, alive and dead. The rules for each time step are described in terms of the current state of the cell and how many of the four cardinal direction neighbors are in the alive state.

Rules for Conway's Game of Life

Current State + Alive Neighbors	New State
Live + 0 or 1 alive neighbors	Dead
Live + 2 or 3 alive neighbors	Alive
Live + 3 or 4 alive neighbors	Dead
Dead + 3 alive neighbors	Alive

An example of a simple cellular automaton that is commonly used to generate procedural areas is a simple system that is able to generate cave-like maps from an initial random grid of walls. This cellular automaton operates on a 2D grid like Conway's Game of Life. The cells can be either walls or open space, and the grid is typically initialized with some percentage of random wall cells.

Example Rules for a Simple 2D Cave Map Generator

Current State + Wall Neighbors	New State
Open + 6–8 wall neighbors	Wall
Wall + 0–4 wall neighbors	Open

These rules, when applied repeatedly, tend to smooth out the stand-alone walls and concentrate the denser clusters, resulting in a cave-like appearance.

Figure 26.11 shows a cave map being iteratively generated by cellular automata in *Caves of Qud*. The field is generated with a two-wide border, and then each interior cell has a 55% chance to contain a wall. The cave rules described above are then executed twice on that random field, resulting in a cave-like set of chambers.

Examples of cellular automata in use are

- Simulating growth patterns for spreading plants and forests

- Simulating spreading fire

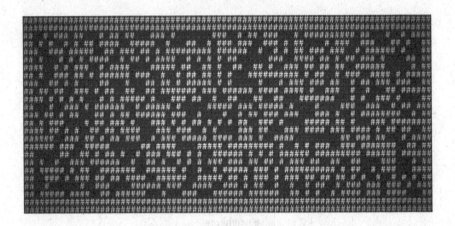

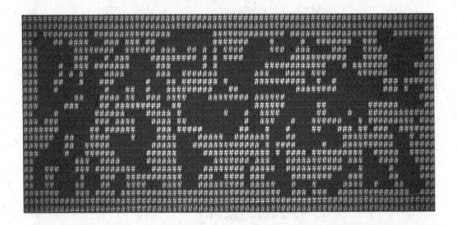

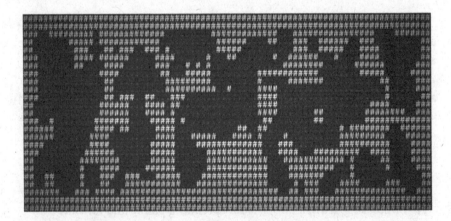

FIGURE 26.11   Stage of cellular automata level generation.

- Simulating migration and proliferation patterns for populations of animals

Settling

A settling algorithm takes a set of assorted shapes that are generated with some overlap. Those shapes are given simple physics rigid body representations, and a physics simulation that causes the overlapping shapes to "push" away from each other is run until they no longer overlap. This provides a straightforward means to arrange a large set of pieces with widely varying sizes and shapes into a set that is connected but not overlapping.

Examples of settling in use are

- Generating a pile of randomly sized dungeon rooms with larger physics colliders than the interior rooms themselves and allowing them to settle out, and then connecting them with hallways

- Generating a pile of very randomly shaped areas and allowing them to settle out, creating a cave system

- Generating a pile of straight and elbow pieces and allowing them to settle out into a sewer system

Wang Tiles

Wang tiles are a mechanism for defining a set of tiles and the way they each connect to each other side by side as they are laid down across a plane. They can be imagined as squares with a color for each side. The tiles are placed so that the color of each side of each newly placed tile matches the color of the sides of each other tile that it touches.

In games, these colors often signify a particular kind of connection between tiles. For example, "blue" tile sides might be those with a door along that side, and "green" tile sides those with a hallway, so that when tiles are aligned based on the color, they produce a properly connected set of areas.

One particularly interesting subset of Wang tiles for procedural games is those carefully select sets of tiles that can tile a plane without creating repeating patterns (aperiodic tilings) (Figure 26.12). Not all possible combinations of tile number and side color will produce aperiodic tiling, but many such sets have been discovered. These aperiodic sets can be as small as 11 tiles (Figure 26.13) (http://arxiv.org/abs/1506.06492).

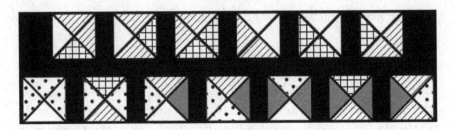

FIGURE 26.12   A 13-tile Wang tile set that will not repeat its pattern across a plane.

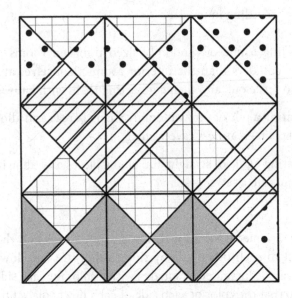

FIGURE 26.13   Example of nine tiles from the set tiled properly in a 3 × 3 block.

Examples of Wang tiles in use are

- The placement of hand-built tiles with predefined edge connections to form large 2D platformer worlds

- Placing hand-built detail tiles inside a room to add detail to the room

- Using Wang tiles to create nonrepeating variation in plant type and tree density in a larger forested area, with each Wang tile having a hand-designed population and density of plants and trees

PARTITIONING SPACE

It's often the case in generating procedural content that you have an open, undifferentiated space that you need to partition into a set of regions. This might be, for example, dividing a landmass or star map into political areas, dividing that country into states, or taking a space and generating a set of units for pathfinding or decision making.

Binary Space Partition

A binary space partition takes a given space and splits it in half, and then takes the two areas that were created and splits those in half, and repeats until some threshold is reached. Some commonly used thresholds are a particular number of splits performed and the average size of the resulting areas (Figures 26.14 through 26.17).

Caves of Qud builds the internal structure of many types of ruins by using a simple binary space partition of that space (Figure 26.18). A simple volume outline for the building is created, and then a random column or row in the building is selected and a wall is created, splitting the area in two. Each time the area is split, a door is placed that connects the two spaces along the splitting line.

Since we know cutting an area in half and placing a door that connects both creates two areas that are definitely connected, and since we know each additional split of those resulting subareas ensures the resulting two

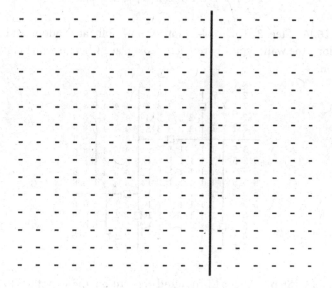

FIGURE 26.14   Step 1: A region is split by a wall along a random column.

```
1 1 1 1 1 1 1 1 1 1 | 2 2 2 2 2
1 1 1 1 1 1 1 1 1 1 | 2 2 2 2 2
1 1 1 1 1 1 1 1 1 1 | 2 2 2 2 2
1 1 1 1 1 1 1 1 1 1 | 2 2 2 2 2
1 1 1 1 1 1 1 1 1 1 | 2 2 2 2 2
1 1 1 1 1 1 1 1 1 1 | 2 2 2 2 2
1 1 1 1 1 1 1 1 1 1 | 2 2 2 2 2
1 1 1 1 1 1 1 1 1 1 | 2 2 2 2 2
1 1 1 1 1 1 1 1 1 1 | 2 2 2 2 2
1 1 1 1 1 1 1 1 1 1 | 2 2 2 2 2
1 1 1 1 1 1 1 1 1 1 | 2 2 2 2 2
1 1 1 1 1 1 1 1 1 1 □ 2 2 2 2 2
1 1 1 1 1 1 1 1 1 1 | 2 2 2 2 2
1 1 1 1 1 1 1 1 1 1 | 2 2 2 2 2
1 1 1 1 1 1 1 1 1 1 | 2 2 2 2 2
```

FIGURE 26.15 Step 2: A portal is placed at random somewhere along the wall. The newly created subregions are marked 1 and 2.

```
3 3 3 3 3 3 3 3 3 3 | 4 4 4 4 4 4
3 3 3 3 3 3 3 3 3 3 | 4 4 4 4 4 4
3 3 3 3 3 3 3 3 3 3 | 4 4 4 4 4 4
3 3 3 3 3 3 3 3 3 3 | 4 4 4 4 4 4
─────────────────□──┤ 4 4 4 4 4 4
1 1 1 1 1 1 1 1 1 1 | 4 4 4 4 4 4
1 1 1 1 1 1 1 1 1 1 | 4 4 4 4 4 4
1 1 1 1 1 1 1 1 1 1 | 4 4 4 4 4 4
1 1 1 1 1 1 1 1 1 1 | 4 4 4 4 4 4
1 1 1 1 1 1 1 1 1 1 └□─────────
1 1 1 1 1 1 1 1 1 1 | 2 2 2 2 2
1 1 1 1 1 1 1 1 1 1 □ 2 2 2 2 2
1 1 1 1 1 1 1 1 1 1 | 2 2 2 2 2
1 1 1 1 1 1 1 1 1 1 | 2 2 2 2 2
1 1 1 1 1 1 1 1 1 1 | 2 2 2 2 2
```

FIGURE 26.16 Step 3: Each subregion is now split at random and a portal placed along the wall, typically restricted to a place where it won't create a T or X junction.

```
7 7 7 7 7 | 3 3 3 3 3 | 4 4 4 | 8 8
7 7 7 7 7 □ 3 3 3 3 3 | 4 4 4 | 8 8
7 7 7 7 7 | 3 3 3 3 3 | 4 4 4 □ 8 8
7 7 7 7 7 | 3 3 3 3 3 | 4 4 4 | 8 8
──────────────────□── | 4 4 4 | 8 8
5 5 5 | 1 1 1 1 1 1 1  | 4 4 4 | 8 8
5 5 5 | 1 1 1 1 1 1 1  | 4 4 4 | 8 8
5 5 5 | 1 1 1 1 1 1 1  | 4 4 4 | 8 8
5 5 5 | 1 1 1 1 1 1 1  | 4 4 4 | 8 8
5 5 5 | 1 1 1 1 1 1 1  └□───────
5 5 5 | 1 1 1 1 1 1 1  | 2 2 | 6 6 6
5 5 5 | 1 1 1 1 1 1 1  □ 2 2 | 6 6 6
5 5 5 □ 1 1 1 1 1 1 1  | 2 2 | 6 6 6
5 5 5 | 1 1 1 1 1 1 1  | 2 2 □ 6 6 6
5 5 5 | 1 1 1 1 1 1 1  | 2 2 | 6 6 6
```

FIGURE 26.17 Step 4: After a third round of partition, the area starts to resemble a set of connected rooms.

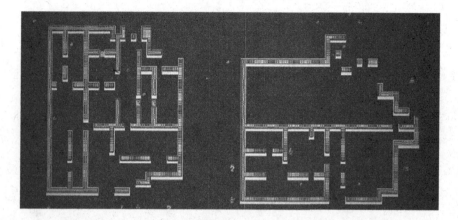

FIGURE 26.18   Set of ruins in *Caves of Qud*, generated primarily via binary space partition.

areas are themselves connected, we can be sure the process guarantees that all the rooms created during the space partition will be reachable from one another.

Examples of binary space partitions in use are

- To create a traditional *Rogue*-style room layout, you can place a smaller rectangular room inside the borders of each generated region and connecting to the adjacent regions with hallways based on portals.

- Filling an area with walls and doors to form connected rooms.

Voronoi Diagrams

A Voronoi diagram is constructed by taking a set of seed points on a plane and partitioning that plane so that the region containing each seed contains only the points on the plane closest to the seed (Figure 26.19). A variety of distance metrics can be used.

Since Voronoi diagrams work to partition a continuous plane of space, they are most useful for partitioning continuous, uninterrupted spaces, like continents; however, there are variations of Voronoi diagrams that take obstacles into account.

Examples of Voronoi diagrams in use are

- Generating the areas of farmed fields from the placement of farmhouses in a countryside

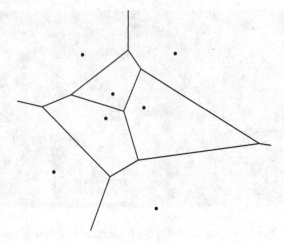

FIGURE 26.19 Simple Voronoi diagram.

- Generating territorial control of dragons from the placement of their lairs

- Generating areas of varying encounter difficulty from the placement of major dungeons

Dijkstra Maps

Dijkstra maps partition space in a manner similar to that of Voronoi diagrams; however, they work on a discrete graph instead of a continuous plane. In our examples, we use a square grid, which is a graph where each node is connected to its four or eight neighbors, but the algorithm supports any graph.

A Dijkstra map is generated by taking a set of seed points and calculating the distance from each node in the graph to the closest seed point. This is typically done via a breadth-first search from each seed point. During the search, each node is typically marked with the seed point it is closest to and the distance to that seed, forming a region surrounding each seed.

Dijkstra maps have wide applicability to terrain analysis and pathfinding. *Caves of Qud* utilizes Dijkstra maps with randomly placed seeds in order to generate a uniform population of uneven spaces (Figure 26.20). Random seeds are placed on the map until the largest region reaches a target size. The resulting Dijkstra map regions are each populated with a similar number of objects, providing an even distribution of map contents irrespective of the map's layout or amount of open space.

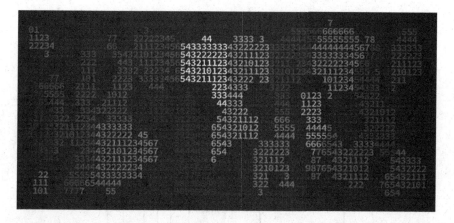

FIGURE 26.20   A 20-seed Dijkstra map regionalization of a cave system in *Caves of Qud* used for terrain analysis and to create an evenly distributed population.

Examples of Dijkstra maps in use are

- Finding the furthest point from the entrance of a cave system to place treasure or a boss encounter

- Evenly distributing encounters throughout a nonuniform space

- Analyzing areas to place internal features, for example, a set of square buildings or tents in a nonuniform space

- Filling national territories around a set of capital cities on a map

Tree Mapping

Tree mapping is a technique used to take a list of values and then partition a rectangular 2D field into a set of rectangular division (Figure 26.21). Each of the rectangular divisions has an area proportional to one of the target values in the list. There are several algorithms for producing tree maps that trade off a consistent visual aspect ratio of the divisions with the stability of the map layout when changes are introduced to the list of values.

Examples of tree maps in use are

- Creating a basic city street grid for a set of buildings and city blocks of known size

- Creating the rooms of a side-view building given a list of room sizes

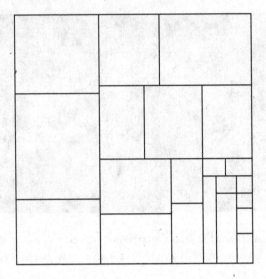

FIGURE 26.21 Typical tree map.

PUTTING IT ALL TOGETHER

Let's use some of the techniques described above to generate an adorable little galaxy!

First, we need all the stars in a galaxy. We can use a normal distribution in 3D to generate the positions of every star in a little globular cluster of a few thousand stars—or a few million stars if we have a little more time to work! While we work, we'll assign each star a random seed. We might just give each one a totally random value, or we might base it on the physical location in the globular cluster, hashing the position to produce a seed.

We don't yet have to generate most of the information about the star, since we can now generate it based on each star's seed whenever we need it. However, we probably want to generate just enough information about the stars to display them. Probably the size and color of the star are enough.

We can use a little weighted distribution for each star in our galaxy to pick the type, temperature, and size.

Weight	Star Type	Temperature (K)	Size
1	Super giant 1a	3,000–30,000	Mega huge!
1	Super giant 1b	3,000–30,000	Huge!
2	Bright giant	3,000–30,000	Big
5	Giant	3,000–30,000	Big
20	Main sequence	1,000–30,000	Medium
2	White dwarf	4,000–30,000	Small

So now we know the size of each star and we can pick the display color based on the temperature.

When the player clicks on a star, we can seed the random number generator with a value like (starseed+hash("starname")) and then use a Markov chain of syllables we've created from a catalog of star names to generate a random name for the star. This is fast enough that we can just do it in real time whenever we mouse over a star.

When the player zooms into the system, we can continue to add detail. A weighted table to tell us if it has one or more companion stars, perhaps a weighted table for the number of inner rocky planets, and then one for the outer gas planets. Then we can select a seed for each planet, perhaps a hash of the system name and orbital ("Algotauri 4") and generate the overall visual aspects of the planet for display.

When the player zooms in to a planet, we can generate more detail, for example, using Perlin noise layers to generate the topography, L-systems to generate the layouts of the cities of the creatures that occupy it, binary partition to create the rooms in an individual building, a weighted table to tell you what the contents of a particular room are, and a Markov chain to tell you what is on the notepad that is in a desk in that particular room.

Procedural generation opens endless doors in endless hallways to endless untracked worlds.

Happy hiking!

CHAPTER 27

Meaning

Dr. Mark R. Johnson

Independent

HOW MIGHT *RANDOMNESS* BE given meaning? Can the placement of elements of a procedurally generated game ever have the kind of meaning present in other games, especially those notorious for deep narrative significance in the nature and location of every component, such as the *Souls* series? Can meaningful thematic elements be offered up to a player through procedural generation? How might deep and implicit connections between procedurally placed game elements be forged? Will the worlds and spaces and gameplay challenges created by procedural generation ever be able to transmit the same kind of meaning as a handmade game?

An increasing number of games are moving toward offering complex stories and depicting detailed worlds, fundamentally dependent on the creation of meaning. Although roguelikes and other procedural games are known primarily for their mechanics and gameplay rather than these less formal elements, there is no reason that designers of procedural games need to fall behind in this aspect of game design. Procedural generation is absolutely capable of producing meaning at a number of scales and with varying levels of designer effort and involvement, depending on the scale and scope of the desired result.

In this chapter, we look at how meaning is created, the concept of meaninglessness, and two methods of how meaning can be produced during play. Players can assign meaning to elements lacking any designer-intended meaning, just as players can readily fail to note the deeper meaning of game content specifically placed by designers with the purpose of creating meaning. Lastly, we'll explore the procedural creation of meaning in *Ultima Ratio Regum* (*URR*) as a case study, the most fundamental underlying component of the game's design. In the process, we'll examine the design goal of emphasizing meaning over more traditional aspects of game design, the use of meaning as a game mechanic and its intriguing relationship to the practice of seeking out game "spoilers," and what I believe the procedural generation of meaning can bring to game design in the future.

MEANING IN GAMES

What is *meaning*? On the most highly abstracted level, meaning in games (and any work of art, fiction, or media) is created through forging connections between elements of that experience. A phrase has meaning when the reader remembers another character uttering the same phrase before; a company name has meaning when the viewer recalls seeing their logo on a van earlier in the film; the visual design of a boss or enemy has meaning when it is similar or comparable to others seen previously. When this is not the case, in-media information serves only a role as background or scene setting. Background is an important role, without doubt, but does not produce elements that are truly meaningful to the experience of the work, because they could be exchanged for other comparable elements (switching the logo on one van seen for a moment with a different logo) and the salient elements of the media artifact would go unchanged, because that element has nothing to do with the message being conveyed. Meaning is fundamentally created through the connection of otherwise disparate elements.

A common source of meaning in games is through the distribution of information about what now tends to be called "lore." This is often textual in-game content that is optional to the player's success over the mechanical challenges of the game, but serves instead to flesh out the fictional world in which the action takes place.

In procedural games, this takes many forms. A game like *Tales of Maj'Eyal* adheres to a model of scattered lore that adds up to a large body of data about a story, and a story can appear at first to be one thing and then morph into something else as more information is acquired. *Dungeon Crawl Stone Soup* instead draws on classical mythology for its lore, positioning its monsters within various mythologies, ranging from ancient Greek to Egyptian and Jewish to Hindu, in many cases giving hints about how these monsters behave based on these classical origins. *The Binding of Isaac* offers puzzling fragments of a story that appear gradually over many playthroughs, and slowly lend increasingly substantial meaning to the different items and monsters found within the game's dungeons, epistemologically repositioning "mere" grotesque monsters and unsettling body horror world design to become part of a deeper, darker, and more profound story about (depending on your interpretation) religion, child abuse, parenting, and imaginary worlds. In each of these cases, meaning exists outside the formal mechanics of the game, as provided by extra narrative and thematic information, and this information both provides an understanding of a story or a setting and changes how the player thinks about those same mechanical elements in their transition from an isolated gameplay element to a component of a greater whole.

Investigation of such lore is contingent upon a kind of "deal" made with the player—players must be persuaded that there is sufficient meaning there to actually merit their time. One could readily imagine a game that procedurally generates cryptic descriptions and utterances of the sort found in *Souls* games, without having the underlying system or hidden narratives required to actually tie these together into a greater thematic whole. Players would discover that these clues actually meant nothing and were just selections of words and phrases selected by an algorithm for their potential for obfuscation, instead of hinting the player toward deeper truths about the game world, and would lose interest in attempting to uncover the game's meaning—because the signifiers of supposed meaning are actually meaningless. There is therefore no meaning to be found by examining them.

However, such forms of meaning do not always only add to the game, as in some cases they can almost serve the opposite role and highlight the constrained nature of a game's world, rather than (or as well as) bringing a player's attention to the wider thematic or historical elements of a fictional space.

As Erik Champion has previously noted in his work *Critical Gaming: Interactive History and Virtual Heritage*, an amusing example can be found in the *Elder Scrolls* games. Although the game's books and the ambient comments of nonplayer characters do much to flesh out the game world and its history, factions and cultures, there is a rather odd observation to be made: the world described in the game's books is almost infinitely richer than the game actually experienced by the player. There are vast numbers of events and occurrences in the game's lore books that cannot be experienced by the player, and reading all the books can come to make the quite repetitive core gameplay of the games themselves feel surprisingly paltry in contrast to the rich world hinted at, but never directly experienced. Lore in this case does bring meaning and background to the game world, but it also undermines that same meaning by highlighting the artificiality of the game world and the limited numbers of interactions that can take place in the game's possibility space, and reminding the player that what they read is pure fiction, one step disconnected from the possible interactions in the world they're currently exploring.

Meaning is therefore about striking a balance between bringing together all the elements within a particular fictional world to come to resemble more than the sum of their parts and avoiding bringing to the player's attention what isn't there—a meaningful game world must be somehow hermetically sealed, giving out just the right amount of information. This is a difficult balance that few games get exactly right, showing that meaning is a complex question that extends into all elements of game design, from the mechanical to the thematic and the narratological to the experiential, as embodied by each individual player.

MEANINGLESSNESS IN GAMES

Meaningless occurrences in games take many forms, but here I'd like to focus on particular kinds in specifically procedural generation—the unnecessary item and the mostly uninteresting map. In games with very explicit and linear differences in the quality of items, where there are rarely interesting decisions to be made about using Weapon A over Weapon B in Context C, for example, then acquiring Weapon A after Weapon B, if Weapon B is undeniably stronger and there are no contexts in which Weapon A will actually be better, makes the acquisition of Weapon A an effectively meaningless moment, and turns Weapon A into a meaningless item (from a gameplay mechanics perspective).

This meaninglessness is not inherent to the item, but rather an emergent property from the elements of the context in which it was acquired— Weapon A might have been deeply meaningful if found at the start of the game and in the process giving the player's character a significant boost, and it was an item the player had become used to using for hours and hours of subsequent gameplay, but at the end of the game, it becomes merely an unnecessary addition. This is perhaps most marked in the *Angband* family of roguelikes—in many of these games, late-game item decisions become almost impossible without actively ignoring or removing from consideration a large volume of the acquired loot.

This problem of the meaningless item arises often in roguelikes and other games that utilize procedural generation, in which items have their statistics (semi-)randomized, and therefore only a small portion will be relevant to the player. Some games try to "tilt" the generation of items toward the player character's strengths and weaknesses in an attempt to raise the volume of found items that will actually have some meaning to the player, but there will always be procedurally generated elements that lack any meaning to the player in the current gameplay context.

Similarly, on a game with a large expanse of procedural terrain, much of the terrain is only present to split up points of interest, such as settlements, dungeons, or events. Several games, including URR (as noted later), have developed various ambient elements of the game world (weather, flora, fauna, random events, etc.) designed to alleviate the disinterest stemming from these large tracts of uninteresting land. It is nevertheless the case that large volumes of these game spaces are meaningless or, at best, derive their only meaning from other elements surrounding them, rather than any gameplay experience they themselves offer.

In my upcoming theoretical monograph on unpredictability in games, I call this the "granularity of interest" possessed by a game, which is to say the volume of experienced or present content that is actually intriguing, relevant, and meaningful to a player. If almost all elements are in some way interesting and meaningful, then the game has an extremely high granularity of interest, since the player doesn't have to look far from one point of interest to find another, for points of interest are closely packed. By contrast, if large volumes of the game space serve little direct purpose other than spacing out the interesting or meaningful aspects, then the game has a low granularity of interest.

All games that integrate procedural content generation can be usefully understood on this scale, as granularity of interest affects the ebb and flow of player action and engagement in the game, ranging from a consistent high level of engagement and interest (high granularity) to a sinusoidal wave of gameplay between moments of rest and moments of interest, more intense as a result of the previous rest (low granularity).

A low granularity of interest therefore does not necessarily mean that the entire game, viewed as a whole, is automatically less interesting than one with a high granularity of interest; indeed, this is a possibility explicitly taken by the developers of the procedural galaxy game No Man's Sky. Rather than attempting to make every single generated planet interesting and every single region of every single planet interesting, they have instead accepted that many regions of many planets will be relatively uninteresting to the player, and that in many cases entire planets will lack any real interest for the player. However, they present this as a positive—the more worlds are bland and ordinarily, the more that the interesting and unique worlds will actually come to stand out. As exploration is one of the game's central draws, it appears that they instead rely on the hopeful appearance of a kind of emergent player behavior, whereby players find interesting worlds and share them with others, and the presence of uninteresting worlds gives compelling meaning to this exploratory pursuit of interesting worlds, and their sharing with other players.

It is often difficult to create handmade worlds where every instant is interesting, and such a problem certainly remains present when dealing with procedural content generation. Meaninglessness is therefore hard to avoid in procedural generation, but can be adapted to one's advantage if presented as a contrast that highlights the meaningful elements, rather than irrelevant aspects of a game experience that, in certain contexts, will simply never be of note.

DESIGNER AND PLAYER MEANING

We can perceive two methods by which meaning can be experienced by a game's player—either it can be specifically placed by a game's designer and then recognized by the player, or elements not intended to have any meaning can be seen as possessing meaning by a player, whether "correctly" or spuriously.

Many games utilizing procedural generation have a large database of fixed content that is placed first (or placed with the highest priority), and then procedural content is set up around it. Excellent examples of this approach include fixed characters and bosses in narrative-driven roguelikes like *Ancient Domains of Mystery* and *Tales of May'Ejal*, and the long chain of secret actions in *Spelunky*—reaching the final boss involves combining specific items, locating a particular area, dying in a particular place, and so forth. This sequence remains the same regardless of what the game's algorithmic generation systems produce, much like the bosses and important characters in other roguelikes, and systems of this sort enable designers to author points of meaning and importance into a game while still making the overwhelming majority of the game procedurally generated. This system requires that the rest of the content works "around" it, as the secret actions must always work and elements must spawn every time—they are not randomly available or unavailable.

A related but distinct system to the one outlined above is the creation of handmade optional content segments worked into otherwise procedural areas. In addition to Chapter 7, you may also take, for example, the "vaults" in *Dungeon Crawl Stone Soup* parlance. In *Dungeon Crawl Stone Soup*, the vaults range from unique and distinctive gameplay challenges to areas designed to give the player a little bit of information about the game's fictional universe. One might encounter a shrine to a particularly bloodthirsty god with the remains of sacrifices strewn around it, or a vault designed to tell a particular story, such as the tragic and rather amusing tale of the deceased bakers, which I encourage all readers to go and seek out. Handmade segments of gameplay such as vaults are typically nonessential, will appear on some playthroughs of a procedural content generation game but not others, are generally used to develop thematic or "background" elements rather than the immediate narrative of a game, and are placed on top of the game's procedural generation systems as an optional and unpredictable extra.

There are also situations in which players will assign their own meaning to particular events. In Chapter 13, we explored briefly how players could come to regard actions of particular artificial intelligence (AI) actors in some roguelikes as being far more "intelligent" than they actually were. Similarly, in a playthrough of a roguelike where the player character has always been weak and been unlucky with procedurally generated items, for example, the sudden discovery of a tremendously powerful weapon or highly effective piece of armor will immediately transform the player's experience of that playthrough and come to be seen as a moment of great meaning in that playthrough.

This is very visible when we look at the player-created practice of writing "Yet Another Stupid Death" or "Yet Another Victory Post" forum posts that offer handwritten narratives of a character's eventual success or death within a permadeath roguelike. These player stories assign their own meaning to particular stages of the game that had no designer intention and were entirely or predominantly procedural, but which came to strongly affect the outcome of the game, such as gaining a powerful item, defeating a particular enemy, or making a critical error.

Meaning is also often assigned in procedural games through encouraging players to take greater risks to achieve greater rewards, and these playthroughs—when successful—are moments for great celebration and pride. In *Dungeon Crawl Stone Soup*, for example, the player must acquire three "runes" to win, but there are 15 available runes in total, and a victory with more runes is seen as more prestigious than one with fewer. *NetHack*, similarly, has a range of "conducts"—such as the vegetarian conduct that forbids the player character from consuming meat. Practices of this sort are another way to give even greater weight and meaning to a player's decisions and to the eventual outcome of victory, if achieved, and to mark out one playthrough of a roguelike from all the other playthroughs that surround it.

Such practices are rare in player cultures surrounding non procedurally generated games (such as speed running and high score tables), whereas it is hard to find a roguelike without a wealth of player-created (or designer-created) extra challenges that give players the feeling that a particular playthrough in a particular style was especially meaningful, and representative of their skill, knowledge, and abilities in the game in question. These many forms of meaning combine to offer players a range of "anchors" for their experiences in these randomized worlds, providing ample sources of meaning and consequence for their activities, and undermining the popular idea that randomness is necessarily devoid of any deeper importance.

MEANING IN QUALITATIVE PROCEDURAL GENERATION

The creation of meaning is a central part of my own game design work, and I'd like to close this chapter with a critical reflection on my own successes (and failures) in this area thus far, and how I've sought to build on previous concepts of both designer-assigned and player-assigned meaning to develop a system for procedurally generating worlds rich with meaning, and making player understanding of that same meaning a central gameplay mechanic. *URR* absolutely hinges on the creation of meaning, but in a way distinct from the techniques outlined in the earlier sections.

Fundamental to *URR*'s world-building processes, and the creation of meaning within them, is the idea of "chains of meaning." Nothing (or at least, very little) is intended to appear in the world that is only related to itself, or only related to one other element.

For example, flora and fauna are not fixed, but rather procedurally generated in such a way as to be meaningful to other elements. There are huge databases of options, in which there are various options that enable and disable other options, for the generation of wildlife and plant life in each region of the planet, and modeling their spread. Thus, each region then ends up with its own distinctive selection of animals and plants, each of which comes with a procedurally generated image based on its "abstract" traits, and a name. These serve to orient the players as they move around the world, and also to produce extra variety as the players move around the planet. Games that generate huge procedural worlds often struggle with making different areas of the world feel different, and although terrain (temperate, desert, tundra, etc.) goes a long way, *URR* deploys this procedural flora and fauna as an additional detail that varies widely as the player moves around the world.

The crucial point, however, is that animals and plants (just one example of a vast number of elements I could have selected for this discussion) do not only serve this purpose—they also create and influence meaning in a range of other in-game elements. The covers of books might depict local animals. Healers in the area will speak of local plants and their regenerative properties. Those encountered in distant lands might speak of the national animals or plants of their homeland.

Perhaps one of the most striking and effective examples of this system thus far implemented is the generation and reproduction of shared aesthetics distinct to each (secular) culture and each religion (with some bleeding of visual styles and practices between the two). Everything within a particular culture is designed to share commonalities of shape and color—everything from chairs to shop signs and city layouts to ornate floor tilings in one civilization will share a particular geometric form (squares, octagons, circles, etc.), while everything in a religion, from religious vestments to altars and prayer mats to holy books, shares particular sets of colors reproduced in different but clearly connected ways across each item.

The point of these systems is to show the player the meaning in the generated world, instead of telling them about it. When viewing a sigil embossed on a shield, for example, the game never says, "This is the coat of arms of House B." Instead, the world is simply presented to the player, along with the understanding that nothing in the game world is disconnected, and that meaning is there to be found if the player is able to identify it, and the player is left to do the rest.

If these elements were generated merely as background information, however, their meaning would be limited, no matter how detailed. However, as well as the technical and artistic interest and challenge of developing a system of this sort, it is also arguably the most fundamental gameplay system in the game. The player's central objective is the uncovering of a global conspiracy, clues to which are distributed through the world's cultures: a hint might be found in the corner of a painting, or a particular line in a particular novel, or hidden in a chest in the quarters of a mercenary, in the stained glass window of an ancient religious building, or in a piece of poetry.

All the interwoven meaning of *URR* is a method for the player to track down these clues. A novel containing a clue doesn't exist in isolation, but might be mentioned by philosophers, influential in public opinion about a recent war, sold in translation in foreign lands, or named after a particular local animal. All these connected elements enable the player to zero in on tracing down a copy of that work, and thereby acquiring the clue in question.

Discovering meaning is therefore the game's core gameplay system, and one that hinges on both designer-led meaning (creating procedural systems to create systems with shared meanings) and player-led meaning (the ability to identify points of meaning, connect them, and extrapolate from them).

When we think about "discovering meaning" as a game mechanic, there is actually an illustrative comparison here to playing roguelikes with and without spoilers. Many classic roguelikes are so complex, and contain so many obscure and sometimes unclear mechanics, that many players elect to play roguelikes "with spoilers"—this means that they have a "wiki" or guide or equivalent source opened up in their Internet browser while they play, and upon discovering a new monster, a challenging boss, or some item they haven't found before, or a decision they haven't previously encountered, they will look up all the relevant information and make their decisions based on that information.

Crucially, therefore, this is information the player is not intended to have—if the game doesn't give out that information upon a first encounter, and this is indeed the player's first encounter, then the game's designers must have intended for this decision to be made without complete knowledge about its potential outcome(s). Some classic roguelikes, probably most noticeably *NetHack*, are popularly thought to be almost impossible to complete without the use of spoilers, and only the tiniest number of people have ever (claimed to have) achieved such a feat.

Playing how the designers intended, therefore, in this case means discovering the meaning behind the game's systems. This is a form of meaning contingent upon understanding more traditional statistical and mechanical game systems—what does this stat mean, what does this item do, and how does this monster attack?—rather than the kinds of meaning I'm describing here in my own work, but it is still asking the player to uncover meaning as part of playing the game.

All games of course have some kind of learning process, but the per-madeath of roguelike games is what encourages many players away from learning "the hard way" that Medusa will immediately petrify you if she is given line of sight, or that certain enemies in *Dungeon Crawl Stone Soup* can banish you to the abyss far before you are ready, and thereby away from the intended gradual discovery metagame and toward immediate knowledge.

There are two different kinds of knowledge at play here—*NetHack* knowledge applies to every playthrough, since Medusa will always be a threat, and *URR* knowledge, which only applies to a single playthrough, aside from the meta-knowledge of how knowledge in *URR* is acquired. In *URR*, players can only take to the next playthrough the understanding that they are meant to acquire knowledge, not what that knowledge is, and thus a wiki or guide becomes almost irrelevant and the centrality of "discovering meaning as a game mechanic" is maintained even with the presence of spoilers.

CONCLUSION

An opposition between *meaning* and *randomness* need not always be present. Unchanging meaning can be easily added into procedural games through the use of static markers around which the rest of the world is generated, while "changing" meaning that is unique to every playthrough can be implemented through utilizing deeply interconnected procedural generation systems that do nothing in isolation, and always draw upon each other when producing their outcomes.

In turn, this final point allows for the development of intriguing and highly unusual game mechanics, focused on discovery, understanding, and problem solving. They are similar to those used in many puzzle and adventure games, but replayable across however many playthroughs are desired. Even the creation of riddles or puzzles whose widely distributed yet closely related elements, ideally, should be indistinguishable from something that was handmade. Meaning can therefore be a central part of procedural generation, but it requires designers to move beyond the mental model of the "random" procedural generation that distributes affordances with little thought to their connections, and instead embrace the ability to distribute moments of meaning within the randomness, and from these build a story, a background, or entire gameplay mechanics.

Index

Printed in the United States
by Baker & Taylor Publisher Services